Battle for
SOVEREIGN GRACE
in the
Covenant

Battle for
SOVEREIGN GRACE
in the Covenant

The
Declaration
of
Principles

David J. Engelsma

Reformed Free Publishing Association

Scripture cited is taken from the King James (Authorized) Version

Reformed Free Publishing Association
1894 Georgetown Center Drive
Jenison, MI 49428

Cover design by Gary Gore
Interior layout and typesetting by Erika Kiel

ISBN 978-1-936054-19-0
LCCN 2013932652

To the honored memory of the two
TOWERING CHAMPIONS OF SOVEREIGN GRACE
who contended valiantly for the Reformed faith in the very dark, almost desperate, days of 1953, Herman Hoeksema and George M. Ophoff, and of the doughty little warrior who fought beside them—Hope's stalwart elder and my old friend, Richard Newhouse

Contents

Preface

This is a book about a document: the Declaration of Principles of the Protestant Reformed Churches.

It is not a history of the schism that the document occasioned, even though some, even a great deal, of this history necessarily enters into the account of the document.

There ought to be a history of the schism within the Protestant Reformed Churches in 1953. Short treatments of the schism have appeared in works on other subjects. But it is time for a thoroughly researched, full-blown history of the event.

Such a history becomes a virtual necessity for members of the Protestant Reformed Churches. No minister survives who took part in the controversy. Members who lived through those agonizing years and can therefore speak to the younger generations from experience become few. And the record of the history is largely buried in old issues of magazines, acts of synods, and the archives containing letters and other documentation of the schism. These sources do not attract the average church member, regardless how interested in the history he or she may be.

The younger generations in the Protestant Reformed Churches ought to know the schism in the history of their churches. The issue was a fundamental doctrine of the Reformed, Christian faith—the truth of the covenant of grace. The outcome of the controversy, in addition to reducing the size of the denomination by two-thirds, powerfully formed the churches into what they are today. This is true not only doctrinally but also in other ways, for instance, their polemical character, that is, their willingness to contend for the faith. Inasmuch as, evidently, there could have been no clear, firm grasp of the doctrine of sovereign grace in the covenant apart from the schism, the schism was the preservation of the Protestant Reformed Churches as Reformed churches confessing salvation by the almighty, irresistible grace of God only.

A history of the schism would serve a good purpose also with regard to members of other Reformed and Presbyterian churches.

The schismatic faction in the Protestant Reformed Churches, particularly the ministers, many of them both able and popular, were successful in convincing the Reformed churches in North America and abroad that the conflict in the Protestant Reformed Churches was mainly about personalities and carnal power. And of course, to hear them, the only offensive personality was Herman Hoeksema.

A history of the schism, based on readily ascertainable and incontrovertible facts, would conclusively demonstrate that the conflict was mainly about doctrine, and that this doctrine is at the heart of the Reformed, Christian faith: the covenant of God in Jesus Christ, or in the words of Hebrews 9:15, the "new testament."

The struggle of the Protestant Reformed Churches in the early 1950s was a battle for the gospel of salvation by the sovereign grace of God, nothing less. It was a struggle to maintain in these churches Augustine's confession of grace against Pelagius; Luther's confession of grace against Erasmus; the Reformation's confession of grace against the Roman Catholic Church; Calvin's confession of grace against Bolsec, Pighius, and Servetus; and Dordt's confession of grace against Arminius.

But the struggle of the Protestant Reformed Churches was a battle for the gospel of grace with specific reference to the covenant of God in Jesus Christ. *Covenant* grace—the Protestant Reformed Churches contended in the early 1950s and confessed in the Declaration—is particular, sovereign, irresistible, and the sole explanation of the salvation of the baptized children of believers.

In thus confessing grace in the covenant and with regard to salvation in the covenant, these churches officially settled a controversial issue that had long troubled the Reformed churches. Again and again, the false doctrine of a conditional covenant in which grace is wider than election and therefore resistible, conditioned by the will and works of baptized babies, has surfaced in the Reformed churches. Today, this doctrine of conditional, resistible grace in the covenant plagues Reformed and Presbyterian churches in the theology of the federal (covenant) vision. It is the overthrow of the gospel of grace.

In the Declaration of Principles, the Protestant Reformed Churches addressed directly the issue of a conditional or an unconditional covenant. They condemned the doctrine of a conditional covenant, not merely as unacceptable to the Protestant Reformed Churches but as heresy—the fundamental heresy of denying that salvation is alone of God who shows mercy and of making salvation—*in the covenant*—dependent on man's willing and running (see Rom. 9:16).

Thus the Protestant Reformed Churches settled the great issue concerning the covenant, just as Dordt settled the issue concerning salvation, whether dependent on God's eternal will of election or dependent on the allegedly free will of the sinner.

The history of this battle, settling an ages-long controversy over covenant grace and covenant salvation, should be written.

But this is not that book, even though some of the history will appear in it.

This book concerns the Declaration of Principles. In the main, it is a history of the Declaration—when, how, and why it appeared in the Protestant Reformed Churches; the controversy surrounding its adoption; and its content.

The book contains five appendices that will assist the reader in comprehending the history, doctrine, and significance of the Declaration. The first is a timeline of important events in the history of the adoption of the Declaration and of the schism that the Declaration occasioned. The second is the Declaration of Principles. The third is my brief commentary on the content of the Declaration, to my knowledge the only such commentary. The fourth and fifth appendices are my critical reviews of two recent books that defend the covenant theology of Norman Shepherd and the federal (covenant) vision. These reviews starkly indicate the heretical fruits that are sprouting in the Reformed community of churches from the root of the covenant doctrine that the Declaration exposes, rejects, and condemns. Thus the reviews demonstrate the significance of the Declaration, as of the great battle that the Protestant Reformed Churches fought in the early 1950s on behalf of sovereign grace in the unconditional covenant.

The occasion for this book is the sixtieth anniversary of the adoption of the Declaration by a synod of the Protestant Reformed Churches in 1951 and the sixtieth anniversary of the schism of the Protestant Reformed Churches in 1953.

I write this book for a popular, as distinguished from a scholarly, theological audience, for young people as well as their parents and grandparents.

Does the Declaration warrant such treatment, sixtieth anniversary or not?

The book itself will have to prove the warrant.

To the questioning member of the Protestant Reformed Churches and to a skeptic outside the churches, I may here respond with questions of my own.

Does an ecclesiastical document about covenant, promise, faith, infant baptism, election, and grace have some importance?

Is a document that occasioned schism in a Reformed denomination of churches significant?

Is a document that was influential to preserve an entire denomination of Reformed churches in the orthodoxy of the three forms of unity, in our doctrinally weak and apostate twenty-first century, worthy of some attention?

And then there is this provocative statement by Herman Hoeksema on the floor of the synod of 1951, which would adopt the Declaration. He spoke in the heat of battle, surrounded by foes who would pounce on the statement to charge pride and folly: "We must not go back, but defend our beautiful and strong position at the head of all the Reformed churches." He added immediately: "And therefore, we must stand on the basis of our Confessions. Let us continue to do this."[1]

"At the head of all the Reformed churches"!

Many will fume at this statement, as many fumed in 1951. Others will laugh, as many laughed in September 1951. But perhaps not so furiously, or so heartily, today, when many of the Reformed churches in North America are permeated with, and helpless before, the heresy of the federal vision.

This is the heresy that at its root was exposed, opposed, and condemned in the Declaration of Principles, some twenty-five years before the heresy surfaced, with virtually irresistible force, in the Reformed churches in North America.

---

1   Herman Hoeksema, "The Synod of 1951," *Standard Bearer* 28, no. 8 (January 15, 1952): 173.

Chapter One

Provisional Adoption
of the Declaration

The Declaration of Principles is a nearly eight-page synodical decision of the Protestant Reformed Churches in America, in the back of the *Acts of Synod, 1951* of these churches.[1] The synodical decision that is the Declaration states certain fundamental truths concerning the Reformed, biblical doctrine of the covenant of grace, as these fundamental truths are authoritatively expressed in the Reformed confessions. These confessions are mainly the Heidelberg Catechism, the Belgic Confession of Faith, the Canons of Dordt, and the Reformed Form for the Administration of Baptism.

In general the principles enunciated in the Declaration are, first, the truth that salvation in the covenant of grace, particularly regarding the baptized children of godly parents, depends wholly on the baptizing and promising God and not at all upon the baptized infants.

Second, the covenant, its blessings, and its salvation have their source in God's eternal decree of election. And covenant salvation is as unconditional as the election out of which it flows.

Specifically, these principles are the truth that God establishes the covenant of grace only with the elect children of believing parents; the truth that the covenant promise (by which the covenant is established with the children of believers and according to which the children are saved) is unconditional, that is, gracious, depending only upon the sovereign grace of the promising God and not upon works of the children; and the truth that the faith by which

---

1   *Acts of Synod, Protestant Reformed Churches in America, 1951*, 201–8.

children, like their parents, are justified and saved is the gracious gift of God to the children and not the work of the children, upon which the covenant and its salvation depend as a condition.

These principles had been known and confessed by the Protestant Reformed Churches from their founding as a separate denomination of churches in 1924. Correctly, the preamble of the Declaration says about the principles of the covenant expressed in the Declaration that "these have always been maintained in the Protestant Reformed Churches."

When ministers in the denomination began opposing these principles of the covenant in the late 1940s and early 1950s, they were rejecting fundamental truths that the denomination had always believed and confessed, even though as yet it had not officially adopted these truths. And the ministers opposing these principles knew it.

The statement of these principles in a "declaration" was occasioned by a request to the Protestant Reformed synod of 1950 from the domestic mission committee of the denomination. The mission committee asked for a "form" that missionaries could use in the organization of groups in Canada as Protestant Reformed congregations.

> Your committee requests Synod to draw up a form that
> may be used by those families requesting organization into
> a Prot. Ref. congregation. We believe that this would serve
> to remove all misunderstanding and aid toward unity.[2]

At the time the Protestant Reformed Churches were working with Dutch immigrants in Canada who had deep convictions concerning the doctrine of the covenant. These convictions differed essentially from the doctrine of the covenant embraced and preached by the Protestant Reformed Churches. These immigrants had themselves inquired of the Protestant Reformed missionaries whether the Protestant Reformed Churches' doctrine of the covenant would be binding on them, were they to organize as congregations in the federation of the Protestant Reformed Churches.

The mission committee presented one such inquiry to the 1950 synod. Identifying his family as "confessing members of the Reformed Church maintaining Article 31 of the Church Order

---

2   *Acts of Synod, Protestant Reformed Churches of America, 1950,* 54.

[commonly known as the liberated Reformed churches]," the author of the inquiry made this request: "As one of the most important points, I would gladly receive elucidation whether you will hold the former liberated Reformed people, when they are received by you as confessing members into the Protestant Reformed Churches, to your conceptions concerning covenant and baptism, or that they need to expect no binding in these [doctrinal] matters from you."[3]

The mission committee assured synod that the letter "is quite typical of repeated requests that we have received from various groups in Canada."[4]

That the Declaration was drawn up and adopted by synod in response to a request for such a "form" by the denominational mission committee became important later, when Protestant Reformed ministers and consistories raised objection to the Declaration as having been adopted by synod without having originated from a local consistory. Synod defended the church political legality of the Declaration by noting the request from the mission committee and by appealing to Article 30 of the Church Order. This article states that in the major assemblies of Reformed churches (one of which is the annual synod) "only such matters shall be dealt with...as pertain to the churches of the major assembly in common."[5] A request from a denominational committee concerning the mission work that the churches in common are doing is a matter with which a synod may rightfully deal.

To the requests from the Dutch immigrants in Canada for enlightenment whether the Protestant Reformed beliefs concerning covenant and baptism would be binding upon them, should they join the churches, the mission committee responded, "We do not feel that it lies within our jurisdiction to give answer to this question."[6]

---

3   Ibid., 52–53. The request was in Dutch. The translation of the Dutch is mine. An English translation of this part of the letter is found in the *Acts of Synod, Protestant Reformed Churches in America, 1953,* 165.

4   Ibid., 52.

5   Church Order of the Protestant Reformed Churches, Article 30, in *The Confessions and the Church Order of the Protestant Reformed Churches* (Grandville, MI: Protestant Reformed Churches in America, 2005), 389.

6   *Acts of Synod, 1950,* 53.

The mission committee therefore turned to the synod for the answer to the question about the binding nature of the Protestant Reformed doctrine of the covenant of grace. In their request to synod for an official statement, or "form," the mission committee added that it "would appreciate having something uniform and definite to present to these groups, particularly when they request organization."[7]

A synodical committee of pre-advice recommended that the 1950 synod "adopt the following clear-cut expression as one which should appear in each request for organization, along with the denial of common grace and the Three Points of 1924, and profession of adherence to the Three Forms of Unity and the Church Order of Dordtrecht and professing the Scriptures to be the infallible Word of God." The "clear-cut expression" proposed by the committee was as follows:

> The promise of the Gospel, both as to the will of God to save His people and the execution of His will to save them, is not general, that is, it does not include all the baptized children of the church, but is particular, that is, it pertains only to the elect of God.[8]

Although this recommended statement was brief, it did express the heart of the Protestant Reformed doctrine of the covenant, as well as address the main points of controversy over the doctrine of the covenant between the Protestant Reformed Churches and the Reformed Churches in the Netherlands (liberated). It would have conveyed to the mission committee and ultimately informed the Dutch immigrants in Canada that it is the confession of the Protestant Reformed Churches that the covenant promise, "I will be your God and the God of your children," applies to the elect children and elect further descendants of believing parents.

The much-longer Declaration would only expand on this short statement. In addition the Declaration would polemically reject the covenant conception opposed to the doctrine of the covenant that the short statement confesses and demonstrate that this covenant doctrine is indeed binding in the Protestant Reformed Churches,

---

7   Ibid., 54.

8   Ibid.

since it is the expression of the binding Reformed creeds.

The two professors at the Protestant Reformed Seminary, who would play a prominent role in the subsequent controversy over the Declaration, Herman Hoeksema and George M. Ophoff, were not members of the committee of pre-advice that drew up and recommended the short "clear-cut expression" in response to the request of the mission committee.

The synod of 1950 was not satisfied with this brief statement. Evidently, synod desired a more detailed statement regarding the covenant doctrine of the Protestant Reformed Churches, with which groups desiring to be organized as Protestant Reformed Churches ought to be familiar and in agreement. The decision of synod was "to re-submit this matter to the committee of pre-advice, and to add the two professors as advisors to this committee."[9]

Charged on Friday with drawing up a "form" that would give direction to the mission committee, the now enlarged committee presented the Declaration to synod the following Monday. The Declaration was drawn up, therefore, in one day—the Saturday between the resubmission to the synodical committee and the following Monday.

The synodical committee of pre-advice called the document that it proposed to synod "A Brief Declaration of Principles of the Protestant Reformed Churches."[10] In the very small print of the *Acts of Synod*, the brief Declaration runs to slightly more than seven pages.[11]

This proposed response to the mission committee was much longer and more detailed concerning the covenant doctrine of the Protestant Reformed Churches than was the original "clear-cut expression." It was also negative, stating and condemning certain teachings concerning the covenant that the Protestant Reformed Churches repudiate, whereas the "clear-cut expression" was only positive.

Synod adopted the "Brief Declaration," as was later acknowledged by all, without much discussion and with hardly any opposition.

---

9   Ibid.
10   Ibid., 83.
11   Ibid., 83–90.

Only one of the sixteen synodical delegates voted against adopting the Declaration.

The trouble-free and almost unanimous adoption of the Declaration was misleading. Immediately after the synod vehement objection to the Declaration would surface throughout the denomination. Controversy would rage. And the result, some three years later, would be schism.

As the committee that had drawn up and presented the Declaration recommended, the synod of 1950 also decided:

1. That synod subject this entire document to the approval of the churches.

2. If no objection is offered, to adopt this at our next synod.

3. To adopt this [Declaration] in the meantime as a working hypothesis for our mission committee and for our missionaries in the organization of churches.[12]

Adoption of the Declaration by the synod of 1950, therefore, was only provisional. The decisive adoption was delayed to the synod of 1951. In the meantime, however, the Declaration had authority in the churches. It was to be "a working hypothesis" for the mission committee.

THE AUTHOR

The author of the Declaration was Herman Hoeksema. He himself acknowledged his authorship. Defending the Declaration soon after the synod of 1950, Hoeksema mentioned that one reason he felt himself responsible for the document was that "the committee asked me to draw up the first Draft of this Declaration of Principles, which then was discussed by them and proposed by them to synod, and finally adopted by this body."[13]

The foes of the Declaration also recognized Hoeksema as the Declaration's author. At their first separate synod upon separating from the Protestant Reformed Churches, they busied themselves

---

12 Ibid., 90.

13 Herman Hoeksema, "Reply to Rev. Blankespoor," *Standard Bearer* 27, no. 1 (October 1, 1950): 4.

Herman Hoeksema, author of the Declaration, foremost defender of the Declaration, leading theologian in the PRC, and "doctor of the covenant."

to vote the Declaration null and void in their communion. In the course of this action, they spoke of "the author of the Declaration, the Rev. H. Hoeksema."[14]

It was only fitting, indeed to be expected, that Hoeksema would compose the Declaration of Principles.

The Declaration must express the fundamental truths of the Protestant Reformed doctrine of the covenant of grace. Not only was Herman Hoeksema the leading theologian in the Protestant Reformed Churches, but he was also the man who had led the churches into the knowledge of the truth of the covenant as the churches confessed it. Reacting against the doctrine of the covenant taught him and all other seminarians in Calvin Seminary by the Christian Reformed theologian Prof. William Heyns when Hoeksema was still a Christian Reformed seminarian, Hoeksema set himself the task of forming a doctrine of the covenant. This doctrine would be both a genuine development of a prominent, indeed *the* prominent, conception in the Reformed tradition, as represented especially by Herman Bavinck, and in harmony with the Reformed creeds, particularly the Canons of Dordt. Early in his ministry in the Protestant Reformed Churches, already in 1927, Hoeksema had spelled out this doctrine of the covenant in a series of articles in the *Standard Bearer*. Later, sometime before 1932, these articles

---

14 *Acts of Synod, 1953*, 353. It is a peculiarity of the *Acts of Synod, 1953* that the minutes of the continued synod of the schismatic faction, March 1954, are bound together in one volume with the minutes of the synod of the still-united churches that met in June 1953 but then recessed until March 1954.

in the Dutch language were published as *De Geloovigen en Hun Zaad* (Believers and their seed).[15]

CONTROVERSY

During the year between the provisional adoption of the Declaration by the synod of 1950 and what was intended to be the decisive adoption of the document by the synod of 1951, there was heated debate about the Declaration in the Protestant Reformed Churches. Controversy raged. Schism was in the air. The two periodicals that served the members of the churches, the *Standard Bearer* and *Concordia*, contended over the Declaration—the *Standard Bearer* defending the Declaration, *Concordia* opposing its adoption. Sermons reflected on the Declaration and the doctrinal issues it addressed. Households discussed the matter, not always amicably.

Those Protestant Reformed ministers who opposed the Declaration were, in fact, defending the covenant doctrine of Klaas Schilder and the Reformed Churches in the Netherlands (liberated).

They had become enamored of this doctrine of the covenant at least in part by the persuasive presentation of it by Schilder himself. In the fall of 1947, at the invitation of the Protestant Reformed Churches, he had spoken on the covenant at conferences with the Protestant Reformed ministers, he had preached his covenant conception in the churches, and he had won them over by personal conversations.

Although the ministers did not forthrightly state that they rejected the prevailing Protestant Reformed doctrine of the covenant

---

15 The original articles in the *Standard Bearer* appeared in volumes 3 and 4 of the magazine. The series began in volume 3, number 14 (April 15, 1927), and concluded in volume 4, number 3 (November 1, 1927). The booklet, published in Grand Rapids by C. J. Doorn, contains no publishing date but was certainly published before 1932, since Hoeksema remarks on the booklet in his editorial in the December 15, 1932 issue of the *Standard Bearer*. The booklet was translated into English by Homer C. Hoeksema and published by the Reformed Free Publishing Association (RFPA) as *Believers and Their Seed* in 1971. A revised edition of this English translation was published by the RFPA in 1997, titled *Believers and Their Seed: Children in the Covenant*.

in favor of the doctrine of the liberated, there can be no doubt that all their opposition to the Declaration was due to, and expressive of, their embrace of the liberated doctrine.

First, the principles of the covenant doctrine that they advanced were fundamental elements of the liberated doctrine of the covenant. These principles were (and are) a severing of the covenant and covenant grace from the decree of election; the extension of the gracious covenant promise to all the baptized children without exception; God's establishment of the covenant with all the baptized children alike; and the conditionality of the covenant promise, as of the covenant itself.

Second, in their defense of a

Klaas Schilder, founding father of and leading theologian in the Reformed Churches in the Netherlands (liberated); vigorous proponent of a conditional covenant, cut loose from election; chief external foe of the Declaration; and influential in converting many Protestant Reformed ministers to his theology of the covenant.

doctrine of the covenant opposed to, and by, the Declaration, the adversaries of the Declaration admitted their attraction to, if not their wholehearted embrace of, the covenant doctrine of Schilder and the liberated. Defending the conditionality of the covenant in the sense that, although there is no condition for a child's entrance into the covenant, there are conditions for remaining in the covenant, Rev. Andrew Petter appealed to Schilder (whose views he was propounding): "Dr. Schilder expressed this in his speeches among us by saying: 'There are no conditions *for* the covenant, but there are conditions *in* the covenant. God does not give the enjoyment of life to His people except under conditions of faith and conversion.'"[16]

16 A. Petter, "The Covenant, XXVII—Dr. Schilder," *Concordia* 6, no. 4 (Thursday, March 31, 1949): 3.

Klaas Schilder (l) and Andrew Petter (r) under the palm trees in southern California on one of Schilder's tours of the Protestant Reformed Churches. During these tours, especially in 1947, he indoctrinated many Protestant Reformed ministers, including Petter, who were evidently susceptible to this indoctrination, in the liberated doctrine of the covenant. Far more was going on under the palms than only the enjoyment of southern California scenery and flora.

That these conditions in the covenant—in the covenant theology of Petter and, as he correctly supposed, in the covenant theology of the liberated—are real, full-fledged conditions, upon which God and his saving work in the child depend, Petter made plain by the example of them that he gave from earthly life. "A settler can home-stead a section of land on condition that he tills so much of it." Petter then asked rhetorically: "Is he a Pelagian heretic, minimizing the counsel and efficacy of God over his tilling, when he calls this government stipulation a condition that is set before him?"[17]

To which question the answer is, "The settler is not a Pelagian settler, if he stands toward the government and demands his rights on the basis of his performing the prescribed condition, for home-steading was by works. But a minister who teaches a child to take his stand toward God with regard to his covenant salvation according to this (revelatory) example is a Pelagian heretic and responsible for the child's eternal damnation. Such a minister denies salvation by grace alone in the covenant and teaches baptized children that covenant salvation is by and on the basis of the child's works."

Writing after the schism had happened, Petter frankly acknowledged the influence of the liberated doctrine of the covenant on

17 A. Petter, "The Covenant, XLIII—Correspondence," *Concordia* 6, no. 20 (Thursday, December 8, 1949): 4.

himself and his colleagues in the churches that now were separated from the Protestant Reformed Churches. Having referred to the "contact with the Liberated of the Netherlands," Petter added: "In that contact most of our ministers tried to form an evaluation of their covenant views and many of us felt that also in our criticism of the conditional element in their theology we must not go to the extreme that would lose our understanding of the conditional expression and relations as they are used in the Bible in the administration of the covenant and in the preaching of the full counsel of God."[18]

Rev. John D. De Jong and Rev. Bernard Kok, both ardent supporters of a conditional covenant and vehement foes of the Declaration, let the cat out of the bag as early as 1949. In that year they traveled to the Netherlands and met with leading churchmen of the Reformed Churches in the Netherlands (liberated). At the meeting they informed the theologians of the liberated churches that

> [Hoeksema's] conception regarding election [in relation to the covenant] is not church doctrine. No one is bound by it. Some are emitting a totally different sound. Their [Kok's and De Jong's] opinion was that most (of the Prot. Ref.) do not think as Rev. Hoeksema and Rev. Ophoff [about the covenant]. And sympathy for the Liberated was great also in the matter of their doctrine of the covenant… For the conception of the Liberated there is ample room.

This was the report of the meeting of the two Protestant Reformed ministers and the liberated theologians by Prof. Benne Holwerda, of the liberated churches, in a letter to a liberated immigrant in Canada.[19]

Contributing to the strife in the churches were two events that were intimately related to the Declaration and its provisional adoption by the synod of 1950. One was the preaching by a prominent Protestant Reformed minister of the covenant doctrine that

---

18 A. Petter, "Was the Split Necessary?" *Reformed Guardian* 1, no. 9 (November 27, 1953): 9.

19 The quotation is from the letter of Professor Holwerda in the article by G. M. Ophoff, "Revs. De Jong and Kok in The Netherlands," *Standard Bearer* 25, no. 20 (August 1, 1949): 470.

the Declaration condemned as contrary to the Reformed confessions. The minister was Rev. Hubert De Wolf, who was prominent by virtue of being one of the pastors of First Protestant Reformed Church in Grand Rapids, Michigan. At the time it was the largest and most influential congregation in the denomination. On April 15, 1951, after synod's provisional adoption of the Declaration and in deliberate contradiction of the Declaration, De Wolf preached a sermon explicitly defending the doctrine of a conditional covenant promise to all who hear the preaching of the gospel. The sermon climaxed in the statement "God promises everyone of you that, if you believe, you shall be saved."[20] This sermon divided the congregation and inflamed the entire denomination. Members of the church protested the sermon to the consistory.

The second event that contributed to the division of the Protestant Reformed Churches during the year between the provisional adoption of the Declaration in June 1950 and its intended decisive adoption in June 1951 was the virtual deposition of a Protestant Reformed minister and an elder by a nominally Protestant Reformed congregation in Canada. This congregation was made up of Dutch immigrants whose strong covenant convictions were contrary to the beliefs of the Protestant Reformed Churches as expressed in the Declaration. In January 1951, again *after* the provisional adoption of the Declaration by the synod of 1950, the nominally Protestant Reformed consistory in Hamilton, Ontario, Canada deposed Rev. Herman Veldman and elder Sam Reitsma for preaching and upholding in the congregation the doctrine of an unconditional covenant with the elect only.[21]

Not only did this action make the debate about the Declaration more heated, but it also lent urgency to the request by the mission committee for a "form" to be used in organizing new churches, particularly new churches whose membership might be Dutch immigrants committed to a doctrine of the covenant diametrically opposite that of the Protestant Reformed Churches. The mission committee of the Protestant Reformed Churches had organized

---

20 *Acts of Synod, Protestant Reformed Churches in America, 1954,* 54.

21 For this history, see Gertrude Hoeksema, *A Watered Garden: A Brief History of the Protestant Reformed Churches in America* (Grand Rapids, MI: Reformed Free Publishing Association, 1992), 173–74.

the congregation in Hamilton as a Protestant Reformed church prior to the adoption of the Declaration and evidently without making the difference over the covenant an issue.

In these circumstances of controversy and open division, the synod of 1951 met. The main matter on its agenda was the adoption of the Declaration, decisively. Also included in the agenda were numerous protests against the Declaration from both ministers and churches. Indeed, Classis West, one of the two classes comprising the denomination, protested the adoption of the Declaration and overtured the 1951 synod "to declare that as churches we are not at all ripe and ready to compose a Declaration, and that the need for it has NOT [sic] been proven."[22]

Because of the opposition to the Declaration on the part of Classis West, which could only be expected to be voted by its delegates at synod, final adoption of the Declaration by the synod of 1951 was doubtful when synod assembled.

---

22 *Acts of Synod, 1951*, 108.

Chapter Two

The Content of the Declaration

The content of the document that was so controversial in the Protestant Reformed Churches between the synods of 1950 and 1951, that would take up so much of the time and energy of the synod of 1951, and that would eventually occasion schism in the Protestant Reformed Churches concerns the doctrine of the covenant of grace. The Declaration is not, nor did it intend to be, a thorough, systematic exposition of the biblical truth of the covenant. As the name of the document expresses, it is the statement of certain fundamental truths concerning the covenant. These are truths that were being contested in the Protestant Reformed Churches at the time of the adoption of the Declaration. They are truths that have been contested in the broader Reformed tradition. Indeed, they are truths that are the subject of controversy in reputedly conservative Reformed and Presbyterian churches at present, due especially to the heresy of the theological movement that calls itself the federal vision.

The Declaration is divided into four main sections, headed by a preamble and by what amounts to an introduction.

PREAMBLE

The preamble establishes the use in the Protestant Reformed Churches of the document. This use is exclusively "for the organization of prospective churches."[1] As the preamble goes on to make

---

1   Declaration of Principles of the Protestant Reformed Churches, in *Confessions and Church Order*, 412.

clear, this use is not that the Declaration is the basis of the organization of churches. The basis of the organization of churches is "Scripture and the confessions."[2] But the Declaration must be used by the mission committee and the missionaries of the Protestant Reformed Churches in the instruction of people who will be organized, so that their understanding of the covenant is in harmony with the principles set forth in the Declaration.

No group may be organized as part of the federation of Protestant Reformed Churches that dissents from the principles concerning the covenant that are declared in the Declaration.

Basic to this use of the Declaration is the conviction of the Protestant Reformed Churches that the truths of the covenant that the Declaration confesses are the teaching of Scripture and the Reformed confessions concerning the gospel itself. The principles of the covenant specified by the Declaration are fundamental truths of the gospel. Deviations from these truths are departure from the gospel of grace.

This conviction explains the willingness of the Protestant Reformed Churches to adopt the Declaration in the face of the threat, indeed likelihood, of schism in the small denomination, with all the grief, pain, suffering, and loss that schism inflicts.

INTRODUCTION

Immediately following the preamble are two short paragraphs that amount to an important introduction to the Declaration, although they do not have this heading. These introductory paragraphs state the basis of the Protestant Reformed Churches as Reformed churches. The basis is "Scripture as the infallible Word of God and...the Three Forms of Unity."[3] The three forms of unity are the Belgic Confession of Faith, the Heidelberg Catechism, and the Canons of Dordt. Reformed Christians readily understand that the meaning is that Scripture is the basis of the churches, but Scripture as summarized and explained by the three forms of unity.

To the statement of the basis of these churches is added that the Protestant Reformed Churches "accept the liturgical forms used in

2   Ibid.
3   Ibid.

the public worship of our churches." These forms are then named. The importance of this addition is that these forms function in the churches as minor confessions. They are regarded as in harmony with and, in certain respects, as elaborations of the three forms of unity, so that these forms also are authoritative. Especially the baptism form is important in the controversy over the covenant and plays an important role in the Declaration.

Establishment of the authoritative creeds and forms enables the Declaration to appeal to these creeds and forms in affirming the basic truths of the covenant.

The force and significance of the Declaration are that the Declaration demonstrates that the Reformed creeds teach a certain definite doctrine of the covenant of grace—the doctrine sketched in the Declaration. Thus the significance of the Declaration is that it brings the creeds to bear on a longstanding debate, even controversy, in the Reformed tradition over two different, and often conflicting, doctrines of the covenant.

The content of the Declaration is not new doctrinal statements. The Declaration only expresses the teachings of the creeds, major and minor. This is the answer to the charge that was leveled against the Declaration by foes within and outside the Protestant Reformed Churches, namely, that the Declaration is a fourth Reformed creed in the Protestant Reformed Churches.

This was the charge against the Declaration by the liberated Reformed theologian Klaas Schilder. Schilder, whose doctrine of the covenant was repudiated by the Declaration as unreformed, watched with great interest as events concerning the Declaration unfolded in the Protestant Reformed Churches. After the synod provisionally adopted the Declaration, Schilder wrote a series of articles in his church paper *De Reformatie* (The reformation) that were later translated into English and published as *Extra-Scriptural Binding—A New Danger.*[4] Protestant Reformed ministers opposed to the Declaration echoed the charge.

But this charge was mistaken. The Declaration is an expression of the teachings of the existing Reformed creeds concerning

---

4   The brochure in English translation is found in Jelle Faber, *American Secession Theologians on Covenant and Baptism* (Neerlandia, Alberta, Canada: Inheritance Publications, 1996), 55–167.

fundamental truths of the covenant. This was the description of the Declaration by the synod of 1951, which adopted the Declaration decisively. The motions adopting the Declaration read either that "there is nothing objectionable to the Declaration of Principles… because it is the truth expressed in our confessions"[5] or that "the Declaration…is the expression of the Three Forms of Unity, with regard to certain fundamental principles."[6]

That this analysis of the Declaration is indeed correct is evident to every reader. The Declaration is mostly quotations of the creeds and the liturgical forms. There is no quotation of Scripture. There is hardly any explanation of the creeds that are quoted, much less argumentation on the basis of them. In the Declaration the Reformed creeds speak concerning the covenant of grace.

To the charge of Schilder and others—a charge that is still raised today—that the Protestant Reformed Churches, on their own, apart from the Reformed community of churches, have added a fourth creed to the Reformed body of confessions or otherwise engaged in illegitimate church political conduct in adopting the Declaration, the response is that the charge is patently false. Finding themselves troubled with controversy over the doctrine of the covenant and in danger of being overrun by a covenant doctrine that contradicts the confession of the Protestant Reformed Churches from the beginning of their history and that the churches judge to be false doctrine, the Protestant Reformed Churches settled the controversy and defended themselves by allowing the creeds to speak to the issues in debate.

Surely this is not only proper Reformed church political behavior, but also the behavior that is demanded of a Reformed denomination of churches. Synods must settle doctrinal disputes, especially when the unity of the denomination is threatened. For a Reformed denomination of churches, the basis of the decisive settlement must be Scripture, as authoritatively summarized by the Reformed confessions.

The only weighty attack on the adoption of the Declaration would be one that contends with the Declaration's statements concerning

---

5   *Acts of Synod, 1951*, 189.

6   Ibid., 193.

the creedal doctrine of the covenant of grace. The attack must show that the principles that the Declaration claims to derive from the confessions are in fact at loggerheads with the confessions, or at the very least, without foundation in the confessions.

The claim of the Declaration to express the teaching of the creeds with regard to fundamental truths of the covenant has implications for other Reformed churches that also subscribe to the three forms of unity and use the Reformed baptism form. If the Declaration is right in its claim to express the truth of the Reformed creeds, all the Reformed churches are bound to confess the doctrine of the covenant according to the principles set forth in the Declaration. For them to differ with the Protestant Reformed Churches regarding the fundamental principles of the covenant is not merely to disagree with a specifically Protestant Reformed synodical decision, but is to be in conflict with the Reformed confessions.

It is not my intention in this chapter to go into the content of the Declaration in detail. I have written a short commentary on the Declaration, which is included in this book as an appendix. To it, I refer the interested reader for a more detailed explanation of the content of the Declaration.

Here I call attention to the principles themselves, indicating that they are indeed fundamental truths of the Reformed understanding of the gospel as framed in the Reformed confessions.

THE COVENANT PROMISE

The first principle is that the promise of the gospel is God's gracious oath to and about his elect, that he will save them by faith in Jesus Christ.[7] The promise of God, specifically the covenant promise, "I will be the God of you and of your children," is particular—to those who believe according to divine election. The preaching, or announcing, of the promise comes to all hearers, unbeliever as well as believer, reprobate as well as elect. But the promise is always addressed to the believer and makes plain that it is for the believer. Canons 2.5 teaches the particular promise: "Moreover the promise of the gospel is, that whosoever believeth in Christ crucified shall not perish, but have everlasting life." The article goes on to

---

7   Declaration of Principles, in *Confessions and Church Order*, 413.

affirm that "this promise, together with the command to repent and believe, ought to be declared and published to all nations, and to all persons promiscuously and without distinction, to whom God out of his good pleasure sends the gospel." But the promise is to and for "whosoever believeth in Christ crucified."[8] The promise is not general. It is not to and for every hearer of the preaching of the promise. It is emphatically not to or for the one who does not believe in Christ crucified.

The preaching of the gospel is neither a gracious offer nor a gracious promise on the part of God to all who hear the preaching, which offer or promise depends for its saving efficacy upon the acceptance of it by the hearer. Such a conception of the preaching is that of the Arminian heresy, which the Synod of Dordt condemned in 1618–19 in the Canons.

The principle of a particular promise applies to the doctrine of the covenant inasmuch as the controversy over the covenant in which the Protestant Reformed Churches were embroiled in the late 1940s and early 1950s concerned the question of whether God graciously, but conditionally, promises salvation to all the physical offspring of believers, or unconditionally promises to establish the covenant with the elect children in Christ Jesus.

COVENANT AND ELECTION

A second principle concerning the covenant in the Declaration is the affirmation that election is "the sole cause and fountain of all our salvation," including *covenant* salvation and including the faith by which those baptized infants who are saved receive covenant salvation.[9]

That election is the sole source of all salvation is the express teaching of Canons 1.9: "Election is the fountain of every saving good; from which proceed faith, holiness, and the other gifts of salvation, and finally eternal life itself, as its fruits and effects."[10]

---

8   Canons of Dordt 2.5, in Philip Schaff, ed., *The Creeds of Christendom: With a History and Critical Notes*, 6th ed. (New York: Harper and Row, 1931; repr., Grand Rapids, MI: Baker, 2007), 3:586.

9   Declaration of Principles, in *Confessions and Church Order*, 416–17.

10   Canons of Dordt 1.9, in Schaff, *Creeds of Christendom*, 3:583.

This truth is applicable to the right doctrine of the covenant inasmuch as the covenant of grace is and bestows salvation. If election is the cause and fountain of all salvation, it is the cause and fountain of *covenant* salvation. Election thus is closely related to the covenant. Election governs the covenant, its grace, its blessings, and its salvation. These truths about election and covenant are denied by the conception of the covenant that the Declaration condemns.

UNCONDITIONALITY

A third principle is that the covenant and the promise by which God establishes and maintains the covenant with one of the elect are unconditional. That is, the promise and the covenant do not depend upon the will or work of the object of the promise and beneficiary of the covenant. This fundamental truth follows from the truth that the covenant and its salvation are gracious and from the truth that the covenant and its salvation flow from and are the effect of election, which is unconditional. By definition, grace means not dependent on the sinner, that is, unconditional. And as election is unconditional, according to the Reformed confession, so also are the covenant and its salvation, which have their source in election.

This principle bears heavily on the doctrine of the covenant by virtue of the fact that the doctrine of the covenant rejected by the Declaration teaches that the covenant is conditional. On this view God graciously promises the covenant and its salvation to all the baptized children alike, and he even graciously establishes the covenant with all of them alike. But the maintenance of the covenant and final salvation in the covenant depend on works that the children must perform, namely, believing and obeying. The covenant is conditional. In the end, it depends on the baptized children, rather than on the baptizing God.

The Declaration observes that the promise of the covenant must be unconditional by virtue of the fact that infants obviously cannot perform conditions. But the promise of the covenant is to and for the infants of godly parents, *in their infancy*: "I will be the God of your seed, that is, your *infant* children."

In support of the unconditionality of the covenant promise, the Declaration appeals to Canons 2.8. This article of the Reformed creed teaches that Christ died only for the elect and that his death's "saving efficacy...should extend to all the elect, for bestowing upon them alone the gift of justifying faith, thereby to bring them infallibly to salvation."[11] The argument of the Declaration on behalf of an unconditional promise to only the elect children is based on the truth that God's promise of covenant salvation can only promise that which Christ has objectively merited by his death. Christ's death merited covenant salvation only for the elect children of godly parents, for Jacob, not for Esau. Therefore, God can promise salvation only to the elect children. This argument rests, ultimately, on the close relation between the acquiring and the bestowing of salvation by a sovereign, righteous God.

But the Declaration also appeals to another prominent, conclusive passage in the Reformed creeds, Question and Answer 74 of the Heidelberg Catechism. Such is the importance of this reference to the confessions that in connection with it occurs one of the rare instances of overt argumentation in the Declaration. Question and Answer 74 contends for infant baptism, partly on the ground that "to them no less than to their parents" is "promised" "the Holy Ghost, who works faith."[12]

This promise to the infants must be unconditional because, as already noted, infants cannot, and cannot be expected to, perform conditions.

But the argument of the Declaration here is still more profound. The question in the great controversy over the covenant in 1950, as also today in the wider community of Reformed churches, is this: Is the covenant promise made conditionally to all the physical offspring or made unconditionally to the elect children, as the true, spiritual seed of Abraham and of godly parents? Those who defend a conditional covenant promise to all the children alike maintain that the condition is faith. But in Question and Answer 74 the Catechism teaches that the promise includes not only the establishment of the covenant and the blessing of covenant salvation—"redemption from sin...through the blood of Christ"—*but also the child's faith*, by which he or she will consciously receive

---

11   Canons of Dordt 2.8, in ibid., 3:587.

12   Heidelberg Catechism Q&A 74, in ibid., 3:331.

and enjoy the covenant, its blessings, and salvation. If God in the covenant promise swears that he will give the objects of the promise—here, the infant children of believing parents—"the Holy Ghost, who works faith." God promises to give the children faith itself. The covenant promise, "I will be the God of your children," must be understood as including giving to them the Holy Ghost, who works faith, and therefore giving them faith itself.

From this teaching of the Catechism, it follows, first, that since God certainly fulfills his promise, the covenant promise refers to the elect children only, for only the elect children receive faith from God as his gift. As the Canons teach, "election is the fountain of every saving good; from which proceed[s] faith."[13]

Second, it follows from this teaching that faith is not a condition unto the covenant and its blessings, upon which a general promise depends for its realization. Faith is the gift of God to the elect children, for whom alone Christ earned faith by his death, according to Canons 2.8.

Defenders of a conditional covenant are unable to answer, and therefore always refuse to answer, the question: Is the gift of faith also included in the covenant promise of God to the children of believers?

Question and Answer 74 of the Heidelberg Catechism answers this question, in the context of infant baptism and the covenant.

> Are infants also to be baptized?

> Yes; for since they, as well as their parents, belong to the covenant and people of God, and both redemption from sin *and the Holy Ghost, who works faith*, are through the blood of Christ promised to them no less than to their parents.[14]

Therefore, the unconditional covenant promise, a fundamental truth of the covenant of grace, is an expression of the Reformed confessions.

---

13 Canons of Dordt 1.9, in ibid., 3:583.
14 Heidelberg Catechism Q&A 74, in ibid., 3:331. The emphasis is added.

CONCLUSIONS

Section III of the Declaration draws conclusions from these and other passages of the Reformed confessions. In good Reformed fashion, in order to make the covenant doctrine of the Declaration unmistakably clear, section III expresses the conclusions of the preceding sections both negatively and positively.

On the basis of the Reformed creeds, the Declaration repudiates the teaching that "the promise of the covenant is conditional and for all that are baptized."[15] Further proof for this repudiation of error is adduced from Canons 1.6–8 and from the doctrinal part of the Reformed baptism form. Here, in the Declaration, the baptism form, which dates from the late 1500s and is the common, authoritative form of all Reformed churches in the Dutch Reformed tradition, rises to prominence.

The baptism form concludes with a prayer of thanksgiving. This prayer thanks God that he "hast forgiven us and our children all our sins through the blood of Thy beloved Son Jesus Christ, and received us through Thy Holy Spirit as members of Thine only begotten Son, and adopted us to be Thy children, and sealed and confirmed the same unto us by holy baptism."[16] What is said here about the baptized children of believers incontrovertibly applies only to the elect children, proving that reference throughout the form to the covenant of God with the children of believers is to the elect children. In keeping with the view of Scripture that only the elect children are the true, spiritual children of the covenant, the baptism form regards the elect children as the children of the covenant and has them in mind when it speaks of our children. This, the prayer of thanksgiving makes indisputably plain.

The Declaration also repudiates two other errors concerning the children of believers. One is that presupposed regeneration is the basis of infant baptism. The Declaration raises this error, in order expressly and publicly to reject it, not because it was or is a real problem in the Protestant Reformed Churches, but because the proponents of the doctrine of a conditional covenant with all the children alike charge that the Protestant Reformed Churches'

---

15 Declaration of Principles, in *Confessions and Church Order*, 424.

16 Form for the Administration of Baptism, in ibid., 260.

covenant doctrine includes the error of presupposed regeneration.

The Protestant Reformed Churches do not teach, and never have taught, presupposed regeneration. They do not suppose, contrary to Scripture and experience, that all their physical offspring are regenerated. Much less do they teach that this false supposition is the basis of infant baptism.

The members of the Protestant Reformed Churches know from both Scripture and bitter experience that some of the offspring of godly parents manifest themselves, when they come to physical maturity, as unregenerated and unconverted unbelievers. They either leave the church or become the objects of Christian discipline. Not all are necessarily elect. Some may be reprobate, as the history of the twin sons of Isaac and Rebekah in Genesis 25 and 27 shows and as is the doctrine of Paul in Romans 9.

In the covenant, God does not bind himself to save every physical descendant of Abraham or of believing parents. God is sovereign in salvation and damnation not only on the mission field, but also in the sphere of the covenant.

An implication is that no Christian parent and no child may *presume* upon the gracious promise of the covenant. Parents may not presume that their children will be saved, regardless that the parents do not rear them in the nurture and admonition of the Lord Jesus, which rearing is the means that God uses to save covenant children. The children may not presume that they are and will be saved, regardless that they do not believe on Jesus Christ with the true faith that produces a life of holiness, which faith is the means God uses to justify and save the elect children of believers.

The covenant promise does not allow for unbelieving presumption, but rather works, addresses, and assures faith.

On the other hand, repudiation of presupposed regeneration does not imply ignorance or denial of God's usual regeneration of elect infants in their early childhood, even in their infancy.

The ground of infant baptism is not presupposed regeneration.

Rather, "The ground of infant baptism is the command of God and the fact that according to Scripture He established His covenant in the line of continued generations."[17]

---

17 Declaration of Principles, in ibid., 430.

The other error regarding the covenant of God with the children of believers that the Declaration repudiates is the teaching that "the promise of the covenant is an objective bequest on the part of God, giving to every baptized child the right to Christ and all the blessings of salvation."[18] This teaching is an aspect of the doctrine of a conditional covenant with all the children alike, which the Declaration condemns on the basis of the Reformed creeds.

The doctrine of a conditional covenant likes to employ the objective/subjective distinction. No, it acknowledges, God does not promise or bestow covenant salvation *subjectively* to and upon every baptized child, that is, God does not promise to regenerate every child. But yes, it insists, God gives every child the covenant and its salvation *objectively*, and this involves giving every child the right to Jesus Christ. The doctrine of a conditional covenant adds that this objective bequest on God's part will become subjective and saving if the child will perform the prescribed and prerequisite conditions.

Everything about this notion is erroneous. First, Scripture and the creeds do not know of an objective bequest of Christ in distinction from, indeed in separation from, a subjective bestowal of the savior.

Second, the covenant promise, "I will be your God and the God of your children," contains all of salvation as its content. The promise is God himself in Jesus Christ and the fullness of salvation in him.

Third, the promise of the covenant is to and for the elect only, whether regarding an "objective" bequest or a "subjective" bequest.

Fourth, neither all humans nor all the physical offspring of believers have a "right to Jesus Christ." Only those for whom Christ died to earn this right have a right to Christ and his salvation. But, as Canons 2.8 teaches, "Christ by the blood of the cross" purchased both the right to salvation and all of salvation for "all those, and those only, who were from eternity chosen to salvation," according to the "sovereign counsel and most gracious will and purpose of God the Father."[19]

Fifth, if any human possesses the objective "right" to Christ by the bequest of God, he will, and must, also subjectively receive the

18 Ibid., 426.
19 Canons of Dordt 2.8, in Schaff, *Creeds of Christendom*, 3:587.

Christ to whom he has a right. Were God not to give him Christ subjectively, by the work of the Spirit in his heart, God would be unjust. According to God's own word, he has a *right* to Christ. To separate subjective (salvation) from objective (salvation) is to charge God with injustice. God must give a person his rights.

Section III of the Declaration is also positive. Positively, section III expresses that the Reformed creeds teach that "God surely and infallibly fulfills His promise to the elect."[20]

An obvious, damning weakness of the doctrine of the conditional covenant is that God fails to fulfill his covenant promise in countless instances, both in the Old Testament and in the New Testament. Promising to be the God of every physical child of believing parents, God nevertheless proves *not* to be the God and savior of many of them. He promises, but he does not *fulfill* the promise.

The reason for this failure, according to the advocates of this covenant doctrine, is the failure of the objects of the promise to perform the conditions upon which the fulfillment of the promise depends. The promise is conditional. Although the explanation of the nonfulfillment is the weakness and sinfulness of the children, the fact remains that God solemnly promises but does not keep the promise. In the language of Question and Answer 74 of the Heidelberg Catechism, God on his part promises to many children that he will give them the Holy Ghost, who works faith, but fails to execute the promise by not giving to them the Spirit and faith.

On the very face of it, this theology portrays God as false and faithless—false and faithless to his word of promise.

Clearly evident at this point in the covenant controversy is the *heresy* of the doctrine of a conditional covenant. The promise of covenant salvation depends on the deed of the sinner who is to receive the covenant salvation. Evidently, God on his part is desirous to establish his covenant with all the children of the godly. Only this explains his extending his gracious promise to all of them. But the refusal of some to perform the condition frustrates the gracious will of God. How this differs from the Arminian theology of universal, resistible grace, which the Reformed faith condemns as heresy, no one has yet satisfactorily explained.

---

20 Declaration of Principles, in *Confessions and Church Order*, 426.

Adding to the gravity of the error is the necessary implication that the reason the promise is fulfilled with some children, in distinction from others, is that these children did perform the prerequisite conditions, in distinction from the others. Covenant salvation therefore is due, finally, to the will and work of the saved sinner. Those children who enjoy covenant salvation have made themselves to differ from those children who remain unsaved. But the Reformed creeds deny this, on the basis of Scripture.

> But that others who are called by the gospel obey the call and are converted, is not to be ascribed to the proper exercise of free-will, whereby one distinguishes himself above others equally furnished with grace sufficient for faith and conversion (as the proud heresy of Pelagius maintains); but it must be wholly ascribed to God, who, as he hath chosen his own from eternity in Christ, so he...confers upon them faith and repentance.[21]

The application of this article of the creed to the children of godly parents is plain. Some children grow up to show themselves unbelieving and disobedient. That other children obey the call of the gospel and are converted is not to be ascribed to their performing the condition of faith, whereby one child distinguishes himself above others equally furnished with covenant grace sufficient for faith and conversion (as the proud heresy of Pelagius maintains); but it must be wholly ascribed to God, who as he has chosen his own from among the offspring of believing parents, so he confers upon them faith and repentance.

Although Canons 3–4.10 does not express the biblical basis for its teaching, the creed confesses the word of the apostle in 1 Corinthians 4:7: "For who maketh thee to differ from another? and what hast thou that thou didst not receive? now if thou didst receive it, why dost thou glory, as if thou hadst not received it?"

Not only does this aspect of the doctrine of a conditional covenant detract from the promise of God by having it depend for its fulfillment on the sinner—in this case, the *infant* sinner—but it also detracts from the promise by eviscerating it of its fulfillment.

A promise, specifically the covenant promise of God, has three

---

21 Canons of Dordt 3–4.10, in Schaff, *Creeds of Christendom*, 3:589–90.

essential elements: the good will of the one who promises to do or to give what is promised; the content of the promise—the promised good; and the realization, or fulfillment, of the promise. The conditionality of the promise of conditional covenant theology strips the covenant promise of its all-important fulfillment. The promise does not include the fulfillment. Its fulfillment is not part of the promise. The fulfillment depends not upon the promise itself, or upon the one promising, who is God himself, but upon something else and upon another.

This stripping of the covenant promise of the element of realization, or fulfillment, is a grievous assault on the covenant promise, which is the promise of the gospel. The divine promise of the covenant is glorious, not only because of the gracious will of the promising God and because of the marvelous content, but also because the promise carries with itself, guarantees, and accomplishes that which is promised.

So important is this third element—the certain realization of the promise, by the power of the promise itself—that, lacking this element, the promise is worthless. What good is it to me that God wills my salvation and vows to give me this great good, if the promise does not assure me the realization of itself—my salvation? And of what worth is this promise, if its fulfillment depends upon highly uncertain me?

Against this grievous attack on the promise of God, the Protestant Reformed Churches confess, in their Declaration, "that God surely and infallibly fulfills His promise to the elect."[22]

RESPONSIBILITY

In section III of the Declaration are found several paragraphs affirming the full responsibility of all who are in the sphere of the covenant, both elect believers and reprobate unbelievers. Much of this was lacking in the original draft of the Declaration, provisionally adopted at the synod of 1950. It was added by amendment at the synod of 1951.

Objection to the original draft of the Declaration included the criticism that, although confessing the sovereignty of God in covenant

---

22 Declaration of Principles, in *Confessions and Church Order*, 426.

salvation, it said little or nothing about covenant responsibility.

Synod 1951 responded to this criticism about a lack of responsibility by inserting three paragraphs affirming and describing responsibility, with the creedal basis.

The original draft was not completely lacking in the confession of responsibility. It contained this paragraph:

> We maintain…that when He so fulfills His promise and establishes His covenant, the elect are not mere stocks and blocks, but obliged and willing to fulfill their part of the covenant, to love the Lord their God with all their heart and mind and soul and strength, to forsake the world, to crucify their old nature, and to walk in a new and holy life.[23]

As the phrase "stocks and blocks" indicates, also this original warning against concluding from divine sovereignty in salvation to human passivity, or worse, is confessional. The third and fourth heads of doctrine of the Canons, which confess that the conversion of the sinner is wholly the work of God the Holy Spirit, maintain human responsibility in these words:

> But as man by the fall did not cease to be a creature endowed with understanding and will, nor did sin, which pervaded the whole race of mankind, deprive him of the human nature, but brought upon him depravity and spiritual death; *so also this grace of regeneration does not treat men as senseless stocks and blocks*, nor take away their will and its properties, neither does violence thereto; but spiritually quickens, heals, corrects, and at the same time sweetly and powerfully bends it, that where carnal rebellion and resistance formerly prevailed a ready and sincere spiritual obedience begins to reign, in which the true and spiritual restoration and freedom of our will consist.[24]

But what was inserted by the synod of 1951 was more complete than the brief, original statement of responsibility.

---

23 *Acts of Synod, 1950*, 89–90.
24 Canons of Dordt 3–4.16, in Schaff, *Creeds of Christendom*, 3:591–92. Emphasis is added.

> We maintain…the sure promise of God which He realizes in us as rational and moral creatures not only makes it impossible that we should not bring forth fruits of thankfulness but also confronts us with the obligation of love, to walk in a new and holy life, and constantly to watch unto prayer.
>
> All those who are not thus disposed, who do not repent but walk in sin, are the objects of His just wrath and excluded from the kingdom of heaven.
>
> That the preaching comes to all; and that God seriously commands to faith and repentance; and that to all those who come and believe He promises life and peace.[25]

This affirmation of covenant responsibility is both thorough and distinctively Reformed.

It is distinctively Reformed in that it does not jeopardize or compromise God's sovereignty in salvation, but accentuates the sovereignty of grace, even as it is based on sovereignty. The relation between divine sovereignty and human responsibility is not this: God is sovereign, *but* the saved sinner is also responsible. Invariably, this account of the relation between sovereignty and responsibility—placing the two in conflict with the adversative "but"—goes on to explain the relation in such a way that human responsibility vitiates divine sovereignty.

Rather, the Declaration states that the "sure promise of God… makes it impossible that we should not bring forth fruits of thankfulness." The promise of the covenant realizes itself in such a way that it makes the covenant child spiritually alive unto God. He or she lives a thankful life of faith and obedience, as the "fruits" of the working of the promise. The child's faith and obedience, therefore, are not conditions upon which the covenant depends—to the overthrow of divine sovereignty—but "fruits of thankfulness."

Such a conception of covenant life and responsibility is in harmony with Lord's Days 24, 31, and 45 of the Heidelberg Catechism; Canons 3–4.12, 16–17; Canons 5.14; Canons 3–4, rejection of Error 9; the Belgic Confession, Article 24; and the forms for

---

25 Declaration of Principles, in *Confessions and Church Order*, 426.

baptism and the Lord's supper, which are adduced in proof of this view of responsibility.

The Declaration adds that the promise produces such fruits in the covenant child not apart from his consciousness and will, but by his thinking and willing: "the sure promise...which He realizes in us *as rational and moral creatures*...confronts us with the obligation of love, to walk in a new and holy life, and constantly to watch unto prayer."

Always, God deals with humans as rational, moral creatures. This is the Reformed confession in Canons 3–4.16, which the Declaration quotes: "As man by the fall did not cease to be a creature endowed with understanding and will...so also this grace of regeneration does not treat men as senseless stocks and blocks."[26]

Also, those children who do not repent but live profanely, like Esau of old, are responsible. They make themselves the objects of God's "just wrath and excluded from the kingdom of heaven." The reason for this guilt, according to the Declaration, is that "the preaching comes to all; and...God seriously commands to faith and repentance."

The promise is not common to all. But the *preaching* of the promise *is* common to all. And the preaching includes the command to all the children without exception, "Believe, and repent."

It adds something important to the Declaration's affirmation of responsibility that the Declaration states in these paragraphs that the promise of salvation is "to all those who come and believe" in response to the preaching. Earlier, the Declaration has laid down the dogmatic truth that the promise is for the elect. But this statement does not assure the individual child of his being the object of the promise personally. Nor does it assure him of salvation. For the only way one can know himself elect is by coming to Christ by a true faith in response to the preaching of the gospel. The form, therefore, that the particular covenant promise takes to all of the elect children is this: "Come to Christ, and to every one who comes, I will give the life and peace of the covenant of grace." Coming to Christ, they thus know themselves also as chosen by God in Christ in eternity.

---

26 Canons of Dordt 3–4.16, in Schaff, *Creeds of Christendom*, 3:591.

AUTONOMY OF THE CONGREGATION

The last section of the Declaration is an anomaly. It concerns church polity, specifically the autonomy of the local congregation. This was not at issue in the Protestant Reformed Churches in the covenant controversy in the early 1950s. Undoubtedly, this was added to indicate an important truth that the Protestant Reformed Churches and the liberated Reformed had in common, despite their doctrinal differences over the covenant. Both maintained the autonomy of the local church against the oppression of a hierarchical form of church government, from which both were convinced they had suffered at the hands of synods and classes.

One surmises that tacking the church political item on at the end of the Declaration may have been motivated by a forlorn hope on the part of the Protestant Reformed Churches that there yet might be ecumenical relationship with the Reformed Churches in the Netherlands (liberated), even though the Protestant Reformed Churches condemned the liberated doctrine of the covenant. That this was the purpose of this last section of the Declaration is suggested by Hoeksema's explanation of the section, shortly before the meeting of synod 1951. "Although we quite fundamentally differ with the Reformed Churches, maintaining Art. 31, of the Netherlands, in respect to the question concerning the promise of the covenant, we are glad to agree with them on the important church-political principle of the autonomy of the local church."[27]

If a lingering hope of preserving a relationship with the liberated Reformed churches is the explanation of the inclusion of the last section of the Declaration, this hope was futile and doomed. As soon as the Protestant Reformed Churches adopted the Declaration decisively in 1951, Dr. Schilder wrote, already in November 1951, that contact of the liberated Reformed churches with the Protestant Reformed Churches was finished.[28]

---

27 Herman Hoeksema, "The Declaration of Principles," *Standard Bearer* 27, no. 14 (April 15, 1951): 318.

28 In characteristic, vividly figurative language, Schilder described the end of the relationship as "*De Kous is Af*" [The stocking is finished]. The article appeared in the November 17, 1951 issue of the Dutch magazine *De Reformatie*. Hoeksema summarized the article and responded to it in an editorial, "The Stocking is Finished" (*Standard Bearer* 28, no. 7 [January 1,

Whatever may have been the motive for insisting on right church polity at the end of a document devoted to the truth of the covenant, the matter itself is important. Christ is not only the savior-priest in the covenant. He is also the governing king. Proper church government is, and ought to be, important to all Reformed churches.

FUNDAMENTAL TRUTHS

One who reflects on the principles of the Declaration concerning the covenant must recognize that these principles are simply the fundamental truths of the gospel of salvation by sovereign, particular grace alone, grounded upon the eternal, unconditional decree of predestination. These are what the Reformed faith, indeed the faith of Protestant Christianity, has always confessed and for which Reformed churches have always contended.

They are not the novel ideas of Herman Hoeksema, although largely to him goes the credit for developing these truths in their application to the covenant of grace. They are not the unique beliefs of the Protestant Reformed Churches, although belief and confession of them are increasingly the unique glory of the Protestant Reformed Churches, as other Reformed churches either become ashamed of the confession of sovereign grace or cravenly permit the denial of it in their fellowship, specifically by the tolerance of the heresy of the federal vision.

Neither are these truths merely abstract, impractical, dogmatical reasonings, far removed from and irrelevant to the preaching of the gospel, unless the confession of sovereign (irresistible) grace by the Protestant Reformation of the sixteenth century, by John Calvin, and by the Canons of Dordt is also arid, abstract theology, of little use to man and obnoxious to God.

But the principles of the Declaration are the fundamental truths confessed especially in the Canons of Dordt. They are part and parcel of the Reformed (logical) system of doctrine embodied in the Reformed confessions. They are the main elements of the biblical doctrine of salvation, from its source in unconditional election to its goal in unconditional preservation. The Declaration applies

1952]: 148–53).

these principles to the doctrine of the covenant and to God's saving work in Christ in the covenant, especially his salvation of the children of believing parents.

The Declaration, therefore, is an important document, not only for the Protestant Reformed Churches but also for all Reformed churches.

As Hoeksema observed about the synod that adopted the Declaration, "It...will undoubtedly go down in history as one of the most important synods—if not the most important—that to date was ever held." He left it an open question whether he meant the history of the Protestant Reformed Churches or the history of the entire Christian church.[29]

---

29 Herman Hoeksema, "Our Synod of 1951," *Standard Bearer* 28, no. 3 (November 1, 1951): 52.

Chapter Three

Decisive Adoption

The Protestant Reformed Synod of 1950 had adopted the Declaration, but only provisionally. The decisive adoption was postponed to the synod of 1951. The decision postponing final adoption to the synod of 1951 is intriguing.

1. That synod subjec: this entire document to the approval of the churches.

2. If no objection is offered, to adopt this at our next synod.

3. To adopt this in the meantime as a working hypothesis for our mission committee and for our missionaries in the organization of churches.[1]

The one who proposed this postponement was Herman Hoeksema. Responding to the charge by an enemy of the Declaration that Hoeksema and Ophoff were forcing the Declaration upon the members of the Protestant Reformed Churches with "foolish haste and rash eagerness," Ophoff wrote: "To avoid even the semblance of hierarchy it [the synod of 1950] advised that before adopting the 'Declaration' the churches take it in study for a year. And the motion was Rev. Hoeksema's."[2]

Two things about the synodical decision postponing decisive adoption of the Declaration to the synod of 1951 are intriguing. First, the phrase "if no objection is offered" indicates the

---

1 *Acts of Synod, 1950,* 90.

2 G. M. Ophoff, "Rev. Petter's 6[th] and 7[th] Instal[l]ments," *Standard Bearer* 27, no. 10 (February 15, 1951): 236.

assumption that there would be no objection to the Declaration at the synod of 1951. In light of the vehement and numerous objections against the Declaration at the synod of 1951, this assumption now appears foolish.

But at the time the decision to postpone adoption was made, there were solid reasons for the assumption. First, the synod of 1950 adopted the Declaration, provisionally, virtually unanimously and with little or no discussion. Second, as a "form" for use in organizing churches among the Dutch, liberated immigrants in Canada, the Declaration had been requested by the very men who later so vigorously objected to it. The Declaration was not the result of a proposal by Hoeksema and Ophoff, but the result of a request from the reverends A. Cammenga, B. Kok, H. De Wolf, and J. Blankespoor. These men were either the missionary or members of the mission committee who came to synod 1950 requesting such a "form."

A third reason for the assumption that there would be no objection at the synod of 1951 against adopting the Declaration had to have been the nature of the Declaration itself. Consisting almost entirely of quotations of the confessions, it expressed what Hoeksema and Ophoff had taught all the ministers in the Protestant Reformed Churches about the covenant from the beginning of the history of the churches and what the Protestant Reformed Churches had always confessed and preached about the covenant in opposition to the covenant doctrine of Christian Reformed theologian Prof. William Heyns. And the covenant doctrine of the liberated Reformed, which the Declaration condemned, is essentially that of Heyns.

Although I reserve a more thorough examination of the covenant theology of Heyns for later in this book, an understanding of the history of the struggle over the Declaration and its doctrine of the covenant requires familiarity with Heyns and the condemnation of his doctrine of the covenant in the Protestant Reformed Churches from the very beginning of their separate existence.

William Wynand Heyns was a longtime, prominent, and influential theologian in the Christian Reformed Church (CRC). He served as professor of theology at the seminary of the CRC from 1902 to 1926. He taught seminarian Herman Hoeksema.

What Heyns taught seminarian Hoeksema and the many other

students who sat under his instruction was that the covenant is a conditional "contract" that God establishes by gracious promise with every baptized child without exception. All the children alike are in the covenant. He also taught that in this covenant grace toward every child God gives every child a certain "subjective," covenant grace *that enables every child to perform the covenant conditions upon which the covenant promise and the covenant itself depend.*

In his *Handboek voor de Catechetiek* (Manual for catechetics), Heyns asked concerning "the subjective significance of inclusion in the covenant for the catechumens" (that is, for Heyns, all the baptized children who are being instructed by the church in the catechism classes). Appealing to John 15:1–8, Jesus' instruction concerning branches of the vine that bear fruit and branches that are fruitless, among other passages, Heyns asserted that God gives to all the children of believers, without exception, an "inner capability" to produce the fruit of good works that God requires of them in the covenant.

William Heyns, the Christian Reformed professor of theology who formed the dominant covenant theology of the CRC, against which Hoeksema developed the covenant doctrine of the PRC, and whose doctrine of the covenant is condemned by the Declaration with that of Schilder and the liberated.
Photograph from Calvin College archives.

> Scripture teaches us the gift of a subjective grace to each child of the covenant, that is, to each child of believers, sufficient to bring forth good fruits. To *each* child of the covenant, not to the elect only, for it is abundantly plain that a grace that cannot be lost is not meant, a grace that flows out of election...Therefore, a subjective grace, which a) is sufficient in connection with spiritual operation by

the means of grace for the producing of good fruits of faith and obedience...[and] b) does not exclude the possibility that the child of the covenant remains unfruitful, even in spite of the most outstanding operations by the means of grace.[3]

By virtue both of the gracious promise to all the children and of subjective, covenant grace within all the children, all the children without exception are "a seed upon which God has performed covenant work and to which God has given capability for [spiritual] impressions. And that [subjective, covenant] grace [which God has given to every child], he [every child] must cherish and cultivate, so that they 'may increase and grow up in the Lord Christ,' in the way of a Christian and godly rearing."[4]

Since this subjective, covenant grace, which can be lost, is supposed to develop gradually into mature Christian faith and life and to end in eternal life, if a child performs the requisite conditions, it is undeniably evident that Heyns taught a saving grace of God that is resistible, and often resisted.

Heyns denied, explicitly, that the covenant, the covenant promise, and covenant grace have election as their source and cause, and therefore that election governs the covenant. Heyns' covenant theology cut the covenant loose from election.

Heyns formed the covenant theology of the Christian Reformed Church.

Against this conception of the covenant, Hoeksema reacted from the earliest days of his public ministry, indeed already when he was a student under Heyns. In one of his earliest published works, *De Geloovigen en Hun Zaad* (Believers and their seed),[5] Hoeksema exposed Heyns' covenant doctrine as

---

3   W. Heyns, *Handboek voor de Catechetiek* (Grand Rapids, MI: Eerdmans-Sevensma, n.d.), 141, 144–45. The emphasis is Heyns'. The translation of the Dutch is mine.

4   Ibid., 146.

5   Herman Hoeksema, *De Geloovigen en Hun Zaad* (Grand Rapids, MI: C. J. Doorn, n.d.). The work has been translated into English by Homer C. Hoeksema and published as *Believers and Their Seed: Children in the Covenant* (Grandville, MI: Reformed Free Publishing Association, 1997). All quotations are from this English translation.

"Arminianism Injected Into the Covenant."[6]

Against Heyns' doctrine of the covenant, Hoeksema early developed his own doctrine of the covenant, building on a prominent theology of the covenant in the Dutch Reformed tradition—a tradition that runs through the Secession theologians Hendrik De Cock and Simon van Velzen,[7] to Herman Bavinck.[8] This tradition of covenant theology originates with John Calvin and other reformers.[9] This doctrine of the covenant acknowledges that election governs the covenant. It regards the covenant as established by God unconditionally with the elect children of believers only, according to God's gracious covenant promise to Christ Jesus, as head of the covenant of grace, and to those children of godly parents who belong to Christ.

Hoeksema not only charged Heyns' doctrine of the covenant with Arminianism and Pelagianism. He also attributed the Christian Reformed Church's adoption of the false doctrine of universal, resistible grace in the preaching of the gospel (the well-meant offer), which resulted in Hoeksema's deposition by the Christian Reformed Church and in the separate existence of the Protestant Reformed Churches, to the influence of Heyns' doctrine of the covenant upon the majority of Christian Reformed ministers, who had been trained by Heyns.[10]

Throughout the history of the struggle of the Protestant Reformed Churches regarding the Declaration, Hoeksema contended that the

6   Ibid., 14–28.

7   For the covenant doctrine of the fathers of the Secession of 1834 (in the Netherlands), see David J. Engelsma, "The Covenant Doctrine of the Fathers of the Secession," in *Always Reforming: Continuation of the Sixteenth-Century Reformation*, ed. David J. Engelsma (Jenison, MI: Reformed Free Publishing Association, 2009), 100–136.

8   For the covenant doctrine of Herman Bavinck, see David J. Engelsma, "Bavinck on Covenant and Election," in *Covenant and Election in the Reformed Tradition* (Jenison, MI: Reformed Free Publishing Association, 2011), 163–176.

9   For Calvin's doctrine of the covenant, see David J. Engelsma, "Calvin's Doctrine of the Covenant: Union with Christ," "Calvin's Doctrine of the Covenant: Covenant and Election," and "Calvin's Doctrine of the Covenant: Elect Infants in the Covenant," in ibid, 83–126.

10   Hoeksema, *Believers and Their Seed*, 14.

covenant doctrine of Schilder and the liberated Reformed, which the foes of the Declaration in the Protestant Reformed Churches were defending, is essentially that of Heyns.

Representative is what Hoeksema wrote in response to a letter by Professor Holwerda of the liberated Reformed churches.

> Now as I have made very plain before, the covenant theology of Heyns is condemned by our churches, when they rejected the First Point of 1924. There is no room any more for Heynsianism in the Prot. Ref. Churches. And unless you can make clear, professor, that the Heynsian theology is not the same as the theology of the liberated, we need no official act of synod to express that there is no room in our churches for their conception.[11]

Were Hoeksema's charge that the covenant doctrine of the liberated is essentially that of William Heyns to have stuck, the result would have been fatal to the cause of the enemies of the Declaration in the Protestant Reformed Churches. They were intent on gaining approval of the liberated doctrine of the covenant as Reformed and, therefore, at least an option for Protestant Reformed ministers and members. It behooved them, therefore, to deny the charge of Heynsianism, which they consistently did, to the deception of the people who followed them.

The main ground for the denial that the covenant doctrine of the liberated is the same as that of Heyns was that the liberated did not teach a subjective grace of God in all the baptized children, enabling them to believe, if only they were willing. Hoeksema pointed out the fallacy of this denial.

> Although this theory of preparatory grace is peculiar to Heyns, yet it is by no means the main principle of his conception of the covenant.

> The conception of Heyns is that the covenant of God is principally and essentially His promise. That promise is a bequest on the part of God to all that are baptized. God bequeaths upon all the children of believers all the

---

11 Herman Hoeksema, "The Open Letter of Prof. Holwerda," *Standard Bearer* 26, no. 1 (October 1, 1949): 9.

blessings of salvation. He gives them the right by testament to the riches of grace. And He solemnly seals His bequest, this testament, this objective right to the forgiveness of sins and eternal life, to them all by baptism. But this promise is conditional. And the condition connected with the promise is faith and repentance. All have the promise. On the part of God the bequest is made to all by promise. God swears to all in baptism that their names are written in His testament. But the blessings promised are applied only to those that accept the promise by faith.

That is Heynsianism....

This is common grace applied to the covenant.

Hoeksema added: "And this conception of the covenant is accepted uniformly by all the Liberated."[12]

Indicating the conviction that the covenant theology of the liberated is the same, essentially, as that of Heyns and his consequent fear that the covenant doctrine of Heyns was gaining ground in the Protestant Reformed Churches, Ophoff called for action to preserve the truth of the covenant in the churches.

We must all be agreed, certainly, that it is high time that we as churches take an official stand in the matter of the covenant-theology of Heyns. It is high time that we as churches officially pronounce that theology heretical and its contrary—the covenant-theology of the Protestant Reformed—Scriptural and true. This has already been done, as was explained. But let us do it again, that all may understand that we do have a covenant-theology that is binding, and that we allow no room at all in our communion to its contrary—the covenant-theology of Heyns and of the Liberated.[13]

---

12 Herman Hoeksema, "Let Us Be Brotherly," *Standard Bearer* 27, no. 10 (February 15, 1951): 224–25. Hoeksema then demonstrated from liberated theologians R. H. Bremmer and C. Veenhof that the liberated doctrine of the covenant is the same as that of Heyns (224–25).

13 G. M. Ophoff, "Revs. De Jong and Kok in The Netherlands," *Standard Bearer* 25, no. 20 (August 1, 1949): 472–73.

Today it is recognized and publicly acknowledged by almost all theologians, including liberated theologians, that Hoeksema's and Ophoff's charge was factually correct: The covenant doctrine of Schilder and the liberated is essentially that of Heyns. Liberated theologian Jelle Faber has recently affirmed the "kinship of [Schilder]... with Heyns."[14] The tradition of the covenant theology of the theological heirs of Schilder, Holwerda, Cornelis Veenhof, and the other founding fathers of the Reformed Churches in the Netherlands (liberated) "is the tradition of especially...Heyns" and others.[15]

In 1950, Hoeksema, Ophoff, and the other sound Protestant Reformed ministers would not have supposed that the confession of the Protestant Reformed doctrine of the covenant, in opposition to a variation of Heyns' doctrine of the covenant, could become as controversial as proved to be the case.

The second intriguing aspect of the decision of the synod of 1950, adopting the Declaration provisionally, is its assertion that "in the meantime" the Declaration would be "a working hypothesis" in the churches. As of the synod of 1950, the Declaration would have some authority in the churches as a synodical decision. It would function as a "working hypothesis" for the missionaries and the denominational mission committee. Although adopted only provisionally in 1950, the Declaration might not thereafter be ignored.

This aspect of the synodical decision bears on the public teaching of a Protestant Reformed minister in the "meantime," that is, between the synods of 1950 and 1951. During this "meantime," a Protestant Reformed minister deliberately, definitely, and provocatively contradicted the doctrine of the covenant adopted by the synod of 1950 in the Declaration of Principles. This public teaching would eventually become the catalyst of the schism in the Protestant Reformed Churches in 1953.

The minister involved could argue that the adoption of the Declaration and its doctrine of the covenant was only provisional. But the provisional Declaration was already a "working hypothesis" in the denomination. The minister had to have known that by preaching the covenant theology condemned by the Declaration,

---

14 Faber, *American Secession Theologians*, 52.

15 Ibid., 53.

he was flouting the wisdom and will of the denomination as expressed by the adoption of the Declaration and thus raising "discord, sects, and mutiny in [the] church."[16]

ATMOSPHERE OF OPPOSITION

Whatever may have been the assumption of Hoeksema and the synod of 1950 concerning a lack of objection to the Declaration, and in contrast to the near unanimity of the decision of the synod of 1950 adopting the Declaration provisionally, the synod of 1951 convened in an atmosphere of strong, vocal, and determined opposition to the Declaration on the part of a large segment of the denomination, both ministers and laity. Ominously for the Declaration, the party of opposition included half of the sixteen delegates to the synod.

During the year between the synod of 1950 and the synod of 1951, a barrage of criticism was leveled against the Declaration. Much of the criticism, although by no means all of it, came from ministers and consistories in Classis West. *Concordia*, one of the two magazines that circulated among the members of the Protestant Reformed Churches, kept up a steady drum-beat of opposition to the proposed adoption of the Declaration by the synod of 1951.

Rev. Petter began a series of articles critical of the Declaration in the October 14, 1950 issue of *Concordia*. The series continued until the meeting of synod in June 1951. In this series Petter objected to the Declaration, "both to its origination and its contents." He held that the document "does not advance the truth and the unity of the church." He condemned the Declaration as "confusing, obstructive, and divisive."[17] In a later article Petter judged the Declaration to be a "hierarchical imposition upon the Churches." Regarding its contents, his "main objection is that it excludes out of our communion brethren who are Calvinistic, Reformed, Biblical."[18]

---

16 This is the language of the Reformed Form for the Administration of the Lord's Supper, describing those who are barred from the sacrament, in *Confessions and Church Order*, 269.

17 A. Petter, "Among Our Treasures: The Brief Declaration (V)," *Concordia* 7, no. 20 (Thursday, December 7, 1950): 3.

18 A. Petter, "Among Our Treasures: The Brief Declaration (VI)," *Concordia* 7, no. 21 (Thursday, December 21, 1950): 3.

Andrew Petter, Protestant Reformed minister who opened up the public controversy over the covenant by writing in defense of the Schilderian, conditional covenant in the church paper *Concordia*. He was soon opposed by Rev. Ophoff, writing in the *Standard Bearer* and thus, the battle was joined. Strangely, Petter was expelled from his pastorate in Chatham, Ontario, Canada by a consistory that was nominally Protestant Reformed, but in reality liberated.

Other ministers joined in the loud chorus of opposition in *Concordia*. To this chorus, liberated immigrants in Canada and liberated writers in the Netherlands added their voices.[19]

Worthy of note, especially in light of the fact that he unexpectedly became a delegate to the synod of 1951, is that the editor of *Concordia*, Rev. Peter De Boer, defended the Declaration, particularly with regard to its content. Immediately after the synod of 1950, De Boer, a minister in Classis West, published the Declaration in full in *Concordia*. Having taken note of the leading objections to the Declaration by many of his colleagues, De Boer wrote: "I am in full agreement with the contents of the document. I am convinced our churches say nothing more than the Three

---

19 Rev. De Jong roundly criticized the Declaration and pleaded for its rejection in a series of articles in which he recounted his recent travels in the Netherlands and visits of liberated Reformed theologians and people. A liberated immigrant in Canada (where the Protestant Reformed mission committee was working at the time with such immigrants) criticized the Declaration for its confession of an unconditional promise only to the elect children. He insisted on the liberated doctrine, that the covenant promise is addressed by God to every child of Abraham and of godly parents without exception and that this promise is conditional (*Concordia* 7, no. 18 [Thursday, November 9, 1950]: 2). Prominent liberated author K. C. van Spronsen wrote in the November 9, 1950 issue of *Concordia* (vol. 7, no. 18, pp. 4–5) and several times afterward sharply criticizing the Declaration and defending the liberated theology of covenant.

Peter De Boer, the Protestant Reformed minister in Classis West whose unplanned delegation to the synod of 1951 and crucial vote in defense of the Declaration were key to the decisive adoption of it by the synod.

Forms state, than they have ever stated, and with which I am in agreement, as I believe our churches, our people and our ministers have ever been."[20]

In a later issue of *Concordia*, De Boer judged the liberated doctrine of the covenant, which the Declaration was opposing and which his colleagues in the West were defending, as "in general the Heynsian covenant view" and as "anti-confessional."[21] These views, publicly expressed, kept De Boer off the delegation of Classis West to the synod of 1951.

Also the *Standard Bearer* published articles and letters criticizing the Declaration and warning against its adoption at the synod of 1951. Even though editor Herman Hoeksema and his colleague, Professor Ophoff, staunchly defended the Declaration and fervently urged its adoption, the pages of the magazine were opened to those who opposed the Declaration, and the opponents seized the opportunity.

As early as the issue of September 15, 1950, barely three months after the provisional adoption of the Declaration, the *Standard Bearer* published criticism of the Declaration in the form of loaded questions by Rev. Blankespoor, a minister in Classis East.[22] Also

---

20 P. De Boer, "Concerning the Declaration of Principles," *Concordia* 7, no. 15 (Thursday, September 28, 1950): 2–3. In subsequent editorials, De Boer defended the principle of the Declaration that confessed that the promise of the covenant is unconditionally to and for the elect children only.

21 P. De Boer, "That Declaration," *Concordia* 7, no. 17 (Thursday, October 26, 1950): 2.

22 J. Blankespoor, "Contribution," *Standard Bearer* 26, no. 22 (September 15, 1950): 516.

Rev. Kok, likewise a minister in Classis East, weighed in against the Declaration in a piece bluntly titled, "The Declaration, A Mistake."[23] So also did several other ministers, several other lay members of Protestant Reformed congregations, and several Dutch, liberated immigrants in Canada.

George M. Ophoff, with his colleague in the Protestant Reformed seminary, Herman Hoeksema, was the main proponent and defender of the Declaration and its theology of the covenant. The fiery Ophoff was, if anything, a fiercer foe of the theology of a conditional covenant than was Hoeksema.

Throughout the year between the synods, in every issue of the *Standard Bearer* both Hoeksema and Ophoff continuously defended the Declaration from all attacks on it and urged the necessity of adopting it at the synod of 1951. Ophoff carried on a running controversy with Rev. Petter, who was criticizing the Declaration and openly defending a conditional covenant in the pages of *Concordia*. Occasionally Hoeksema and Ophoff had support in the *Standard Bearer* from colleagues who shared their convictions about the Declaration and its theology of covenant.

This controversy in the church papers alone would have assured a difficult and tense synod in 1951, as well as tough going for the Declaration. But there were other factors that contributed to the certainty that synod would be a hard-fought, bloody, doctrinal and ecclesiastical battlefield. One factor was the reality that the large and influential First Church in Grand Rapids had been stricken and divided by controversy over the issues of the doctrine of the covenant addressed by the Declaration. This was due to the public preaching of the covenant doctrine condemned by the Declaration

23 B. Kok, "The Declaration, A Mistake," *Standard Bearer* 27, no. 7 (January 1, 1951): 153–56.

by one of the pastors of First Church in a sermon on April 15, 1951. Members had protested the sermon, but the matter was as yet unresolved when synod met in 1951. The entire denomination was well aware of this conflict in First Church between Hoeksema and Ophoff on the one hand and Hoeksema's co-pastor, Rev. De Wolf, on the other hand.

Another factor was the deposition of a Protestant Reformed minister by the consistory of his nominally Protestant Reformed, but actually liberated Reformed, church in Canada. In January 1951, the consistory of the Protestant Reformed church in Hamilton, Ontario, Canada suspended from office its minister, Rev. Herman Veldman. The official charge was insubordination, but the real cause was the opposition to Veldman's teaching on the covenant by those who were, and intended to remain, liberated in their doctrine of the covenant. Veldman preached and taught the doctrine of the unconditional covenant, that is, the covenant doctrine confessed by the Declaration.[24]

A third factor was a letter from Benne Holwerda, professor at the liberated seminary in the Netherlands and a leading liberated theologian and churchman, to the immigrants in Canada with whom the Protestant Reformed Churches were doing mission work—the mission work that occasioned the adoption of the Declaration. Holwerda had written that at a meeting with liberated ministers, including Holwerda, two Protestant Reformed ministers who had been visiting the Netherlands had assured the group that Hoeksema's "conception regarding election, etc. is not church doctrine [in the Protestant Reformed Churches]. No one is bound by it. Some are emitting a totally different sound." Holwerda added that "their [the two Protestant Reformed ministers'] opinion was that most (of the Prot. Ref.) do not think as Rev. Hoeksema and Rev. Ophoff. And sympathy for the Liberated was great also in the

---

24 See Herman Hoeksema, "The Rev. H. Veldman Suspended From Office," *Standard Bearer* 27, no. 9 (February 1, 1951): 198–200. Elder S. Reitsma was deposed from office for his support of Veldman. For Veldman's own account of his suspension and subsequent deposition, as well as of the deposition of Reitsma, see Herman Veldman, "Hamilton's Letter to All Our Consistories" and "The End of Hamilton," *Standard Bearer* 27, no. 10 (February 15, 1951): 231–34; no. 11 (March 1, 1951): 251–254.

matter of their doctrine of the covenant...For the conception of the Liberated there is ample room."

Holwerda then advised the Dutch immigrants to affiliate with the Protestant Reformed Churches, on the following conditions:

> Let them then as Liberated preserve their contact with Holland [that is, with the liberated theologians] by all means, and also spread our literature...If Rev. Hoeksema's conception was binding, I would say, Never join. Now I believe, however, that accession is calling; and then so that the Liberated also help to disseminate the dogmatical wealth of Holland [that is, the liberated covenant theology] in the Prot. Ref. Churches.[25]

Although this letter was discovered and publicized in 1949, it and the controversy and distrust it engendered continued to disturb and divide the churches up to the synod of 1951.

A fourth factor was the warning from the Reformed Churches in the Netherlands (liberated) that adoption of the Declaration would mean the end of the relationship between them and the Protestant Reformed Churches. This relationship was dear to Protestant Reformed men on both sides of the issue of the Declaration. Immediately following the provisional adoption of the Declaration by the synod of 1950, Schilder himself had sent a warning shot across the bow of the Protestant Reformed Churches with regard to the adoption of the Declaration. In the series of articles in *De Reformatie* that were later translated and published as "Extra-Scriptural Binding—A New Danger," Schilder made perfectly plain that adoption of the Declaration would spell the end of the relationship between the two denominations. "Our members who emigrated to America or Canada cannot and may not bind themselves to the *Brief Declaration*...For as long as possible we want to keep the newly developed ties from being needlessly severed."[26]

---

25 The letter of Professor Holwerda was published, whether wisely or unwisely, by Professor Ophoff in an article titled, "Revs. De Jong and Kok [the two Protestant Reformed ministers referred to in Holwerda's letter] in The Netherlands: A Report," *Standard Bearer* 25, no. 20 (August 1, 1949): 470.

26 Schilder, "Extra-Scriptural Binding—A New Danger," in Faber, *American Secession Theologians*, 72–73.

In fact, a classis of the Canadian Reformed [liberated] Churches sent a letter to the Protestant Reformed synod of 1951, calling on the synod to "retract the Declaration of Principles." The letter warned that if synod adopted the Declaration, "we see the way to you indeed barred, so that we in this situation, to our great grief, would not be able to have relations with each other." The letter concluded by describing the Declaration as merely "theological constructions," in contrast to the "simple Word of our God."[27] The end of church relations with the liberated churches in the Netherlands and with the Canadian Reformed Churches would also mean the end of the work of the Protestant Reformed Churches with the Dutch immigrants in Canada and therefore also of the growth of the Protestant Reformed Churches that this work promised.

As if all of these factors were not enough, synod met in the knowledge, or at least the well-grounded fear, that adoption of the Declaration would almost certainly result in schism. Ministers and consistories opposed to the Declaration gave warning that they and their supporters would not submit to a decision adopting the Declaration. In the statement of objection to the Declaration that the consistory of Hull, Iowa, sent to synod 1951, the consistory warned:

> Adopting this Declaration will unquestionably mean division in our churches and, hence, may well lead to a deplorable schism and a separation of brethren who belong together. We are convinced that, as of today, we as Protestant Reformed people can live peaceably and harmoniously under one ecclesiastical roof. It is extremely doubtful that this would be possible if we should adopt this Declaration.[28]

The president of Hull's consistory was Rev. De Jong, who was an especially outspoken adversary of the Declaration. In his personal protest against the provisional adoption of the Declaration by

---

27 Letter to the 1951 synod of the Protestant Reformed Churches from the April 1951 classis of the Canadian Reformed Churches (*Acts of Synod, 1951*, 99–100). The translation of the Dutch is mine. Adding insult to injury, upon adopting the Declaration the 1951 synod had to inform the Canadian Reformed Churches that synod had lost its letter and therefore could not respond (*Acts of Synod, 1951*, 196–97).

28 *Acts of Synod, 1951*, 121–22.

synod 1950 and long, vehement objection against decisive adoption of the Declaration by synod 1951, De Jong threatened schism if his and others' objections to the Declaration were not heeded.

> I can not suppress the fear that an adoption of this Declaration now, and as it is proposed by the Synod of 1950, would bring great disruption, tear our churches, divide our constituency, and separate brethren who belong together.[29]

Under such pressure did the 1951 synod of the Protestant Reformed Churches assemble and take up its work of adopting (or rejecting) the Declaration, which had been adopted provisionally by the previous synod.

A DIVIDED SYNOD

On the agenda of the synod was an overture from Classis West, one of the two classes making up the denomination. The overture informed synod that Classis West objected to the Declaration and asked synod not to adopt it.

> In view of the overwhelming documentary criticism presented by the various consistories in re the Proposed Declaration of Principles, Classis [West] overtures synod to declare that as churches we are not at all ripe and ready to compose a Declaration, and that the need for it has NOT [sic] been proven.[30]

By adopting and making its own the protest and overture of the Bellflower, California, consistory, Classis West overtured synod 1951 "to repudiate the action of syn.[od] of 1950," adopting the Declaration provisionally.[31]

Oddly, in view of its adamant opposition to the Declaration, Classis West also expressed agreement with the content of the Declaration, a striking feature of almost every objection against

---

29 Ibid., 155.

30 Ibid., 108. The complete overture from Classis West against the Declaration runs from pages 108 to 162. It contains all the documents from members and consistories for and (mostly) against the Declaration.

31 Ibid., 112.

the Declaration by ministers and consistories: "We agree with the essential teaching of the principles [in the Declaration] and express our willingness to fulfill our calling to formulate this teaching when instructed to do so being presented with error within our churches."[32]

The fact that virtually every adversary of the Declaration, whether minister or consistory, felt constrained, in his or its statement of opposition, to acknowledge agreement with the truths expressed by the Declaration allows for only one explanation. All knew well, and thus admitted, that the doctrine of the covenant contained in the Declaration was the doctrine that the Protestant Reformed Churches had confessed throughout their history. All of them, in this way, admitted also that the covenant doctrine that the Declaration condemned was diametrically opposed to the doctrine that the Protestant Reformed Churches had confessed from the very beginning of their history as a separate denomination of Reformed churches.

Nevertheless, Classis West as a body rejected the Declaration. The decision of Classis West repudiating the Declaration meant that all eight delegates of Classis West to synod 1951 were committed opponents of the Declaration. They were sure to vote to denounce and overturn the provisional adoption of the Declaration by the synod of 1950.

The eight delegates of Classis East, in contrast, were known, ardent supporters of the Declaration. These delegates included Rev. Herman Hoeksema, who had written the Declaration, and his colleague in the Protestant Reformed Seminary, Professor Ophoff, who was, if this was possible, a fiercer foe of the conditional covenant of the liberated Reformed than was Hoeksema.

Classis East had taken a decision "that we adopt the Declaration and overture synod to do likewise."[33] Significantly, Classis East had also decided "that what the Declaration expresses is the truth and language as believed and spoken by our P. R. C. since the beginning of its history."[34] Several ministers and elders of Classis East

---

32 Ibid.
33 Ibid., 107.
34 Ibid.

had recorded their negative votes on the motions to adopt the Declaration.[35] But none of them was delegated to synod.

There can be little doubt that Rev. De Boer's cynical analysis of the synod of 1951 as a "packed Synod" was correct. Writing in *Concordia* shortly before the meeting of the synod of 1951, De Boer predicted, "without hesitation," that "this Synod will be, and sadly I write this, a 'packed' Synod." He explained:

> A packed Synod is a Synod whose delegates have been deliberately chosen with a view to their particular stand in regard to the one main matter of interest. It is my opinion that the delegation of Classis West was voted largely with a view to the way they would vote on the Declaration [and therefore De Boer himself was bypassed]…I presume that the same will be true of the delegation Classis East will have chosen by the time this article appears in print.[36]

It would not have been the first time. It will not be the last.

A REMARKABLE SERMON

In view of the extreme tension, indeed division, at synod with regard to the Declaration, the pre-synodical sermon by Herman Hoeksema was remarkable. Without commenting explicitly on the great issue before the synod, Hoeksema, being Hoeksema, nevertheless gave direction from Scripture concerning the issue.

That he preached the sermon at all is noteworthy. The custom, if not rule, is that the president of the previous synod leads the pre-synodical worship service and preaches the sermon. The president of the previous synod—the synod of 1950—was Rev. Richard Veldman. A prominent, influential minister in the churches in those days, Veldman was also a delegate to the synod of 1951. But he did not preach the sermon. Hoeksema did. How this came about was reported in the *Standard Bearer*. "Rev. H. Hoeksema had been requested by the president of the Synod of 1950 to preach this pre-synodical sermon."[37] Veldman deferred to Hoeksema, and

---

35 Ibid.

36 P. De Boer, "The Synod of 1951," *Concordia* 8, no. 5 (Thursday, April 12, 1951): 2.

37 J. Howerzyl, "The Synod of 1951," *Standard Bearer* 27, no. 18 (June 15,

Hoeksema did not hesitate, indeed was, no doubt, glad for the opportunity.

Deliberately, in view of the looming debate and decision regarding the Declaration, Hoeksema chose his text, 2 Timothy 2:19: "Nevertheless the foundation of God standeth sure, having this seal, The Lord knoweth them that are his. And, Let every one that nameth the name of Christ depart from iniquity."

With the courage, zeal for sound doctrine, and sense of responsibility for the welfare of the churches characteristic of the man, Hoeksema instructed the synod concerning the doctrinal issue at stake in the coming debate over the Declaration and pointed out the right direction that the synod should go. He did this without mentioning the matter of the Declaration, except in passing and then jocularly.[38]

The Veldman brothers, Rev. Herman (l) and Rev. Richard (r), both of whom featured largely in the history of the adoption of the Declaration. Herman vigorously defended the Declaration and its theology of the covenant in the *Standard Bearer*. For proclaiming sovereign grace in the covenant, he was summarily deposed from office by the liberated consistory of the Hamilton Protestant Reformed Church in Canada. Richard was president of the synod of 1950 that adopted the Declaration provisionally, and he voted for its final adoption as a delegate to the synod of 1951. He deferred to Hoeksema, his uncle, regarding preaching the pre-synodical sermon at the synod of 1951, thus enabling Hoeksema to preach the powerful, though ignored, sermon on 2 Timothy 2:19. With his consistory R. Veldman advised the consistory of First Church in 1953 to suspend Rev. De Wolf and to depose the elders who supported him.

1951): 431.

38   At one point, midway through the sermon, knowing that on the minds of

But Hoeksema made clear that the foundation of the church is Jesus Christ as revealed in Scripture and that Scripture is defined for us by the Reformed confessions. In this connection, Hoeksema made bold to claim that "the truth which has been defined and expressed by the Protestant Reformed Churches is the purest delineation of the sure foundation of God that standeth!"[39]

He emphasized that God has laid this foundation of the church and that man had nothing to do with it.

Upon this foundation, exhorted the hardly beset founder of the Protestant Reformed Churches, the synod of 1951 must build. He warned that those who build, or attempt to build, "on the foundation of man, on the foundation of Arminian grace or any other common grace, do not build on the foundation of the church. They do not. Only the foundation that has this seal, 'God knows those that are his,' has the sign of authority."[40]

The delegates of Classis West, determined to repudiate the Declaration, must have been squirming in their seats. None, however, was convicted. None changed his vote.

THE UNPACKING OF SYNOD

It was apparent to the entire synod, as also to the entire Protestant Reformed denomination that was looking on with hope or fear, that the synod was divided into two equal groups and therefore seemingly deadlocked. The eight delegates of Classis West would repudiate the Declaration and refuse to adopt it decisively. The eight delegates of Classis East would vote to adopt the Declaration. But every motion receiving a tie vote fails. The Declaration, therefore, seemed doomed to rejection.

In recognition of the division between the two sets of delegates, the matter of the Declaration was given to a pre-advice committee of four. This committee of pre-advice would bring the matter of

all in his audience was the Declaration of Principles, Hoeksema said, "And if I may make a declaration, beloved, (I don't mean the Declaration of Principles. I mean if I may make a personal declaration.)" (*Acts of Synod, 1951*, 13).

39 Ibid., 13.
40 Ibid., 17.

the Declaration to the floor of synod and advise synod concerning its treatment of the Declaration. Reflecting the division of the synod, this committee of four consisted of two delegates of Classis East (favoring the Declaration) and two delegates of Classis West (objecting to the Declaration).

As could have been, and undoubtedly was, expected, the committee of pre-advice brought two radically different pieces of advice to the synod. The two committee members of Classis West advised synod to "heed the protest of Classis West…and to declare: That the action of the 1950 Synod in reference to the Declaration of Principles is contrary to our Protestant Reformed way and regulations and to Reformed principles of ecclesiastical actions," that is, to repudiate the Declaration.[41]

The two committee members from Classis East advised, "Synod should…adopt the Declaration."[42]

Synod responded to the two differing recommendations by considering first the advice to repudiate the Declaration. The motion to adopt this advice was made on Tuesday afternoon, June 12. On Friday afternoon, June 15, some three days later, synod voted on the motion to repudiate the Declaration. The motion failed. The *Acts of Synod, 1951* informs us that the vote was nine to seven.[43]

Obviously, the vote was close. One vote made the difference between doubtful deadlock and decisive rejection of the overture of Classis West to repudiate the Declaration.

But how is this one vote to be explained? All eight of the original delegates to synod from Classis West were opposed to the Declaration and in favor of repudiating it. Did one change his mind at the last minute?

The explanation is the extraordinary providence of God governing the synod of 1951. Men may pack a synod. God can unpack it. And in 1951 he did. One of the minister delegates of Classis West, Rev. M. Gritters, who was openly and adamantly opposed to the Declaration, took sick. His alternate was one of the two ministers in the West who approved the Declaration, Rev. De Boer (which

---

41   Ibid., 168.

42   Ibid., 170.

43   Ibid., 182.

was undoubtedly the reason he had not been chosen as a primus delegate to the synod).

De Boer had made his approval of the Declaration known publicly. Writing in *Concordia*, of which magazine he was editor, soon after the synod of 1950 had adopted the Declaration provisionally, he declared to the membership of the Protestant Reformed Churches, "I am in full agreement with the contents of the document [the Declaration]."[44] In a subsequent issue of the magazine, De Boer judged the liberated doctrine of the covenant, which the Declaration condemned, as "Heynsian" and "anti-confessional."[45] At the Friday morning, June 15, session of synod, at which the first and decisive ballot would be cast regarding the Declaration, "Rev. De Boer [took] the place of Rev. M. Gritters."[46] De Boer voted with the eight delegates of Classis East to reject the overture of Classis West repudiating the Declaration. Hence the majority: nine to seven.

Having considered and rejected the advice of one part of its divided committee of pre-advice, synod was ready to consider the advice of the other part. These two men, both delegates of Classis East, advised adoption of the Declaration, in accordance with the recommendation to synod of Classis East.

But before it would take up this advice, synod decided to

---

44 P. De Boer, "Concerning the Declaration of Principles," *Concordia* 7, no. 15 (Thursday, September 28, 1950): 3.

45 P. De Boer, "That Declaration," *Concordia* 7, no. 17 (Thursday, October 26, 1950): 2. De Boer also noted, shrewdly, that the leadership of the Protestant Reformed Churches, which included Hoeksema, was responsible for giving the membership of the Protestant Reformed Churches the impression that the Protestant Reformed Churches and the Reformed Churches in the Netherlands (liberated) were doctrinally one. The synodical Committee for Correspondence with Other Churches had opened the pulpits of the Protestant Reformed Churches to Schilder when the Dutch, liberated theologian had visited the United States in 1947. De Boer also faulted the leadership of the churches for informing both the members of the liberated churches and the members of the Protestant Reformed Churches, on more than one occasion, that the differences between the covenant doctrine of Schilder and the doctrine of the Protestant Reformed Churches were not confessional and essential (P. De Boer, "It's All Your Fault," *Concordia* 9, no. 1 (Thursday, February 14, 1952): 2–3.

46 *Acts of Synod, 1951*, 181.

"adjourn until the last Wednesday of September." The reasons given for this postponement of further action on the Declaration were that "1/ we must still enter into the main part of our agenda, that is the contents of the Declaration; 2/...some of the delegates cannot remain and must go home; 3/...especially Classis West did not finish the material that was before it, that is the protests against the Declaration."[47]

Synod reconvened on September 26, 1951. Almost at once, it was moved to declare "that the Declaration of Principles as amended by Classis East is the expression of the Three Forms of Unity, with regard to certain fundamental principles, as these Confessions have always been maintained and interpreted by the Protestant Reformed Churches."[48] This motion would have had synod adopting the Declaration as a whole. In the end, however, synod decided to treat the Declaration "point by point," adding, "to determine whether the Declaration is in harmony with the confessions."[49]

In this careful, thorough manner, the synod of 1951 adopted the Declaration decisively. Again and again, with regard to all the major points of the Declaration, synod declared that the Declaration is the "expression of the Three Forms of Unity, with regard to certain fundamental principles."[50]

The word "expression," describing the relation of the Declaration to the creeds, was carefully chosen. Synod guarded against the perception that the Declaration was an additional creed—a "fourth form." It also warded off the charge that the Declaration is merely an "interpretation" of the creeds regarding the doctrine of the covenant—the idiosyncratic "interpretation" of the creeds by the Protestant Reformed Churches, or by Herman Hoeksema.

On the contrary, such is the claim of the Protestant Reformed Churches, the Declaration is only the "*expression*" of the creeds, that is, the teaching of the creeds themselves with regard to certain fundamental truths of the covenant of grace. This claim is subject to testing, of course. One can, and should, compare the principles

---

47 Ibid., 182–83.
48 Ibid., 185–86.
49 Ibid., 186.
50 Ibid., 193.

concerning the covenant that the Declaration declares with the creeds that are quoted as the source and basis of the principles.

In the course of adopting the Declaration, synod took certain noteworthy decisions. Synod rejected an amendment that would have had synod declaring that "there are conditions in God's Word… which God annexes to the promise." This amendment, moved by a bitter foe of the Declaration, would have been a death-blow to the document. Having given the delegate who proposed the amendment time to "submit the confessional grounds for his motion," synod defeated the amendment, thus saving the Declaration.[51]

COVENANT RESPONSIBILITY

Another significant decision by synod was the revision of the original formulation of the Declaration by the insertion of material that affirms the responsibility of man in the covenant. This addition to the version of the Declaration that the synod of 1950 had adopted provisionally was the recommendation of Classis East, in response to the criticism that the Declaration was strong on divine sovereignty but weak on man's responsibility. The passage on human responsibility added by the synod of 1951 is III, B, 2, with the grounds, in the final form of the Declaration.

> The sure promise of God which He realizes in us as rational and moral creatures not only makes it impossible that we should not bring forth fruits of thankfulness but also confronts us with the obligation of love, to walk in a new and holy life, and constantly to watch unto prayer.
>
> All those who are not thus disposed, who do not repent but walk in sin, are the objects of His just wrath and excluded from the Kingdom of Heaven.
>
> Grounds:
>
> 1. Baptism Form Part 3
>
> 2. Form for the Lord's Supper—Third Part beginning with "All those" up to "But this is not designed."

---

51 Ibid., 191, 193. The vote was a tie: eight to eight.

3. Heidelberg Catechism, Question[s] 64, 84, 116; Canons
3 and 4:12, 16, 17; 3 and 4 B:9; 5:14; Belgic Confession
Article 24...

That the preaching comes to all, and that God seriously
commands to faith and repentance, and that to all those
who come and believe He promises life and peace.[52]

So strong was the criticism of the Declaration as not doing justice to man's responsibility and so noisy was the clamor at that
time that the Protestant Reformed Churches were failing to preach
man's responsibility that Hoeksema, never of a mind or disposition to skirt sensitive, controversial issues, responded to the criticism and clamor directly and publicly. He did this in his address
at the graduation exercises of the Protestant Reformed Seminary
during the synod of 1953.

At this synod, a number of protests were lodged against the
adoption of the Declaration by the synod of 1951. Tensions in the
churches over the Declaration and the doctrine of the covenant
were at their height. Ministers and members were openly threatening or predicting a split in the denomination.

Since the synod was still in session, Hoeksema would have been
addressing not only the seminary graduates and their families
and friends but also the synodical delegates, half of whom were
opposed to the Declaration as one-sided in its affirmation of divine
sovereignty and critical of the Protestant Reformed Churches as
failing to do justice to human responsibility. In attendance also
would have been many visitors, some of whom shared these criti-
cisms of the Protestant Reformed Churches, of which they were
still members.

The topic of Hoeksema's graduation address was "Man's Freedom
and Responsibility."[53] He began by criticizing the emphasis in the
churches on human responsibility. He observed that "there is quite
a different sound in our churches" from earlier history. "That

---

52 Ibid., 194.

53 Herman Hoeksema, "Man's Freedom and Responsibility," *Standard Bearer*
29, no. 17 (July 1, 1953): 412. The full text of the speech is printed on
pages 412–17 of this issue of the *Standard Bearer*. All the quotations of the
speech that follow are taken from these pages of the *Standard Bearer*.

different sound...principally concentrates around a new emphasis in our churches on Man, instead of on God." Ministers and members of the Protestant Reformed Churches charge that the churches have been "one-sided. And that the one-sidedness consist[s] in this, that they laid too much emphasis on God, and not sufficient emphasis on Man." Hoeksema expressed his fear "that there is a split in our churches when I hear sounds that speak of and emphasize *responsibility of man,* and a *moral choice.*"

Hoeksema denied what he called "double track" theology. This is the teaching that "conceive[s] of God and the responsibility and moral freedom of man as two parallel lines,—a double track, two parallel lines that never meet as far as eye can see." "The real and Scriptural conception of the relation between man's responsibility and man's freedom, on the one hand, and the sovereign counsel of God, on the other hand, is this, that the freedom and the responsibility of man are hemmed in from every side by the counsel of God." "[Man] is not sovereignly free. Man can never be sovereignly free. God only is sovereignly free! And man is forevermore dependent, even as a moral creature, upon God!"

With regard to the responsibility of man in the state of grace and salvation, the justified sinner is not responsible for his sins. This is the meaning of God's justification of the ungodly by faith alone. "I am not responsible for my sins before God. I am not! Christ is! Christ is responsible for my sins. I cast all my guilt on Him by faith. And don't you ever tell your congregation that they are responsible for their own sins. God forbid!...You must tell the congregation to cast their sins upon Christ. Tell them that they are no more responsible for their sins. Tell them that, by all means!"

The objection is always that this is a "dangerous doctrine...It seems that way, but it isn't...Just this doctrine of absolutely free justification, that casts all the responsibility of my individual sins upon Christ, does not make me careless and profane. It answers: That is impossible! Why is it impossible? Because he that is justified by faith is also sanctified by faith, and, therefore, says spontaneously when you tell him that now he can sin as he pleases: 'God forbid! How shall I who am dead to sin live any longer therein?' That is the answer, the only answer.

"That is the Christian's responsibility. The Christian is free in the highest sense of the word…

"His freedom is rooted no longer in his own free will, but is rooted in the Son of God. And if the Son of God shall make you free, then you are free indeed…

"Freedom and responsibility! And in that everlasting freedom man, the redeemed man, shall forever thank God for His sovereign grace, and respond and say: 'O God, I love Thee.'"

This soundly Reformed conception of freedom and responsibility was incorporated into the Declaration by amendment at the synod of 1951. But it did not quiet, much less convert, the critics. In reality, what the critics wanted was not human *responsibility* in the covenant, but human *sovereignty*.

Synod also added a preamble to the Declaration. This preamble prescribed the use of the Declaration by the Protestant Reformed Churches. The preamble reads as follows: "Declaration of Principles, to be used only by the Mission Committee and the Missionaries for the organization of prospective churches on the basis of Scripture and the Confessions as these have always been maintained in the Protestant Reformed Churches and as these are now further explained in regard to certain principles."[54]

This use of the Declaration answered to the occasion of its creation and adoption, namely, the request of the mission committee for a "form" that could be used in organizing churches.

In addition, the preamble served other important purposes. It denied the charge commonly raised against the Declaration by its enemies that it constituted a "fourth form," or creed, alongside the three forms of unity.

The preamble was intended to allay the fear that the Declaration would be used as a creed, particularly in the discipline of officebearers.

And against the charge that the content of the Declaration was something new in the Protestant Reformed Churches regarding the covenant, the preamble expressed that the content is the teaching of the confessions as these have always been understood and taught in the Protestant Reformed Churches. The official statement of the fundamental truths of the covenant is new. The

---

54 *Acts of Synod, 1951*, 195–95.

fundamental truths themselves have always been the heritage of the denomination.

One other motion deserves attention. In a moment of "comic relief" in the tense proceedings, synod decided "to instruct all to abstain from smoking in this room."[55] Fifty years before the politically correct, liberal churches finally arrived at the conclusion that smoking, even secondhand smoke, is detrimental to health, and sinful, the Protestant Reformed Churches gave the lie to the canard that they are hide-bound traditionalists. Breaking with a Dutch Reformed tradition that goes back at least to the great and holy Synod of Dordt (1618–19), which debated and decided the great issues of salvation by grace in a thick cloud of tobacco smoke, the synod of the Protestant Reformed Churches banned smoking in an ecclesiastical assembly. There is no record that any delegate registered his negative vote.

Having gone through the Declaration point by point, deciding that the Declaration is "the truth expressed in our confessions,"[56] synod adopted "this Declaration of Principles."[57]

Three ministers, determined foes of the Declaration to the bitter end, had their negative vote on this motion to adopt the Declaration recorded.[58]

CONTINUING OPPOSITION

Following the synod of 1951, which adjourned on October 3, debate on the Declaration and on the related issues of the unconditionality or conditionality of the covenant and of relations with the liberated churches continued in the church papers, *Concordia* and *Standard Bearer*, as well as in the pulpits of the churches and in discussions among the members.

Soon a new voice joined in the cacophony. Those opposed to the Declaration started a new periodical, the *Reformed Guardian*. The first issue of the *Guardian* was dated July 21, 1953, shortly after the synod of 1953 had begun considering protests against the

---

55   Ibid., 187.

56   Ibid., 193.

57   Ibid., 196.

58   Ibid.

Declaration. The first issue was devoted to condemnation of the consistory of First Church, Grand Rapids, for its discipline of one of its pastors, Rev. De Wolf, for heretical sermons promoting the doctrine of a conditional covenant. The issue also condemned Classis East for advising this discipline. It vigorously defended De Wolf and the elders who supported him. The *Guardian* called the discipline "ruthless and illegal." It judged the action to be "hierarchic."[59]

Both the discipline of De Wolf and the *Guardian*'s public condemnation of the discipline in this inflammatory language guaranteed that the churches would not remain united much longer.

Because the synod of 1951 adjourned so late in the year—October—it was agreed that those who were determined to protest the adoption of the Declaration might wait until the synod of 1953. Would-be protestants did not have time to compose protests to the synod of 1952.

This meant that the Declaration and the doctrine of the covenant it espoused remained a lively, divisive issue in the Protestant Reformed Churches for more than a year after the synod of 1951, for the opponents of the Declaration continued their public criticism of the document and of its adoption. They announced their intention to protest the adoption of the Declaration at the synod of 1953.

Other factors also contributed to the continuing disturbance of the Protestant Reformed Churches after the synod of 1951. Two consistories in Canada, Protestant Reformed in name but liberated in theology—and lawless in tactics—had summarily deposed or dismissed their ministers because the ministers did not toe the liberated line. The ministers were Rev. H. Veldman and Rev. Petter. The release of Petter was ironic, since Petter had taken the lead in the Protestant Reformed Churches to defend the liberated conception of a conditional covenant.

Another factor was the preaching of the doctrine of a conditional promise and a conditional covenant by one of the pastors of the First Protestant Reformed Church in Grand Rapids, Michigan.

---

59 H. De Wolf and A. Cammenga, "Schism in the Church," *Reformed Guardian: For Protestant Reformed Membership* 1, no. 1 (July 21, 1953).

In two sermons, the first preached after the provisional adoption of the Declaration in 1950 and the second preached after the decisive adoption of the Declaration in 1951, Rev. De Wolf not only preached the doctrine of a conditional promise and conditional covenant but also deliberately contradicted the settled and binding decisions of the synods of 1950 and 1951 adopting the Declaration and thus affirming that the doctrine of an unconditional covenant is the teaching of the creeds. These sermons caused division and turmoil not only in First Church but also throughout the denomination.

The discipline of this minister by the consistory of First Church, with the advice of Classis East, would coincide with the meeting of synod in 1953. It would become the catalyst of the schism that was already working in the Protestant Reformed Churches.

Chapter Four

Challenged at the Synod of 1953

The synod of 1951 of the Protestant Reformed Churches had adopted decisively the Declaration of Principles concerning the covenant of grace. The synod had decreed that any church formed by the work of missions could be admitted into the Protestant Reformed federation only if the church was one with the Protestant Reformed Churches in confessing the doctrine of an unconditional covenant with Christ and the elect in him. The decision required the denominational mission committee and the missionaries to use the Declaration in their work of organizing new churches.

By the adoption of the Declaration, the Protestant Reformed Churches confessed and bound themselves to the doctrine of an unconditional covenant, which has its source in and is governed by eternal election. The churches also rejected the doctrine of a conditional covenant, cut loose from election.

Even though the Declaration was not, indeed denied being, a fourth confession, as a synodical decision it was binding upon all members of the denomination, including those members who opposed it. As Hoeksema would point out to a minister who continued publicly to oppose the Declaration after its adoption in 1951, if the Protestant Reformed Churches required agreement with the Declaration on the part of persons and groups that intended to join the denomination, the Protestant Reformed Churches themselves maintain the Declaration and confess its doctrine of the covenant. In addition, the document is a "settled and binding" decision, according to Article 31 of the Church Order: "Whatever may be agreed upon by a majority vote [at a major ecclesiastical assembly] shall be considered settled and binding, unless it be proved to conflict with the Word of God or with the articles of the Church Order."[1]

> I give the Rev. Kok a fair warning that he must refrain from continuing in this disorderly way of agitating against the *Declaration of Principles*, which is now officially adopted by our churches, thus keeping our churches in constant turmoil and attempting to corrupt them by the Liberated errors.
>
> My ground for the above statement is art. 31 of the Church Order...
>
> Although the Declaration is not a fourth form, binding as such upon our ministers or other officebearers, so that they could be disciplined on the basis of it, nevertheless, the *decision* of synod to declare the Declaration the expression of the Confessions, and to use it as an instrument for the organisation of churches, that *decision* is settled and binding upon all our churches, and upon all our officebearers.[2]

Nevertheless, the battle over the Declaration in the Protestant Reformed Churches was not yet over. Not only did the ministers opposed to the Declaration continue to agitate against the Declaration in the public press and in their sermons, as well as privately, but also the opponents had the right of appeal against the decision adopting the Declaration. Many announced that they were resolved to exercise this right.

Ordinarily, these appeals would have come to the following synod, that is, the synod of 1952. But because the synod of 1951 had extended late into the year, adjourning in October 1951, the decisions of the synod were not published in time for appeals to be brought to the synod of 1952. Therefore, it was agreed that appellants would be permitted to bring their objections against the adoption of the Declaration to the synod of 1953.

---

1   Church Order Article 31, in *Confessions and Church Order*, 390.

2   Herman Hoeksema, "To Be or Not To Be," *Standard Bearer* 28, no. 16 (May 15, 1952): 365.

The only reference to the Declaration at the synod of 1952 was synod's agreement with the decision of Classis West that documents objecting to the adoption of the Declaration "can be brought to the synod of 1953."[3]

This state of affairs meant that the denomination would be torn by controversy over the Declaration for yet another year, and longer. And the controversy was raging, not only in sermons and in the magazines of the churches (which by this time were exchanging such insults as *Slander Bearer, Discordia,* and *Deformed Guardian*), but also in the congregations, dividing members of the same church, families, and even married couples.

When the schism would occur (and by the time of the meeting of the synod of 1953, all were certain that it would occur), the division would have had the time to become deep and wide. Some six years of bitter struggle continuously ripped the small, otherwise tightly knit denomination, from the beginning of the controversy by the defense of a conditional covenant in *Concordia* in 1947, to the schism in 1953.

These circumstances must be taken into account when one evaluates the actions of the Protestant Reformed Churches at once after the schism had taken place. The schismatics damned these actions as hasty and harsh. The churches were concerned to put an end to the ongoing controversy, already drawn out over far too long a time, and to protect and solidify what was left of the denomination.

A PERTINENT SERMON AT THE SYNOD OF 1952

Other than a decision recognizing the right of objectors to bring appeals to the synod of 1953, nothing concerning the Declaration appeared on the agenda of the Protestant Reformed synod of 1952.

But this does not imply that the doctrinal issue racking the churches did not confront the delegates to the synod of 1952. Not only was it on the mind of all, but also the pre-synodical sermon, the sermon preached at the worship service that always precedes the meeting of synod, raised the issue that was at the heart of the Declaration—the unconditional covenant promise of God to

---

3   *Acts of Synod, Protestant Reformed Churches in America, 1952,* 82.

Abraham and his seed. The preacher was the venerable pastor of the Hudsonville Protestant Reformed Church in Hudsonville, Michigan, Rev. Gerrit Vos. Perennially a delegate to synod, Vos was a delegate to the synod of 1952. He had been the president of the preceding synod, the important synod of 1951 that had adopted the Declaration decisively. Upon him by custom, if not by rule, fell the duty of leading the worship service the night before the convening of the synod of 1952.

Gerrit Vos, prominent pastor and perennial delegate to synod, was mightily used of God for the adoption of the Declaration and for the preservation of the PRC in the years of the battle of the PRC on behalf of the gospel of sovereign grace in the covenant. His pre-synodical sermon at the synod of 1952 was compelling with regard to the biblical soundness of the Declaration and the unconditional covenant. Vos served, usually as chairman and often thanklessly, on many burdened, important committees in the days of the Declaration and schism.

Deliberately, in view of the great doctrinal struggle convulsing the churches, Vos picked as his text Hebrews 6:17–20:

> Wherein God, willing more abundantly to shew unto the heirs of promise the immutability of his counsel, confirmed it by an oath: That by two immutable things, in which it was impossible for God to lie, we might have a strong consolation, who have fled for refuge to lay hold upon the hope set before us: Which hope we have as an anchor of the soul, both sure and stedfast, and which entereth into that within the veil; Whither the forerunner is for us entered, even Jesus, made an high priest forever after the order of Melchisedec.

Few passages of Scripture address the main issues treated by the Declaration more directly and clearly than does this passage. Hebrews 6:17–20 concerns the covenant promise to Abraham. Verse 13 establishes this: "For when God made promise to Abraham, because he could swear by no greater, he sware by himself." About this covenant promise, the passage is speaking.

The passage teaches that the covenant promise is particular: "heirs of promise."

It describes the covenant promise as oath-bound: "When God made promise to Abraham...he *sware* by himself." The Declaration's description of the covenant promise as "an oath of God that He will infallibly lead all the elect unto salvation and eternal glory through faith" had been criticized by the enemies of the document as one of the Declaration's main errors.

The Hebrews passage relates the promise of the covenant, and thus the covenant itself, closely to the decree of election: "confirmed it [the immutability of His counsel] by an oath [attached to the covenant promise]," something the defenders of a conditional covenant vehemently denied. It is fundamental to the theory of a conditional covenant that the covenant is cut loose from the eternal decree of election.

The text does not explicitly state that the covenant is unconditional, that is, dependent only upon the electing, promising, swearing God and not at all upon the heirs of the promise. But it cannot be explained as, or as in harmony with, a doctrine of a conditional, breakable, uncertain covenant promise and thus a conditional, breakable, losable covenant.

And the text on which Vos preached in his inimitable style, that night in the midst of the battle of the Protestant Reformed Churches for the truth of salvation by grace with regard to the covenant, makes the "consolation" of the believing, hoping Christian dependent on this sure, particular promise, whose source is the eternal decree of election: "that...we might have a strong consolation."

This text Vos preached to the doctrinally divided synod, and to the numerous visitors, also divided.

Enlisting the other New Testament passage that most directly and clearly addresses the great doctrinal issues treated in the Declaration—Galatians 3:16 and 29—Vos struck to the heart of the question whether the covenant promise is conditionally for all who hear the preaching of the gospel and all who are baptized or unconditionally for the elect. Vos asserted, "That promise is centrally, according to Galatians 3:16, not for us, but for Jesus Christ Himself. That is why Christ Himself is centrally the Heir of promise."[4]

With appeal to Galatians 3:29, Vos added that those who are in Christ—the elect—are co-heirs with Christ of the promise. And "we become heir actually and historically because of the generating power of the promise."[5]

If all had heard this word of God that night, the strife over the covenant, over the covenant promise, and over the Declaration as the expression of the creeds would have ended the evening of June 3, 1952, in the small, white, wood-frame building of the Protestant Reformed church in the onion fields of the village of South Holland, Illinois, where the

The little white church building of the South Holland, Illinois, Protestant Reformed Church in 1952. In this building, as part of the synod of 1952, Rev. Vos preached a sermon on covenantal salvation by sovereign grace that ought to have settled the controversy over the covenant then raging in the churches. However, that word of God confirmed only some in the Reformed faith concerning the covenant. It hardened others in the "other gospel," which is no gospel, of covenantal salvation by the willing and working of baptized babies.

---

4   Ibid., 9.
5   Ibid., 10.

synod of 1952 met. The ministers and members of the denomination would have remained united. And countless generations that were soon to be scattered would have been raised in the soundly Reformed truth and antithetical life of the Protestant Reformed Churches.

If any human messenger might have commended the glorious message of Hebrews 6 to the delegates from Classis West, Gerrit Vos was that messenger. At that late date in the controversy, if any minister in the churches still retained the respect and love of both parties, it was the patriarchal, snowy-haired, genial Vos.

But neither Vos nor his message was of any avail to heal the breach and ward off the schism. Men hardened their hearts against the message and the winsome messenger. Satan saw to the continuation of the strife. And God willed otherwise than the cessation of the doctrinal conflict by reconciliation.

APPEALS TO THE SYNOD OF 1953

Appeals against the adoption of the Declaration by the synod of 1951 flowed in to the synod of 1953.

The Protestant Reformed synod of 1953 was extraordinary in several respects. First, it was unusually long. Its first session lasted from June 3 to June 23.

Second, the synod recessed. It adjourned its first session on June 23, 1953, deciding to resume its meeting in March 1954.

The reason for the recess was the third unusual aspect of the synod: It was hopelessly deadlocked. On all the motions related to the Declaration, the eight delegates of Classis West and the eight delegates of Classis East were opposed. Motion after motion is recorded in the *Acts* as having failed on a tie vote. Unable to accomplish anything regarding the appeals against the Declaration, therefore, synod decided:

> To give all the documents addressed to this Synod regarding the Declaration of Principles and also those expressions recorded in the minutes regarding the same matter, into the hands of a Study Committee to report to this

same Synod [which, it was decided, would reconvene the second Wednesday in March 1954].[6]

The first ground for the decision to recess was that "the present tie situation makes it impossible to proceed at this time."[7] The third ground was significant in that it indicated the tense atmosphere in which the synod deliberated the appeals against the Declaration: "This [recessing] may avoid a separation and give us opportunity for further discussion while we remain a communion of churches."[8]

Later, some importance would attach to the decision of the June session of the 1953 synod to hold the reconvened, March 1954 session of synod "in Fuller Avenue Church."[9] The schism having taken place in the meantime, the schismatic faction retained possession of the Fuller Avenue church building. It held a synodical meeting in the appointed building, whereas the Protestant Reformed Churches had to hold their meeting elsewhere. The schismatics' holding their synod at the appointed place became part of their argument that they were, in fact, the genuine continuation of the Protestant Reformed Churches.

In connection with the postponement of its consideration of the appeals against the Declaration, the June 1953 session of synod also appointed a committee whose mandate was to "give definite recommendations [on the appeals against the Declaration]" to the session of synod that was to reconvene in March 1954.[10]

Oddly, the president of synod, Rev. R. Veldman, appointed three ministers to this committee, all of whom were delegates from Classis West and resolutely opposed to the Declaration: Rev. James Howerzyl, Rev. Walter Hofman, and Rev. J. D. De Jong.[11] How their advice on treating the appeals against the Declaration might have been expected to be helpful to the synod is a mystery.

---

6 *Acts of Synod, 1953*, 177–79.
7 Ibid., 178.
8 Ibid.
9 Ibid., 179.
10 Ibid.
11 Ibid.

The fourth unique characteristic of the synod of 1953 was that it was the last synod of the undivided denomination. That is, its June 1953 session was the last meeting of the synod of the undivided churches. Before synod could reconvene in March 1954, the schism took place. The entire, long, twenty-day, June session was conducted under this cloud. The close fellowship and cooperation of some twenty-five years was about to be shattered and forever lost.

The third ground of the motion to recess the synod indicated the awareness that schism was imminent: avoiding a separation and giving opportunity for further discussion while we remain a communion of churches.[12]

Cornelius Hanko, faithful co-pastor with Hoeksema of First Protestant Reformed Church, Grand Rapids, in the difficult days of the schism caused by their colleague at First Church, Rev. H. De Wolf.

Adversaries of the Declaration had been threatening schism at least as early as the months preceding the synod of 1951.

At the beginning of a long address to the synod of 1953, which was made part of the record of the synod, Herman Hoeksema motivated his speech by stating that "it begins to look to me as if we are at the end of the road. That's not hoping that that is so; but it looks very much as if we are not going to stay together. And therefore, this may be my last opportunity to address you and to have anything for the record."[13]

---

12 Ibid., 178.

13 Herman Hoeksema, "Transcript of address delivered...to the Synod of 1953 on June 18, to be entered into the record," in *Acts of Synod, 1953*, 264. The transcript of the address, mainly demonstrating that he—Hoeksema—had always preached against a conditional promise and a conditional covenant, in response to the constant charge that earlier in his min-

The peril of schism was really the burden of the pre-synodical sermon by Rev. Cornelius Hanko, co-pastor with Hoeksema and De Wolf of First Church, Grand Rapids, Michigan. Hanko exhorted the delegates to "mind the same things," from Philippians 2:1–2. He acknowledged the sinful division in the Protestant Reformed Churches.

> When strife and vain pride creep into the church, when one esteems himself above the others, and when every one haughtily minds his own things rather than the things of others, the Spirit that dwells within the church is grieved to silence. The Word of God ceases to have a free course. Love is at a premium. The fellowship is wanting. Bowels and mercies are shut up. In one word, the spiritual life of the church suffers, hatred and bitterness, backbiting and slander run a free course.

> That has been the experience in our own churches during the past few years. Our Christian assemblies have suffered. Our fellowship is disrupted. It has become increasingly difficult, even well-nigh impossible to meet in classical and synodical gatherings.[14]

At the synod of 1953, as the main business of the synod although not the only important business, were a number of protests against the Declaration and appeals against the adoption of the Declaration by the synod of 1951. Some of the official objections against the decision of the synod of 1951 adopting the Declaration were from ministers; others were from consistories. The protesting ministers, all in Classis West, were Rev. J. W. Van Weelden, Rev. Lambert

---

istry he had taught differently, extends from page 264 in the *Acts of Synod, 1953* to page 277. In the address, Hoeksema quoted himself from a sermon he preached in a Christian Reformed church in 1915 or 1916. He had said concerning the doctrine that faith is the "condition" of salvation that if his congregation accepted this doctrine, "we have absolutely departed from the paths of Reformed truth [and]...have become Arminian in principle" (267). Hoeksema concluded his long speech to the synod of 1953 with the assertion, "Conditional theology is not Protestant Reformed, and has never been" (277).

14 Ibid., 16.

Doezema, and Rev. Hofman. The consistories, likewise in the West, were Bellflower, California; Pella, Iowa; and Oskaloosa, Iowa.

Adding to the gravity of the objection against the Declaration was the notification of synod by Classis West that "Classis West... cannot be satisfied with Synod's treatment of the protest of Classis West [to the 1951 synod]...Classis therefore maintains its original position and considers the Declaration to be illegal." In addition, Classis West informed synod that it agreed with the objections by various protestants (who brought their objections against the Declaration to synod by way of Classis West) against the content of the Declaration, especially the Declaration's condemnation of a conditional covenant. Classis West insisted that the "promise is put in conditional form in the Confessions."

Basically, Classis West made the appeals and protests against the Declaration at the synod of 1953 its own—no small matter in that Classis West represented half the denomination.[15]

The objections of the appeals and protests against the Declaration at the synod of 1953 were especially two. First, it was charged that the Declaration was illegally adopted. Second, all the protestants, including Classis West, criticized the content of the Declaration.

Regarding the alleged illegality, the objectors at the synod of 1953 insisted that the Declaration did not arise "out of the bosom" of the churches. Their point was that no congregation had overtured synod for a Declaration of Principles. Rather, the synod of 1950 had drawn up the Declaration, and provisionally adopted it, at the request of the mission committee for a "form" that could be used in organizing new churches. Classis West voiced this aspect of the objection to the Declaration this way: "Synod of 1951, in its adoption of the Declaration of Principles, violated Article 30 of our Church Order which states that 'ecclesiastical matters shall be transacted in an ecclesiastical manner.'"[16] The argument of those who shared this objection was that the adoption of a document "regarding confessional material" may only be the action of a synod if the matter originates in a "concrete case" and has been initiated by a consistory. Because this was not true of the

---

15 For the objections against the Declaration at the synod of 1953 by Classis West, see ibid., 148–150.

16 Ibid., 148.

Declaration, the adoption of the Declaration by the synods of 1950 and 1951 was "hierarchical."[17]

The response to this charge of illegality by the defenders of the Declaration and its adoption and by the synod of 1951, which was confronted by the charge of illegality, was the same. Because the mission committee of the churches is a committee of synod, it was proper both that the mission committee bring directly to synod its request for a "form" to be used in organizing churches (in light of the urgent problem with organizing groups of Dutch, liberated immigrants as Protestant Reformed congregations) and that the synod responded to the request from its committee concerning denominational mission work by the adoption of such a "form" as had been requested.

Although the synod of 1951 simply rejected the appeals against the Declaration that charged illegality, without specifying the ground of synod's judgment that the Declaration was adopted legally,[18] defenders of the legality of the Declaration expressed the ground repeatedly, both in the synodical discussions and in the public debate in the magazines. The ground was Article 30 of the Church Order, specifically the provision of the article that "in major assemblies...such matters shall be dealt with...as pertain to the churches of the major assembly in common."[19] Since the request for and adoption of the Declaration were matters pertaining to the mission committee and mission work of the churches of the major assembly in common, that is, of the entire denomination, the adoption of the Declaration by the synod was legal, regardless that the request for the Declaration had not arisen "out of the bosom of the churches."

Regarding the other main objection to the Declaration at the synod of 1953, objection to the content of the document, the protestants were cautious. Most of them were careful to affirm that they

---

17 The words in quotation marks in this analysis of the objection against the Declaration, that it was illegal, are those of Rev. Howerzyl, one of the protestants against the Declaration at the synod of 1953 and the opponent of the Declaration who most vigorously raised the objection of illegality from the very beginning (ibid., 144–45).

18 *Acts of Synod, 1951*, 182.

19 Church Order Article 30, in *Confessions and Church Order*, 389.

were not "in disagreement with the basic thrust of the Declaration [or] in disagreement with the current covenant conception in our churches," that is, with the doctrine of an unconditional covenant with the elect in Christ only.[20]

In spite of their protestation of agreement with the "basic thrust" of the Declaration, which is certainly the confession of an unconditional covenant, having its source and cause in the decree of eternal election, the objectors pleaded against the Declaration that it does not allow for the teachings that "the promise of the Gospel is conditional" and that "faith is a condition."[21]

A DIVIDED COMMITTEE OF PRE-ADVICE

Like the synod itself, the committee of pre-advice that was to guide the synod in its treatment of the appeals was divided. Synod assured this result by its appointment of the committee.

---

20 The statement that is quoted was that of Rev. J. W. Van Weelden in his protest to the synod of 1953 (*Acts of Synod, 1953*, 136). Similar expressions of basic agreement with the covenant theology of the Declaration, or at least disavowal of commitment to the doctrine of the covenant that the Declaration condemns, appeared in many of the protests against the Declaration to the synod of 1951 and to the synod of 1953. Classis West, for example, in its objection to the synod of 1953, assured the synod that "we are not pleading for the ushering in of the term condition" (*Acts of Synod, 1953*, 149). It gave this assurance in the midst of its specific objection against the Declaration's rejection of a conditional covenant. A few sentences later, Classis West asserted that "the promise is put in conditional form in the Confessions." Thus Classis West did not merely display that it was halting between two opinions. But it demonstrated that it refused to recognize that the controversy over the covenant, which the Declaration settled, was between two diametrically opposed and irreconcilable theologies of the covenant of grace.

21 Ibid., 138. The quoted statements are those of Van Weelden, in his protest against the Declaration to the synod of 1953. This is the protestant who assured the synod that he was not "in disagreement with the basic thrust of the Declaration." Where his heart was, he made plain two years later. In 1955, barely two years after the synod of 1953, Van Weelden achieved the disbanding of his Protestant Reformed congregation in Sioux Center, Iowa, and entered the ministry of the Christian Reformed Church, whose covenant theology is that of conditions with no room for the doctrine of an unconditional covenant, as it made plain in the deposition of Herman Hoeksema in 1924.

Two were delegates of Classis East; two, of Classis West.

That part of the committee made up of the delegates of Classis West advised synod to express that the action of the synods of 1950 and 1951 adopting the Declaration was illegal. The committee added, regarding the content of the Declaration, that synod should decide that it is proper to teach a conditional covenant and covenant promise because "the promise is put in a conditional form in the Confessions."[22] Such an about-face by synod, of course, would have meant the condemnation of the Protestant Reformed confession of an unconditional covenant and the approval of the doctrine of a conditional covenant, cut loose from election, as taught by Klaas Schilder, Benne Holwerda, and the Reformed Churches in the Netherlands (liberated).

The other part of the committee, consisting of two delegates of Classis East, advised the opposite, in respect both to the legality and to the content of the Declaration.[23] The two members of this committee were Rev. Vos and Elder Gerrit Pipe. This report was a thorough, well-thought-out, and solidly grounded refutation of the arguments against the Declaration, especially the arguments presented to synod by Classis West. In the event, this report was never treated. Soon after defeating the recommendation of that part of the committee of pre-advice that advised nullifying the Declaration, especially on the basis of its having been illegally adopted, synod recessed, without having considered the advice of that part of the committee that advised maintaining the Declaration as a legal decision of synod and as sound theology. Before synod could resume its deliberations, the schism in the churches occurred. Unfortunately, the reconvened synod of the Protestant Reformed Churches did not take up and adopt the advice of this part of the committee.

I say "unfortunately" because the advice of Vos and Pipe responded pointedly and convincingly to all of the objections raised by the appellants. In addition to defending the Declaration, the advice went on the offensive against the appellants, especially Classis West. Charging illegality, Classis West had boldly, if not with a

---

22 Ibid., 154.

23 Ibid., 154–58.

revolutionary attitude, stated to the synod that "Classis...maintains it original position and considers the Declaration to be illegal."[24] The committee of pre-advice would have had synod decide that this statement by Classis West

> is a serious breach in our ecclesiastical life from a church political point of view. The Declaration is legally adopted also by Classis West...Synod of 1951 adopted the Declaration by a majority vote. Hence, the decision in re the Declaration of Principles is settled and binding, unless it be proved in conflict with the Word of God and the articles of the Church Order, etc. Art. 31 [Church Order of Dordt]. And this has not happened to date. And therefore the docu-ment [the Declaration] is legal, also for Classis West.[25]

In characteristically Vosian language, the report of this part of the committee of pre-advice stated the *necessity* of the churches' adoption of the Declaration, something that the synods had hitherto failed to do, even though protestants had criticized the Declaration as being unnecessary.

> Synods of 1950 and 1951 considered the adoption of the Declaration of Principles very necessary and hence adopted same. Before the Synod of 1950, and after-wards this necessity was plainly evident: Our Protestant Reformed Churches were in danger of being swallowed up alive by the Liberated emigrants who entered and would have continued to enter our Church denomination. At our classical meetings they argued against and voted against our beloved Protestant Reformed truth. They cast our ministers on the streets of their Canadian cities as so much dirt under their feet, contrary to all order and decency. How can anyone, being acquainted with the past history ask whether or not the Declaration of Principles was and is necessary? We are 3 or 4 years late with it. If our Synod of 1947 had adopted same it would have saved the Revs. H. Veldman and Andrew Petter untold heart-ache.[26]

---

24 Ibid., 155.

25 Ibid.

26 Ibid., 156. Rev. H. Veldman and Rev. Petter had been summarily deposed

Responding to the common accusation against the Declaration that it did not appeal to Scripture for its doctrine of the covenant, but only to the confessions, the report of the two delegates of Classis East advised synod to declare that

When new confessions are made, they are built on the Word of God.

When a gravamen against the Confessions is lodged, it is lodged on the basis of the Word of God.

But when the Confessions are interpreted or applied, as was the case with the Declaration of Principles, appeal is made and should be made solely to the Confessions.

When a question arises in Reformed Churches as to what is Reformed, no one is supposed to appeal to Scripture, but appeal is made solely to the Reformed Symbols. They and they only decide what is and what is not Reformed.[27]

The synod of 1953 was now confronted by two conflicting pieces of advice concerning its treatment of the appeals and protests against the Declaration. Synod proceeded by voting first on the recommendations of that part of the committee of pre-advice that advised repudiation of the Declaration as illegally adopted. The motions to adopt this advice failed by tie votes—eight for and eight against the motions.[28]

So conflicted was the synod that the attempt to send an explanation of synod's rejection of their protests against the Declaration to all the protestants and to Classis West failed—on a tie vote. Synod was reduced to informing the protestants and Classis West that "we cannot give an answer because of the tie situation."[29]

Having rejected the advice that synod approve the protests against the Declaration, and thus in reality having rejected the protests and appeals, synod decided to adjourn until March 1954.

---

by nominally Protestant Reformed, but in actuality liberated, consistories in Canada, for maintaining the doctrine of an unconditional covenant.

27 Ibid., 157–58.

28 Ibid., 161–62.

29 Ibid., 166.

This tactic was motivated more by the present haplessness and hopelessness of the synod, because of its deadlock, than by hope of a brighter future. It did appoint a committee of three ministers from Classis West with the mandate to study all the documents addressed to synod regarding the Declaration, in order to give "definite recommendations" to synod when it would reconvene.[30]

All that the synod of 1953 had been able to accomplish in its long June session regarding the protests against the Declaration, before synod recessed for several months, was to reject the advice of a committee to repudiate the Declaration as illegally adopted. This rejection was by a tie vote.[31]

SPEECHES AT THE SYNOD

At the synod of 1953, during the deliberations on the Declaration, several ministers gave significant speeches on the Declaration, its theology of the covenant, and its adoption (or rejection). Some were of great length. Evidently the rule limiting speeches to ten minutes was waived. These speeches were recorded and included in the *Acts*, by synodical decision.

---

30 Ibid., 177–79. The committee members were Howerzyl, Hofman, and De Jong. The first two were themselves protestants against the Declaration at the synod of 1953; the last was a very vocal, vehement adversary of the Declaration. That they should have been appointed to give advice to guide the synod at its reconvened session in March 1954 regarding its handling of the protests and appeals against the Declaration was passing strange. That their advice proved to be a recommendation that synod uphold the protests and appeals and thus repudiate the Declaration could not have been surprising to anyone.

31 This deadlock of the synod was nothing short of an embarrassment to Herman Hoeksema. That a Protestant Reformed synod could not take a stand for what in his mind was fundamental Protestant Reformed, indeed Reformed, doctrine injured him cruelly. How those tie votes, which hamstrung the synod, stuck in his craw came out years later in a conversation with the present writer. As a seminary student in the fall of 1960, I was sent by Hoeksema to the special synod of the schismatics that met in October 1960. At that synod the great issue was their return to the Christian Reformed Church. The motion to return failed (at the synod of 1960; the motion would prevail the next year) on a tie vote—eight to eight. When I reported this to Hoeksema, he growled, "That was the judgment of God! By that tie vote they crippled our synod of 1953."

One of the long, significant speeches was by Herman Hoeksema. He demonstrated that, although on occasion he had used the term "condition" in his voluminous writings, he had never taught a conditional covenant but had always opposed it as false doctrine, especially in connection with his controversy with the conditional covenant theology of his former, Christian Reformed, seminary professor William Heyns. Displaying a touch of irritation with those of his colleagues who persisted in advancing the absurd notion that he—Hoeksema—had once taught the doctrine of a conditional covenant that they were now defending, Hoeksema quoted, among other items, a passage from a sermon he had preached in 1917, when he was still a minister in the Christian Reformed Church.

> The covenant of grace…is established not with all the individual members, but with the Head. And that one Head is Christ Jesus. Let us also clearly see this fact. We do not belong to this covenant…because of our personal consent. That is an idea which lives often in the hearts and minds of the people of God. But this is wrong… Nor must you have the idea that you must fulfill certain conditions in order to enter into that covenant. For that would again place the burden of the covenant upon your personal responsibility. And this is not so at all. Surely, there are obligations also in the covenant of grace. But these obligations flow forth from our being in the covenant. Christ, therefore, has fulfilled all the conditions. The covenant was established with Him as the Head in all eternity. And therefore He came in time to fulfill the conditions at the Head of His people. And as their Head He suffered, as their Head He died, as their Head He fulfills the law. And having fulfilled all, His people have nothing at all to fulfill anymore. There are no conditions in the covenant of grace. They are saved by grace.[32]

Hoeksema interjected at this point in his address, "That I preached in 1917. Don't ever say that I changed, please!"[33]

---

32 Ibid., 270.
33 Ibid.

Hoeksema concluded his speech with these words:

> Conditional theology is not Protestant Reformed, and has never been…Conditional theology and Liberated theology is certainly quite different, fundamentally different, from our Protestant Reformed truth. And therefore, if you want to be Protestant Reformed, you must adhere to these principles [the principles of the covenant expressed as the teaching of the confessions in the Declaration].[34]

Also Rev. Vos requested that he be permitted to speak for the record. His speech is notable for its pungency, for its indication that all the Protestant Reformed clergy, even the most longsuffering, were weary of their colleagues' advocacy of the conditional theology of Heyns and Schilder, and for its blunt description of the history of the doctrinal division in the Protestant Reformed Churches. For these reasons, Vos's speech at the synod of 1953, although long, is worthy of quotation.

Vos was directly responding to a similarly long speech by Rev. Doezema, also recorded in the *Acts*, defending conditions in the covenant. Doezema had quoted many Reformed theologians who used the term "condition," including Herman Bavinck, as proof that the Declaration of Principles is in error in rejecting a conditional covenant. Vos responded as follows:

> I, too, have something for the record.

> First, a question: Is that conglomeration of unrelated material of the Rev. Doezema an attempt to give us a scientific justification of the tenets that the promise of God is conditional and that faith is a condition unto salvation?

> If it is, then I would like to make several observations. I will not take much of your time, neither is it necessary.

> 1. Rev. Doezema could have saved himself much time and effort and the Synod also, for, with apologies to Proctor and Gamble, since it is a travesty on the purity of their product, his manifold quotations were 99 44/100% idle, void, and useless, and that for the simple reason that they

34 Ibid., 277.

are anachronistic. The careful and attentive listener to his reading of those quotations noted how one of his quotations which he very conveniently quoted in a very imperfect way, destroyed the force of 99 44/100% of them. Here is the quotation both in Dutch and in English. [Here Vos, a native Dutch speaker and fluent in the language, quoted Bavinck in the Dutch. The English translation, which was not available at the time in published form, follows.] In English and I [Vos] translate, "At first the Reformed Theologians spoke freely concerning conditions of the Covenant. But when the nature of the Covenant of Grace received more profound study, and had to be defended against Roman Catholics, Lutherans, and Remonstrants, many theologians objected against it and shunned this usage" (Dr. H. Bavinck, [*Gereformeerde Dogmatiek*], vol. 3, pp. 241–42).[35]

2. It would have been scientific and true if he would have outlined how all our men were reared and educated in the sound Protestant Reformed principles, and that we were happy in the preaching and teaching of them, until we came in contact with the Liberated, at the cessation of World War II, when in the person of the late Dr. Schilder, the Liberated theology made its descent upon us, both by personal contact, conferences, literature and visits to the old country.

3. It would have been scientific and true if he had said that the late Dr. Schilder traveled from the Atlantic to the Pacific and from the Pacific to the Atlantic and re-indoctrinated many of us.

---

35 With the translation and publication of Bavinck's dogmatics in English, this important statement by Bavinck about the covenant is available in published form to all who read English. See Herman Bavinck, *Reformed Dogmatics*, vol. 3, ed. John Bolt, trans. John Vriend (Grand Rapids, MI: Baker, 2006), 229. Bavinck adds in the next sentence, "In the covenant of grace, that is, the gospel, which is the proclamation of the covenant of grace, there are actually…no conditions…Christ has accomplished everything…and the Holy Spirit…applies them" (230).

4. It would have been scientific and true if he had said, proving it with numerous quotations from Concordia, that the impact of the Liberated theology proved too strong for many of our ministers and people, so that they forsook our own beloved principles and began an apology for the Liberated theology and tenets.

5. It would have been scientific and true if he further had proven his case by citing the determined and organized attack on our beloved and prized Declaration of Principles, which document was conceived and born as a dam against the hordes of Liberated emigrants threatening to invade our churches.

6. It would have been *very* scientific and true if he had pointed out how our own Reformed brethren in the Netherlands, one million strong, in the "Vervangingsformule" have expressed very definitely that unconditionality of the Covenant of Grace, and that as a dam against the same Liberated error that is threatening to engulf us on these shores.[36]

7. Finally, it would have been scientific and true if he had stated that both Dr. Schilder and Prof. Heyns, resurrected and re-incarnated, had appeared at the Synod of the Protestant Reformed Churches, Anno Domini 1953, in order to make a plea for their beloved error: "The promise of God is conditional" and "Faith is a condition unto salvation."[37]

---

36 Vos here reminded the synod that in the early 1940s, the Reformed Churches in the Netherlands (GKN) had engaged in a doctrinal struggle over the very issues concerning the covenant that were involved in the controversy in the Protestant Reformed Churches over the Declaration. The *Vervangingsformule* [Replacement, or substitution, formula] was a synodical decision of the Reformed Churches in the Netherlands (GKN) condemning the doctrine of the covenant taught by Schilder and the liberated (who had by the time of the decision been separated from the Reformed Churches in the Netherlands [synodicals]) and confessing a doctrine of the covenant that related the covenant closely to election, a truth that the liberated abhor. For this *Vervangingsformule* in Dutch, see E. Smilde, *Een Eeuw van Strijd over Verbond en Doop* [A century of conflict over covenant and baptism] (Kampen: Kok, 1946), 358–61.

37 Especially noteworthy is Vos' identifying the covenant doctrine of Schil-

Mr. President and worthy members of Synod, do you not see that we have come to the end of the road? If the brethren are so in love with Liberated theology and tenets; and if they dislike the Protestant Reformed truth so much and so consistently that they actually stifle the very institutional life of our churches, assembled in Synod, so that all we can achieve is a tie vote, why in the name of all that is good and upright and true, do they not separate from us, organize a Liberated Church denomination, seek contact with the likeminded both in Canada and Holland, and, please, please, leave us alone?

---

der with that of the Christian Reformed theologian William Heyns. Hoeksema and the other defenders of the Declaration condemned the liberated doctrine of the covenant as essentially that of Heyns, long-time professor at the seminary of the Christian Reformed Church. It was necessary that the foes of the Declaration deny this identity, since the Protestant Reformed Churches had condemned Heyns' doctrine of the covenant from the very beginning of their history—had condemned Heyns' doctrine as, in fact, the source of the doctrine of the well-meant offer, rejection of which was fundamental to the existence of the Protestant Reformed Churches. The foes of the Declaration could not admit that the covenant theology of the liberated, which they were defending, is identical to that of Heyns without exposing themselves as apostates from truths that the churches had confessed as fundamental from their earliest days, and as defending a covenant theology that the Protestant Reformed Churches had always condemned as essentially Arminian and Pelagian. Schilder himself expressed reservations about the covenant doctrine of Heyns. Today, even the liberated theologians freely acknowledge the essential oneness of the covenant doctrines of Schilder and Heyns. Dr. Jelle Faber, liberated theologian at the seminary of the Canadian Reformed Churches in Canada, has written of the "kinship of the fifth dogmatician of Kampen [Schilder] with the American Secession theologians, also with Heyns" (Faber, *American Secession Theologians*, 52). Faber added that the sound tradition of the doctrine of the covenant includes "Schilder, and Veenhof...and Heyns" (ibid., 53). Making unmistakably plain the true nature of this tradition of covenant theology, Faber dismissed Heyns' teaching that God bestows covenant grace internally to every baptized child, so that every child is capable of fulfilling the conditions upon which the covenant with every child depends if only the child is willing, as "only a minimal point" and undeserving of the charge of "Aminianism" (ibid., 52).

Yes there is a better way. It is this: Return unto your first love: the Protestant Reformed truth, embodied in the Declaration of Principles. Verily, those days were better than these![38]

The reconvened session of the deadlocked synod, representing churches on both sides of the controversy over the Declaration, would never meet.

In the months between June 23, 1953, and March 1954, the Protestant Reformed Churches would suffer schism.

---

38 Gerrit Vos, recorded speech at the synod of 1953, in *Acts of Synod, 1953*, 305–6.

Chapter Five

Upheld by the Protestant Reformed Churches

Even though this book is not a history of the Protestant Reformed Churches in the years during which the Declaration of Principles was composed, adopted, attacked, and defended, nor a history of the schism in the churches in 1953, some of this history is pertinent, indeed necessary, to the further history of the Declaration.

SCHISM

While the synod of 1953 was in session, June 3 to 23, events related to the controversy over the Declaration were unfolding that would climax in a schism in the denomination and thus put an end to the strife over the Declaration. These events must have affected the delegates of the 1953 synod, harden-ing them in their determination to abolish the Declaration on the one hand and confirming their determination to uphold the Declaration on the other hand.

Hubert De Wolf, one of three min-isters in First Protestant Reformed Church, Grand Rapids, at the time of the struggle over the Declaration. His preaching of the theology of a conditional covenant was the direct cause of schism in his congregation and in the denomination. His name, therefore, lives in infamy in the PRC.

The main event was the condemnation of a foe of the Declaration, Rev. De Wolf, for preaching heresy and thus causing schism in his congregation. The congregation was the large, influential First Protestant Reformed Church in Grand Rapids, Michigan.

In September 1952, in the heat of the struggle over the Declaration, De Wolf preached a sermon on Matthew 18:3. In the course of the sermon, he said, "Our act of conversion is a prerequisite to enter into the kingdom." Members of his consistory protested this statement to the consistory. Like the synod of the churches, the consistory of First Church found itself deadlocked. Half condemned the statement; half defended it—and the minister who made it, one of their pastors.

In April 1953, the protestants appealed to Classis East for judgment and help. They brought to classis not only their objection to the teaching of De Wolf in his sermon of September 1952 but also their objection to his teaching in a sermon of April 1951. In this sermon on Luke 16:19–31, De Wolf had declared to the congregation, "God promises everyone of you that, if you believe, you shall be saved." Men had protested also this statement to the consistory, but the divided consistory of First Church had not upheld the protests. For about a year and a half, the case regarding the sermon of April 1951 had languished—and festered—in the consistory.[1]

At its continuing session in May 1953, Classis East condemned the two statements as "heretical." It explained this weighty decision. With regard to the first statement, that of April 1951 concerning a universal, conditional promise, Classis East declared that the statement

> teaches a general promise of God unto salvation to all that externally hear the preaching of the gospel, head for head and soul for soul, limited by a condition which man must fulfill, while Scripture and our confessions plainly teach: 1. That, indeed, the proclamation of the gospel comes to all to whom God in His good pleasure sends it. 2. That, however...the promise itself is particular, unconditional, of and only for the elect.[2]

---

1   For the two statements, see *Acts of Synod, 1954*, 54.
2   Ibid., 55.

Regarding the second statement, that of September 1952 concerning man's act of conversion being a prerequisite to his entering into the kingdom, classis explained that the statement

teaches that our act of conversion is a prerequisite to enter the kingdom of God, which means that we convert and humble ourselves before we are translated from the power of darkness into the kingdom of God's dear Son, while Scripture and the confessions plainly teach: That the whole work of our conversion…[in] which we humble ourselves, is sovereignly wrought by God, by His Spirit and Word through the preaching of the gospel in His elect…This entire work of conversion is our translation and entering into the kingdom of God. Hence, it is not, cannot be before but THROUGH our conversion that we enter the kingdom…Our ACT of conversion is never antecedent to our entering in, but always is performed IN the kingdom of God, and there are no prerequisites.[3]

Although the case was not ostensibly about the Declaration of Principles and although the classical decision did not mention the Declaration, in fact the classis condemned the covenant theology that the Declaration repudiated and upheld the doctrine of the covenant that the Declaration confessed as the teaching of the Reformed creeds.

De Wolf himself, the ministers who supported him, and members of the Protestant Reformed Churches later complained that De Wolf was condemned by his consistory and by Classis East on the basis of only two statements. In a private conversation with the present writer, in fact in the course of instruction he was giving at the Protestant Reformed Seminary at the time, Rev. Vos, a leading minister at the time of the troubles in the churches and deeply involved in all the struggles of the churches, said that "although De Wolf was judged on the basis of the two statements, which were bad, the real issue in the case was the doctrine of a conditional covenant, and we all knew it."

---

3   Ibid., 55. Classis gave abundant proof from Scripture and the confessions for its judgment of the statements and theology of De Wolf (see ibid., 55–57).

This was the decision of Classis East in May 1953—barely one month before the meeting of the synod that had to treat protests against the Declaration from half the denomination.

Not only did Classis East condemn the teachings of one of the pastors of First Church, but it also advised the bitterly divided consistory of First Church "to demand that the Rev. De Wolf make a public apology for having made the two statements in question" and "that the Consistory also publicly apologize for having supported the Rev. De Wolf with respect to the two statements in question."[4]

> Classis further advise[d] the Consistory of First Church: a. that in case the Rev. De Wolf should refuse to apologize, which our God graciously forbid, the Consistory proceed to suspend him from the office of the ministry of the Word and the Sacraments, according to the pertinent articles of the [Church Order]. b. that in case any elder or elders should refuse to submit to the proposed action as stipulated...which God graciously forbid, such elder or elders be disciplined according to the articles of the [Church Order] pertaining thereto. Grounds: Art. 79, 80 [Church Order].[5]

On June 1, 1953, two days before the synod of 1953 was to convene, a committee of Classis East met with the consistory of First Church to deliver, explain, and exhort upon the elders these classical decisions. The consistory of First Church adopted the decisions of classis as its own, but by a close vote. By adopting the decisions of Classis East, the consistory of First Church required a public apology from De Wolf. The consistory also composed the apology the minister was to make. It called for him to confess that he was "sorry" for the two statements he had made in his sermons, since they taught "contrary to all our Confessions." It also would have had him promise "henceforth to refrain from such statements and to teach that the promise of God is unconditional and for the elect only."[6]

---

4   Ibid., 55.

5   Ibid., 57–58

6   Gertrude Hoeksema, *A Watered Garden*, 182.

Consistory of First Protestant Reformed Church, Grand Rapids, in the early 1950s prior to the schism of 1953. The consistory was bitterly divided over the Declaration and the heretical sermons of Rev. De Wolf.

On Sunday evening, June 21, during the time the synod of 1953 was in session, De Wolf gave the appearance of complying with the consistory's demand that he publicly apologize for his heretical teachings. However, he disregarded the genuine apology that the consistory had stipulated and merely expressed sorrow that the statements were not clear and therefore left room for a wrong interpretation.

This was not the apology called for by Classis East, the apology required by the consistory of First Church, or an apology at all.

Concerning both his controversial statements, which Classis East had condemned as heretical and for which his consistory had required an apology, Rev. De Wolf worked this pseudoapology into his sermon: "If I did not make myself clear, and if in some way I gave occasion to draw a wrong conclusion, I am sorry. I wouldn't want you to draw a wrong conclusion from my preaching."[7] The

---

7   Hubert De Wolf, from a transcription of his sermon of Sunday, June 21, 1953. It is significant that, although De Wolf denied that this was what he

apology that the consistory of First Church had drawn up for Rev. De Wolf and that he had agreed to make would have had De Wolf confessing that the two statements were "errors," "contrary to all our Confessions." Had he read out the apology required of him, he would also have promised to "refrain from such unscriptural and unreformed teaching."[8]

At the meeting of the consistory of First Church the following evening, a motion to reject De Wolf's remarks from the pulpit as unsatisfactory failed on a tie vote. The consistory was deadlocked.

Thereupon, those elders who were in compliance with the advice of Classis East claimed to be the sole lawful consistory. They met, apart from the elders that supported De Wolf, on June 23 (the last day of the summer 1953 session of synod) and, with the advice of a neighboring consistory, suspended De Wolf from his office. They also deposed the elders of First Church who, rejecting the advice of Classis East, supported De Wolf and his theology.

Because Rev. Hoeksema, Rev. Hanko, and the elders of First Protestant Reformed Church who favored the Declaration and its covenant theology met for the suspension of De Wolf and the deposition of the elders opposed to the Declaration without notifying De Wolf and the elders who supported him, this consistory meeting and its actions drew fierce criticism.

The foes of the Declaration charged that the actions of Hoeksema, Hanko, and the elders who participated were "illegal," "schismatic," "hierarchic," and "contrary even to the jurisprudence of men of the world."[9]

---

meant by the statements, he himself acknowledged, in his pseudoapology, that the statements were, in their literal meaning and in the context of the doctrine of a conditional covenant (which De Wolf was proclaiming), the Arminian heresy: "I have never preached such Arminianism to you." The complete sermon, containing the pseudoapology, has surfaced only recently and is available on the website of the Reformed Free Publishing Association (See "The Gospel: The Power of God unto Salvation" based on Romans 1:16 at http://rfpa.org/pages/remembering-the-schism-of-1953.) The recent obtaining of an original tape of the sermon has made possible the knowledge of the exact terminology of the pseudoapology for the first time.

8 For the full apology required of De Wolf by his consistory, which he failed, and then refused, to make, see G. Hoeksema, *A Watered Garden*, 182.

9 See the representative letter of Rev. Cammenga, in *Acts of Synod, 1954*,

Reconstituted consistory of First Protestant Reformed Church, 1953. This is the consistory of First Church of which Rev. H. Hoeksema and Rev. C. Hanko were the pastors, greatly reduced in size, which suspended Rev. De Wolf and deposed the elders who supported him at its controversial meeting of June 23, 1953. After the schism in the congregation, Classis East recognized this consistory as the legitimate consistory of First Protestant Reformed Church, Grand Rapids.

Classis West of the Protestant Reformed denomination condemned this consistory meeting as "illegal…since many of the legal officebearers of that consistory were not notified of this meeting."[10]

Even the neighboring consistory, whose advice was required for the suspension of De Wolf and the deposition of the elders— Fourth Protestant Reformed Church, Grand Rapids—had reservations about the legality of the consistory meeting at which the suspension and deposition were executed. Having acknowledged the right of the consistory of First Protestant Reformed Church to proceed with discipline, Fourth Church added: "However, we are not prepared to say: a. That the consistory meeting can be called legal when half of its members were not notified that it should be

36–39.

10   Ibid., 63.

held. b. That a suspension can be called in order when the involved were not notified that the double consistory meeting would be held and the suspension be decided on."[11]

The decimated consistory of First Church vigorously defended its action of meeting without De Wolf, one of the pastors of the church, and without about half the elders, all of whom would be either suspended or deposed at the meeting.

Classis East had advised the consistory of First Church "that in case the Rev. De Wolf should refuse to apologize [for his heretical teaching, which the classis had condemned]...the Consistory proceed to suspend him from the office of the ministry of the Word and the Sacraments." At a consistory meeting on June 22, 1953, De Wolf had refused to apologize as the classis had advised. Classis East had also advised the consistory "that in case any elder or elders should refuse to submit to the proposed action [by Classis East, requiring an apology for De Wolf's heretical statements and advising his suspension, should he refuse to confess his sin]...such elder or elders be disciplined according to the articles of the [Church Order] pertaining thereto."[12] The elders who were deposed at the consistory meeting of June 23, 1953, had refused to submit to the decisions of Classis East at the full consistory meeting held on June 22, 1953.

By his refusal to apologize for his heretical teaching and by their refusal to require an apology of their pastor, De Wolf and the elders who supported him placed themselves in opposition to the decisions not only of Classis East but also of the consistory of First Protestant Reformed Church. At a consistory meeting held on June 1, 1953, which was attended by all the elders of the church, those supporting De Wolf and his theology as well as those opposing him and his theology, the consistory of First Church by majority vote had adopted a motion to adopt the advice of Classis East in the case of the heretical doctrine of De Wolf. This consistorial decision determined that De Wolf would be suspended for impenitent persistence in heresy and that all the elders who defended him, contrary to the advice of Classis East, would be deposed.

---

11 Ibid., 61.

12 Quoted, as part of the complete decision of Classis East regarding the matter of De Wolf's controversial covenant doctrine, in ibid., 57–58.

Defending their holding of a consistory meeting without the presence of one of the pastors of the church—De Wolf—and without the presence of half the elders—all those who had refused to honor a decision of the consistory and to submit to the settled and binding advice of Classis East—Hoeksema, Hanko, and the elders who were part of the June 23 consistory meeting added this:

> It is alleged that this meeting was illegal, because the guilty brethren were not present and were not even notified of the meeting. But the meeting was perfectly legal. Consider: a. That the guilty brethren had been present at every meeting in which their case was treated. b. That they had plainly proved that they were worthy of suspension and deposition. c. That they had no longer any place in the consistory of the First Prot. Ref. Church. d. That their case was completely finished. e. That their presence would only have resulted in more illegal voting and chaos. f. That the Church Order does not require that officebearers that are to be suspended or deposed, must be present at their own suspension and deposition.[13]

The consistory of First Church also contended that the minister who was suspended and the elders who were deposed at the consistory meeting of June 23, 1953, had no right to vote in their own case: "As soon as he [an officebearer] is no longer in good standing, either as the accused, or as guilty, he loses his right to vote."[14]

Confirming this defense of the consistory meeting of June 23, 1953, was the testimony rendered to Classis East by the committee of classis that had been appointed to assist First Church in carrying out the decisions of classis. This committee was present at the consistory meeting of June 23, at which Rev. De Wolf was suspended and roughly half the elders of First Church were deposed. The committee of classis consisting of Rev. Vos, Rev. M. Schipper, Rev. G. Vanden Berg, and elders N. J. Yonker and D. A. Langeland, reported to Classis East that they "witnessed all that took place

---

13 Report to Classis East, October 6, 1953, by the consistory of the First Protestant Reformed Church. Herman Hoeksema, "What Happened at Classis East," *Standard Bearer* 30, no. 2 (October 15, 1953): 31.

14 Ibid.

at this [consistory] meeting and can give testimony that in our judgment the entire proceedings were legitimate."[15]

It is no negation, or even weakening, of this defense of the extraordinary consistory meeting of June 23, 1953, to see it also as Hoeksema's cutting the Gordian knot of the vexatious tie vote of the First Church consistory. This tie vote, for a long time, had permitted the promotion of the false doctrine of a conditional covenant in the mother church of the Protestant Reformed Churches—Hoeksema's own congregation—and had repeatedly frustrated efforts to condemn and eradicate this false doctrine. By radical action (which is not the same as church politically disorderly action), Hoeksema saw to it that the tie vote, which had bedeviled the church for years, would not hinder the church in the crisis of the controversy.

Classis East ratified the consistory meeting of June 23, 1953, and its actions suspending Rev. De Wolf and deposing a number of elders.

At its meeting in October 1953, Classis East was confronted with two sets of delegates asking to be recognized and seated as delegates of First Church, Grand Rapids. Classis received the credentials of the consistory whose pastors were Hoeksema and Hanko.

---

15 Ibid., 29. The entire fascinating report of the committee to Classis East, October 6, 1953, concerning all their actions is found in this editorial on pages 28–29. The editorial concludes with the complete text of the moving speech that Rev. Vos, spokesman of the committee of classis, gave to the full consistory of First Church at the meeting of June 1, 1953, in explanation of the advice of Classis East. Although the speech breathed love for De Wolf ("'Hubert'…because I love the boy"), all the consistory, and First Church ("the mother church…I was awed by you always"), it pulled no punches. It laid out the heresy of the controverted statements by De Wolf. It warned the consistory, "As far as the classis is concerned this is a fundamental matter for us and we will never go back on this stand; and therefore it may be the end of the road." It ended with a plea to De Wolf and the elders who were supporting him: "If you…will throw those statements away, God only knows how many you will save in your church. The whole movement…will be broken… and we can go on…[in] unity." That consistory meeting of the still-united First Church with the speech of Gerrit Vos had to have been one of the momentous occasions in the history of the church of Christ, momentous occasions being determined not by size and publicity, but by the drama of the event and by its significance with regard to the truth of the gospel and the way of the true church of Christ in the world.

It rejected the delegation that included De Wolf. The grounds for this decision of the classis regarding recognition and seating of the delegates of First Church were "that the Rev. De Wolf and his elder were legally under censure, and that therefore they could not function as delegates to Classis, that they refused to submit to their censure and rebelled against their Consistory and that therefore they had become schismatic and severed themselves from the communion of the Prot. Ref. Churches."[16]

At this decision by classis, several ministers and elders who supported De Wolf, foes of the Declaration all, withdrew from the classis. Thus the schism became a reality throughout Classis East of the Protestant Reformed Churches.

Classis West also reacted to the significant events in First Church. No one could have doubted what the reaction of that classis would be.

Classis West met in September 1953. All the ministers and elders were well aware of the happenings in First Church. In addition to rumor, which truly had wings in those days, First Church had notified all the churches in the denomination of its suspension of De Wolf and its deposition of the elders who supported him, rejecting the advice of Classis East.

In response to the decisions of Classis East and the actions of First Church, Classis West behaved disorderly. Rather than to protest the decisions and actions in church orderly fashion, Classis West took decisions condemning the decisions of Classis East and the actions of First Church and supporting De Wolf and the schismatic faction in Classis East.

> We [Classis West] cannot recognize the suspension of the Rev. De Wolf and the deposition of the elders supporting him, but on the contrary must consider the Rev. De Wolf with his consistory and congregation as the legal and proper continuation of the First Prot. Ref. Church of Grand Rapids, Michigan.[17]

By this decision of Classis West, the schism that began in First Church in June 1953 became a grievous reality throughout the

---

16   *Acts of Synod, 1954*, 62.

17   Ibid., 62–63.

entire Protestant Reformed denomination.

The schism effectively put an end to the controversy over the Declaration in the Protestant Reformed Churches. All those opposed to the Declaration separated from the denomination. The Protestant Reformed Churches would maintain the Declaration without dissent.

NULLIFICATION OF THE DECLARATION BY THE SCHISMATICS

Those who had separated from the Protestant Reformed Churches would, unanimously, declare the decisions adopting the Declaration null and void and consign the document to the wastebasket. They would do this as quickly as possible. They began this process already at their first synodical meeting after the schism of 1953.

The reader will recall that the 1953 synod of the still-united churches, hopelessly deadlocked over the Declaration, had recessed until March 1954. To this reconvened session of synod had been given the task of deciding on the many appeals against the Declaration by its determined opponents. The site of this session of synod had been designated as the building of First Protestant Reformed Church in Grand Rapids. At the time of the reconvening of synod, the property was in the possession of the consistory whose pastor was Rev. De Wolf. The schismatic churches, still claiming the name Protestant Reformed, therefore assembled in First Church on the designated date as the continued synod of the Protestant Reformed Churches.

At this meeting of synod, the study committee of three ministers that had been appointed by the June 1953 session of synod, to advise on treatment of the protests against the Declaration, gave their report. Unsurprisingly, in view of the fact that all three were well-known adversaries of the Declaration, their report condemned the Declaration as "illegally before Synod and...illegally adopted by Synod."[18]

---

18 *Acts of Synod, 1953*, 362. Because the synodical stated clerk of the Protestant Reformed Churches at the time was a minister allied with the schismatic faction, the minutes of the continuation of the 1953 synod by

With regard to the content of the Declaration, against which the protests also objected, the report of the study committee upheld the objectors by advising that the Declaration is not the "expression of the Confessions [but] extra-confessional."[19]

It is significant that, to the bitter end of their opposition to the Declaration as the cause of all evil in the Protestant Reformed Churches, the schismatic faction nevertheless felt constrained to qualify their criticism of the Declaration by acknowledging that "all the Protestants expressed their general agreement with the basic thrust and general doctrinal content of the Declaration of Principles."[20] But the "basic thrust" of the Declaration was its expression of the teaching of the creeds that the covenant of grace, its promise, and its promised salvation are unconditional. With this, the objectors publicly expressed agreement.

Their opposition to the Declaration, to the extent of splitting the denomination, to say nothing of their defense of the conditional covenant theology of the liberated churches and of their quick return to the Christian Reformed Church, where not the general doctrinal content of the Declaration but the diametrically opposite covenant doctrine of Heyns reigned, gives the lie to their public statement of agreement with the content of the Declaration. It was important at that stage of the schism that the ministers convince their people that the ministers were still Protestant Reformed in their doctrine of the covenant.

A committee of pre-advice recommended that the reconvened synod of those churches that had separated from the Protestant Reformed Churches "declare that the Synod[s] of 1950 and 1951 erred in originating, treating and adopting the Declaration of Principles and that, therefore, the Declaration is without force as a Synodically approved expression."[21]

---

the schismatics were included in the *Acts of Synod, Protestant Reformed Churches in America, 1953.* Unfortunately, the minutes of the continuation of the 1953 synod by the Protestant Reformed Churches were never printed in a published *Acts.* The minutes of the March 1954 synod of the Protestant Reformed Churches must be sought and are available in the archives of the denomination.

19 Ibid., 362–63.
20 Ibid., 352.
21 Ibid., 363.

The synod, however, declined to adopt this recommendation at the meeting in March 1954. The reason was not any softening of opposition to the Declaration. Rather, the synod took note that the entire delegation from Classis East at the June 1953 session of synod, of which the March 1954 session was a continuation, was missing. All the delegates of Classis East were part of the synod of the Protestant Reformed Churches, which was meeting elsewhere. The absence of the delegates of Classis East cast doubt on the legitimacy of the synod of the schismatic faction. The synod therefore postponed adoption of the advice to repudiate the Declaration to the synod of June 1954.[22]

The schismatic synod of June 1954 decided that, because the original adoption of the Declaration was illegal, "the Declaration of Principles is without force as a Synodically approved expression."[23] It added, concerning the content of the Declaration, that the Declaration "may not be adopted as an expression of our Basis of Unity on certain doctrinal points."[24] The minutes of the synod state that these decisions repudiating the Declaration were unanimous.[25] The Declaration with its confession of an unconditional covenant had not a single friend among the delegates to the synod of the churches that separated from the Protestant Reformed Churches.

Thus perished the Declaration for the schismatic faction. They had officially freed themselves from what was for them, evidently, an intolerable yoke. And then, within a few years, they returned to the Christian Reformed Church, where they willingly took on the yoke of the doctrine of common grace, which, like the Declaration, purported to be the expression of the Reformed confessions.

In addition, they made themselves responsible for the prevailing doctrine of the covenant in the Christian Reformed Church— Heyns' teaching of a gracious but conditional covenant promise to all the baptized children alike; of a gracious but conditional covenant actually established with all baptized children alike; and of

---

22 Ibid., 370–71.

23 *Acts of Synod, Protestant Reformed Churches of America [schismatic], 1954,* 41.

24 Ibid.

25 Ibid.

a covenant grace bestowed upon all baptized children alike—conditionally.

INACTION OF THE PRC

Consideration of the protests against the Declaration was also on the agenda of the reconvened synod of the Protestant Reformed Churches, by virtue of its being the continuation of the synod of 1953. This continued session of synod met from March 10 to 18, 1954, at the Fourth Protestant Reformed Church in Grand Rapids. As all the original delegates of Classis East were missing from the schismatic synod, so all the original delegates of Classis West were missing from this synod. There were newly appointed delegates of "the reorganized Classis West."

Richard Newhouse, stalwart elder of Hope Protestant Reformed Church in western Michigan from the beginning of the existence of the PRC in 1924; and often a delegate to Classis East and to synod. Newhouse, a fervent disciple especially of Rev. Ophoff (former pastor of Hope Church), rose to prominence not only in the preservation of his own congregation, but also in the adoption of the Declaration and in the condemnation of the sermons of Rev. De Wolf as heretical—no doubt, to the complete surprise of the "little Dutchman."

At the synod was the report of the study committee that the deadlocked synod of 1953 had appointed with the mandate to advise the reconvened synod concerning all the materials regarding the Declaration, which were mostly protests against its adoption. This committee, consisting as it did of three ministers opposed to the Declaration, of course advised repudiating the Declaration as illegally adopted and as unnecessary binding, if not as an inaccurate expression of the confessions regarding the covenant. One might have expected the reconvened synod of the Protestant Reformed Churches to reject the advice of the special committee of three ministers and thus, without further ado, to reject all the protests and appeals against the Declaration. Instead, the action of the

March 1954 synod of the Protestant Reformed Churches regarding this report of the study committee was the appointment of yet another committee, whose mandate was "to study this report and advise [synod] concerning it." This committee was instructed to report to the synod of 1955.[26]

This committee never carried out its mandate. Yearly, beginning in 1955, it reported to synod that it had not done the work assigned to it by the synod of 1954. Finally, the committee reported to the 1958 synod that the committee judged itself "out-dated and consequently has nothing to report." Synod then terminated the committee.[27]

The synod of the Protestant Reformed Churches therefore never completely treated the protests against the adoption of the Declaration that appeared on the agenda of the synod of 1953. The sole action was that of the 1953 synod at its June 1953 session, rejecting advice from its committee of pre-advice that would have judged the adoption of the Declaration as illegal. This decision was a tie vote.

Evidently, the thinking of the synods of the Protestant Reformed Churches after the schism in 1953 was that answering protests against the Declaration from ministers and consistories that had separated from the churches had become senseless. The now unified mind of the Protestant Reformed Churches was approval of the Declaration as sound and necessary and its adoption as legal,

---

26 "Minutes of the Continuation of the Synod of June 1953…at the Fourth Protestant Reformed Church, Grand Rapids, Michigan," 3–4. As explained in a previous footnote, these minutes were never printed in a published *Acts*. They are available in the archives of the denomination. The committee that was to advise on the report of the study committee concerning the Declaration consisted of Hoeksema, Ophoff, and the stalwart elder from Hope Protestant Reformed Church, Richard Newhouse. Newhouse was prominent in the struggle over the Declaration. Often a delegate to Classis East and to synod, he was a member of that part of the committee of pre-advice (with Elder Peter Lubbers, from Hudsonville) that recommended to Classis East that it condemn the two statements of De Wolf as heretical. A short man, Newhouse was the embodiment of the Dutch phrase "*klein maar dapper*" (small but brave).

27 *Acts of Synod, Protestant Reformed Churches in America, 1958*, 62.

without any dissent. Further action regarding protests against the Declaration would be a waste of time and energy.

After the schism of 1953, the Declaration of Principles receded into the background of the churches' consciousness. Little more was heard of it. No doubt it functioned according to its expressed purpose, namely, in the organization of new churches. Even in this regard, however, it fell off the churches' radar. For the work with the Dutch, liberated immigrants in Canada came to an abrupt halt with the adoption of the Declaration by the Protestant Reformed Churches. The Declaration was anathema to the liberated. There would be no church of liberated Reformed to organize with the use of the Declaration.

Over the years the Declaration became a neglected, even forgotten, document in the Protestant Reformed Churches. It is not impossible that some members of the Protestant Reformed Churches have regarded the Declaration with disfavor, as the cause of exceedingly painful troubles and even a split in the churches.

This would change with the rise of the theology of the federal vision in the conservative Reformed and Presbyterian churches in North America about the year 2000. The federal vision, a grievous heresy denying sovereign grace, is, and advertises itself as being, the development of the doctrine of a conditional covenant and covenant promise. More specifically, it is the logical, inevitable development of the covenant theology of Schilder, Holwerda, Veenhof, and the Reformed Churches in the Netherlands (liberated).[28]

Thus the federal vision raises once again in the history of the Reformed church the issue of the covenant of grace's being unconditional or conditional—the very issue fought out by the Protestant Reformed Churches in the late 1940s and early 1950s and the very issue addressed by the Declaration.

The Declaration has once again become an important document. But now it is not only an important document for the Protestant Reformed Churches. The heresy of the federal vision has made it an important document also for all Reformed and Presbyterian

---

28 On the theology and root of the federal vision, see David J. Engelsma, *Federal Vision: Heresy at the Root* (Jenison, MI: Reformed Free Publishing Association, 2010).

churches in North America. It should compel the churches that
struggle with the federal vision to consider whether the doctrine
of an unconditional covenant, rooted in the decree of election
and governed by the decree, is not, in truth, the expression of the
Reformed confessions and the only safeguard against the heresy of
the federal vision.

Chapter Six

Effects of the Adoption of the Declaration

The adoption of the Declaration of Principles by the Protestant Reformed Churches had enormous consequences for the denomination.

Even though the schism in the churches did not take place until some two years after the adoption of the Declaration by the synod of 1951 and even though the catalyst of the schism was heretical sermons by a Protestant Reformed minister, in fact the occasion of the schism was the Declaration.

All the ministers in the Protestant Reformed Churches recognized that the Declaration, once adopted, would be a binding decision in the churches. And those who separated from the Protestant Reformed Churches were determined not to be bound to the doctrine of an unconditional covenant.

The two objectionable, heretical statements by De Wolf were public, defiant rejection of the doctrine of an unconditional covenant. The issue before Classis East in 1953 was not only the matter of two statements but also, and especially, the matter of the doctrine of a conditional covenant.

The adversaries of the Declaration warned that adoption of the Declaration would precipitate a split in the churches.

By adopting the Declaration, therefore, the Protestant Reformed Churches knowingly, if unwillingly, subjected themselves to suffering schism, a uniquely painful experience for the church in the world. Lost to the churches were about two-thirds of their members, ministers, and congregations. In the summer of 1953, immediately prior to the schism, the membership of the denomination stood

1953 Protestant Reformed Young People's Convention. Severely battered and grievously wounded in the battle for the covenant resulting in the schism of 1953, the PRC were, nevertheless, not destroyed or defeated. They persevered in their normal church life, holding the annual convention of young people. These young people, meeting just two months after the schism, represent the future of the victorious denomination—victorious by virtue of its maintaining, uncorrupted, the Reformed faith of the creeds, particularly the Canons of Dordt.

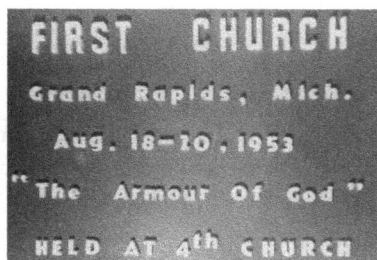

FIRST CHURCH
Grand Rapids, Mich.
Aug. 18–20, 1953
"The Armour Of God"
HELD AT 4th CHURCH

at slightly more than 6,000.[1] After the schism, the membership was reduced to about 2,300.[2] It would take fifty years for the churches to regain the size they had before the schism.

Mere loss of membership was not the worst. Friendships of many years broke up in hot debates and bitter hostility. Families were divided. The normal work of a Reformed denomination of churches suffered. The Protestant Reformed Christian schools, with the loss of the many children of those who left the churches, struggled for their existence and made no advancement.

In addition, the Protestant Reformed Churches, always a pariah

1   *Acts of Synod, 1953*, 335.
2   *Acts of Synod, 1954*, 82.

in the wider church community because of the influence of the prestigious, influential Christian Reformed Church, became increasingly the object of suspicion, scorn, and reproach on the part of other Reformed and Presbyterian churches. The schismatics were largely successful in painting the church troubles of the Protestant Reformed Churches as mainly, if not exclusively, due to "personalities" (especially the personality of Herman Hoeksema, it was always suggested), as a mere power struggle, and therefore as completely unnecessary.

Few outside the denomination examined the doctrinal issue at stake in the controversy. One who did was the Christian Reformed theologian James Daane. Daane recognized what should have been apparent to all, namely, that the doctrine of a conditional covenant promise to all baptized children alike is essentially the teaching of the well-meant offer of the gospel, on account of his rejection of which Hoeksema had been ejected from the Christian Reformed Church twenty-five years before the controversy in the Protestant Reformed Churches in the early 1950s. Writing in the *Reformed Journal* magazine in 1951, Daane weighed in on the Protestant Reformed controversy over the Declaration, that is, over the issue of an unconditional or conditional covenant.

> The *Declaration* defines the Protestant Reformed view of the Covenant, in contrast to Schilder's view—and ours [the Christian Reformed Church's; here, Daane observes that the doctrine of Heyns, which prevailed in the Christian Reformed Church, and the doctrine of Schilder

are the same]. It is the denial of common grace as applied to the Covenant... According to Hoeksema and the *Declaration*, the denial of common grace means that there are no "conditions" in the Covenant...Hoeksema believes that if their churches subscribe to the position that God operates with conditions, and takes them seriously, their churches have lost their reason for separate existence. Rejection of the *Declaration* would be an announcement that it is time to return to the Christian Reformed fold. A number of Protestant Reformed ministers are not in favor of the *Declaration*. Some...openly contend for conditions within the Covenant. They maintain that such a view of the Covenant does not do violence to Protestant Reformed theology. In this, I believe these protesting Protestant Reformed ministers are plainly wrong, and Hoeksema, on his basis, is entirely correct...These Protestant Reformed ministers...face two alternatives. They will either have to reject conditions within the Covenant, or insist upon their retention, and become Christian Reformed.[3]

Daane commented again on the Protestant Reformed controversy over the Declaration and its doctrine of the covenant after the schism. He was even more blunt concerning the significance of the rejection of the unconditional covenant by professing Protestant Reformed ministers.

Although they do not admit it, those of the Protestant Reformed Churches who now disagree with the Rev. H. Hoeksema have taken at least one theological step back toward the Christian Reformed Church...Those who differ from Hoeksema and affirm the rightful place of "conditions" within Reformed theology have thereby theologically conceded that grace can after all be offered inasmuch as a condition is in its very nature of the essence of an offer.[4]

So long as the conflict over the Declaration was raging in the Protestant Reformed Churches, the ministers opposing the

3 James Daane, "Timeless Logic?" *Reformed Journal* 1, no. 2 (April 1951): 10.
4 James Daane, "Theology and Schism," *Reformed Journal* 3, no. 9 (September 1953): 3–4.

Declaration and favoring a conditional covenant vehemently denied Daane's analysis of the controversy and virtual prophecy of their return to the Christian Reformed Church. Within a few years, however, they were negotiating their return. By 1960 their synod deliberated a motion to return to the Christian Reformed Church. They returned, *en masse*, in 1961.

The return of the entire schismatic denomination to the Christian Reformed Church a mere eight years after they separated from the Protestant Reformed Churches—in 1961—is itself significant regarding the readiness, if not desire, of many of the leading ministers to abandon the confession of the Protestant Reformed Churches concerning sovereign, particular grace and to embrace, or at least tolerate, the Christian Reformed Church's confession of universal, resistible (saving) grace in its doctrine of common grace.

TREACHERY

But there was more to this readiness to return to the Christian Reformed Church on the part of the schismatic ministers than met the eye in those days, or than has yet come to light to the present time. Already within two years of the schism, one of the ministers who had separated from the Protestant Reformed Churches had successfully sought entrance into the Christian Reformed Church. In 1955 Rev. Van Weelden was accepted into the Christian Reformed Church. His defection involved the disbanding of his congregation in Sioux Center, Iowa. Entrance into the ministry of the Christian Reformed Church for the erstwhile Protestant Reformed minister required of him that he confess his "guilt that he was co-responsible in both misrepresenting the Christian Reformed Church and in engaging in un-Christian practices against [the Christian Reformed Church]."[5]

Within a year of the schism, in 1954, Rev. Howerzyl was publicly asking about his churches' "right of existence." In an editorial in *Concordia*, Howerzyl asked, "Do we have the right to continue as Protestant Reformed Churches? What does God mean to tell us by our recent history? Is it our calling to return to the Christian

---

5   Reported and quoted in the *Reformed Guardian* 1, no. 12 (November 10, 1955): 179.

Reformed Church? We may not like the question put so bluntly and in so pointed a manner, but it must be faced."[6] Howerzyl's answer, at that time, was that his churches had a right of separate existence, but what was significant was his asking the question at all, in dead earnest, and so soon in their history.

In an article in the *Reformed Guardian* of November 1955, Rev. Edward Knott found it necessary to admonish his colleagues and the members of their churches against seeking admission into the Christian Reformed Church. In words that must have come back to haunt him six years later, when he himself went back to the Christian Reformed Church, Knott admonished his colleagues: "Any minister and/or common member who comes back [to the Christian Reformed Church] denies that the stand that we as churches have held throughout our history has any validity or is in any sense correct...There is no more room in that church [the Christian Reformed Church] for us today than there was then [in 1924]." He then exhorted his troops: "Let us rally, then, about the standard of truth."[7]

In 1957, within four years of the schism, Rev. De Boer advocated that his denomination return to the Christian Reformed Church, regardless of the doctrine of common grace. Pleading for "serious consideration of return to the Christian Reformed Church," De Boer confessed his change of heart concerning the doctrine of common grace and its implications and fruits: "I personally do not believe that the matter of common grace alone warrants our continued separation [from the Christian Reformed Church] or that the denominations ought to live separately because of it."[8]

The 1957 synod of the churches that had broken with the Protestant Reformed Churches addressed a letter to the Christian

---

6   J. Howerzyl, "The Church's Right of Existence," *Concordia* 11, no. 15 (Thursday, October 7, 1954): 2. This editorial is not signed, but the succeeding editorials make plain that the author was Howerzyl.

7   E. Knott, "No Change," *Reformed Guardian* 1, no. 12 (November 10, 1955): 179. Knott could not restrain himself, even then, from an angry—and ill-advised—challenge to the Protestant Reformed Churches: "Time will tell who are truly Protestant Reformed...not by the decree of a court, but in the confession of the truth and a walk in love" (180).

8   P. De Boer, "As I See It," *Reformed Guardian* 3, no. 7 (August 25, 1957): 100.

Reformed Church expressing desire for "ecumenical contact with the Christian Reformed Church."[9] In fact, the overture opened the way for these churches to return to the Christian Reformed Church.

By 1960 a majority of consistories of the schismatic Protestant Reformed Churches, under the leadership of their pastors, expressed that the three points of common grace adopted by the Christian Reformed Church in 1924 were either sound or tolerable, so that there was no reason for those churches to remain separate from the Christian Reformed Church. Writing in the April 1960 issue of the *Reformed Guardian*, Rev. Hofman announced to his churches that "many among us willingly grant and accept much of what is taught by 1924 [that is, the Christian Reformed Church's doctrine of common grace]...With but few exceptions, our Consistories have expressed or implied a willingness to acknowledge as brethren and exercise fellowship with those who would maintain common grace also as expressed in the Three Points."[10] At that time, those churches were in official correspondence with the Christian Reformed Church, negotiating their way back to that denomination.

The schismatic churches held an early, special synod in October 1960—a mere seven years after their separation from the Protestant Reformed Churches—in order to consider the Christian Reformed response to these churches' appeal for acceptance into the Christian Reformed Church. At the synod of 1960, the motion to return to the Christian Reformed Church failed on a tie vote.

But the motion would prevail at their synod of 1961. What was left of the schismatic denomination (for individual ministers and congregations had been leaving for the Christian Reformed Church for some time before the synod of 1961) returned to the Christian Reformed Church, out of which Christ had led them (they had long professed) in 1924. The separate existence of the schismatic denomination lasted barely eight years.

Their end was ignominious.

In returning to the Christian Reformed Church, the separated

9   See J. Howerzyl, "The Letter of Testimony and Our Attitude toward the Christian Reformed Church," *Reformed Guardian* 3, no. 10 (October 10, 1957): 147.

10 W. Hofman, "Some Trends—II," *Reformed Guardian* 6, no. 1 (April 25, 1960): 3–4, 7.

Protestant Reformed Churches renounced their history, sacrificed their heritage, approved the doctrine of common grace as biblical and Reformed, promised not to oppose the doctrine of common grace, and committed themselves and their generations to the deleterious effects of common grace with regard to both doctrine and life. These concessions the schismatic churches published in their magazine for all the membership to read and to become responsible for.

> We no longer charge the "Three Points" [of common grace] with being Arminian and Pelagian nor are we pleading for freedom to agitate and cause turmoil and strife in the churches...[We] agree that the Three Points are neither Arminian nor Pelagian; that in the light of the official interpretation given by our [Christian Reformed] Synod of 1959, the objection that the Three Points are in conflict with the Scriptures and the Forms of Unity is not valid; and that [we] will agree not to agitate against official interpretations.[11]

These were the concessions and actions of churches, especially of the ministers of the churches, who throughout the controversy over the Declaration were loudly insisting that they were, and intended to remain, Protestant Reformed.

If this softness of the schismatic faction toward the doctrine of common grace and openness toward reunion with the Christian Reformed Church are evidence of nothing more, they show that the schismatics did not debate the issues at stake in the Declaration in good faith. They were themselves weak regarding sovereign grace in salvation, open to the Christian Reformed and Heynsian compromise of grace. They carried on the controversy with the secret resolve that if the Protestant Reformed Churches were destroyed by the controversy, or if their own ecclesiastical position became untenable, they would seek refuge in the Christian Reformed Church.

But there is reason to believe that matters were even more reprehensible, at least with regard to the ministers of the schismatic

---

11 "Resolution of Reunion Protestant Reformed [sic] and Christian Reformed," *Reformed Guardian* 7, no. 4 (July 25, 1961): 56.

churches. At their synod of 1961, at which those churches would decide to return to the Christian Reformed Church, permission was given to all officebearers and former officebearers to speak on the motion to go back to the Christian Reformed Church. A former elder of First Protestant Reformed Church, a man who had been elder at the time of the schism, addressed the synod and the audience. Obviously angry and obviously opposed to the prospect of ceasing to be Protestant Reformed and becoming Christian Reformed, he informed the synod and the audience that "within six months of our leaving the Protestant Reformed Churches, Rev. De Wolf was urging our young people to go back to the Christian Reformed Church. We elders [the consistory of the schismatic First Protestant Reformed Church] had to reprimand him for this."[12]

And then there is this largely unknown fact. Within two or three months of the schism, the schismatic ministers were holding secret meetings with leading theologians and ministers of the Christian Reformed Church. At these meetings, the men discussed the various doctrinal issues that historically have divided the Protestant Reformed Churches and the Christian Reformed Church, certainly with a view to the eventual return of the schismatic churches to the Christian Reformed Church.

There is in the possession of the present writer, from the library of one of the ministers of the churches that separated from the Protestant Reformed Churches in 1953, a collection of theological papers written by these ministers and by theologians of the Christian Reformed Church. These papers were the basis of monthly meetings of the ministers and theologians from the

---

12 The present writer attended this synod at the behest of Herman Hoeksema, who, of course, was vitally interested in its proceedings but could not himself appear at the synod. I took copious notes of the speeches, which are in my possession and from which this quotation is taken. Of interest concerning the speech of the aggrieved former elder is that no one challenged his report, although the minister concerned and other elders were present. The only challenge was objection by the president of synod to the elder's reference to the schism as their leaving "the Protestant Reformed Churches." The president corrected the elder, interrupting him, by suggesting instead, "the Hoeksema group." Whereupon, more loudly than before, the elder repeated himself: "within six months after we left *the Protestant Reformed Churches.*" The president said nothing more.

two denominations. At these meetings, the men discussed these issues with a view to the reunion of the two denominations. One of the papers begins, "The subject for this evening's discussion, it should be said at the outset, is not an easy one."[13] Another begins, "In order that our discussions may be carried forward somewhat, we have been asked to introduce the subject of the teaching of the Christian Reformed Church as formulated in the second point of the decisions of 1924."[14]

Yet another paper opens with this statement: "The topic assigned by the committee which organized this conference was presented to me as follows: 'Favorable Attitude, True or False.'"[15]

Concerning the nature and purpose of the discussions, in addition to what can be inferred from the participants and subjects, one paper, in handwriting atop the first page, has, "Given at our last mtg. with C.R. men."[16] Another paper, written evidently by one of the nominally Protestant Reformed ministers, concludes with these words, making the purpose of the meetings and discussions explicit:

> Exactly in our present stadium of contact with the Chr. Ref. and with a view to possible re-union, we must seriously consider how much these things mean. If we cannot and may not bring this stream to a convergence we will have lost an opportunity to testify of a very important and vital area of the Word of God and that we may not do… God places both us and the C. R. Churches before these things again, not that we may seek our self-advantage, or

---

13 Peter Y. De Jong, "What is the Meaning of the Hatred of God?" A privately printed paper dated March 17, 1954, in the library of David J. Engelsma (the page on which the quotation is found is the first page of the paper, although the page is numbered 19).

14 Peter Y. De Jong, "Notes on the Second Point of 1924." A privately printed paper, undated, in the library of David J. Engelsma (the page on which the quotation is found is the first page of the paper, although the page is numbered 48).

15 "Favorable Attitude: True or False?" A privately printed paper, undated, in the library of David J. Engelsma, 1. No author is indicated.

16 J. Blankespoor, "The Third Point of 1924." A privately printed paper, undated, in the library of David J. Engelsma, 1.

whatever, but to make every possible effort to be one as God is one in truth and love.[17]

The names of the authors of the papers read and discussed at the secret conclave identify at least some of the participants in the meetings for "reunion." They are: "Concerning Equal Ultimacy of Election and Reprobation," by Rev. M. Gritters; "What is the Meaning of the Term 'World' in John 3:16," by Rev. H. Vander Kam; "The Concept 'World' in John 3:16," by Rev. James Howerzyl; "What is the Meaning of the Hatred of God?" by Dr. Peter Y. De Jong; "God's Purpose to Save Only the Elect, and the Sincere, General Offer of the Gospel," by John Geels; "God's Intention in Preaching the Gospel to the Unsaved," by Rev. M. Gritters; "What is the Meaning of the Term Grace in the Scripture and in What Sense is it Common?" by C. R. Veenstra; "Notes on the Second Point of 1924," by Dr. Peter Y. De Jong; "The Second Point of 1924," by Rev. James Howerzyl; "The Third Point of 1924," by (Rev.) J. Blankespoor; "Favorable Attitude: True or False," the author of which is not indicated, although it is evident from the paper that he was one of the purportedly Protestant Reformed ministers involved in the meetings; and "Is the Preaching an 'Offer'?" by (Rev.) W. Hofman.[18]

What is of special significance about these papers and meetings, and extremely troubling with regard to the behavior of the schismatic ministers during the controversy over the Declaration, is that one of the papers is dated "January 15, 1954." This was also, evidently, the date of the meeting of the ministers who had just separated from the Protestant Reformed Churches and the theologians of the Christian Reformed Church. Even if this was the earliest conference of the men, the meeting was held not more than two or three months after the schism in the Protestant Reformed Churches had become final. Classis West of the Protestant Reformed Churches had extended the schism to the churches of the West in September 1953; ministers and elders had separated from Classis East in October 1953.

---

17 "Favorable Attitude: True or False?" 21.
18 All of these papers are in the library of David J. Engelsma.

CONCERNING EQUAL ULTIMACY OF ELECTION AND REPROBATION

Rev. M. Gritters

January 15, 1954

WHAT IS THE MEANING OF THE TERM "WORLD" IN JOHN 3:16?

Rev. H. Vander Kam

February 19, 1954

NOTES ON THE SECOND POINT OF 1924

Dr. Peter Y. De Jong

The Third Point of 1924 _by J. Blankespoor_

I. The Third point adopted by the Synod of Kalamazoo in 1924 reads
as follows:

Concerning the third point, touching the performance of
so-called civic righteousness by the unregenerate, the Synod
declares that according to Scripture and Confession the unregenerate, though incapable of any saving good (Canons of
Dordt, III,IV,3), can perform such civic good. This is evident
from the quoted scripture-passages and from the Canons of Dordt
III,IV,4 and the Belgic Confession, where it is taught that
God, without renewing the heart, exercises such influence upon
man that he is enabled to perform civic good; while it is
evident from the quoted declarations of Reformed writers of
the period of florescence of Reformed theology, that our
Reformed Fathers from of old have championed this view.

II. What it teaches.
A. That it in a measure is a matter of interpretation can readily
be understood in the light of the fact that the Synod did not define
its own terms. Perhaps the biggest question has always been, what is
meant with the word good.
First of all we want to see how the Prot. Reformed have
interpreted this point. And let it then be said immediately that our
big objection has not been to the term civic righteousness. The
Scriptures themselves speak of Jehu doing well, and of Jehoash and
Amazia that they did that which was right. But there undoubtedly is
much more involved here than a few terms or words. Dr. Berkhof in
his "De Drie Punten in alle deelen Gereformeerd"readily admits the
same thing:
"Ook hier moeten we tot onzen spijt een soortgelijke opmerking
maken als bij de bespreking van het tweede punt. Strict genomen,
verklaart de Synode alleen, dat de onwedergeborenen, hoewel onbe-
kwaam tot eenig zaligmakend goed, toch burgerlijk goed kunnen
doen. Het blijkt echter wel uit het verband, waarin dit put gezet
is tot het eerste punt, uit het feit, dat al de elementen uit
het oorspronkelijke voorstel ook in de uitspraak der Synode opge-
nomen zijn, en uit de verklaring, dat het uit de aangehaalde be-
wijsplaatsen blijkt, 'dat God zonder het hart te vernieuwen zoo-
danigen invloed op den mensch oefent, dat deze in staat gesteld
wordt burgerlijk goed te doen; --- dat het besluit der Synode
feitelijk meer inhoudt.'

In our opinion this point teaches at least three different
things. 1/ That God exerts an influence upon man. No doubt, this is
the work of the Holy Spirit as is evident from the second point. This
influence man receives by the common grace of the Lord. True, the
word grace is not mentioned here, but in every explanation of the
doctrine set forth in the third point, regardless in which time it was
written, such civic righteousness or good is attributed to the work
of God's common grace. 2/ This work of the Spirit enables man to do
some good. The idea surely is that by the Spirit He is empowered and
also made willing to do this good. And what is it that enables him to
do this? Surely, the common grace of God. Notice, in the first point
the favorable attitude or disposition of God is taught. However,
a gracious attitude surely does not enable people to do something.
Therefore we read here, as we see it, that the Holy Spirit influences
man, works in him, so that he is able to do this good. Doesn't the
unregenerated man then in some way possess grace, which is not saving?

Four of the numerous papers presented at the secret conclave of schismatic
ministers—very recently separated from the PRC—and leading Christian
Reformed ministers. Note the date of one of the papers: "January 15, 1954."
The purpose of the meetings, as early as January, 1954, was the return of the
schismatic ministers and their churches to the CRC. The fact of these secret
meetings and the theological papers negotiating a return to the CRC have
become known only of late.

It is possible that such a high-powered conference be arranged, conferees be agreed upon, and a paper be written for the first meeting in the short time of two or three months—between October 1953 and January 1954—but it is unlikely. What is likely is that arrangements for a conference between the disaffected ministers in the Protestant Reformed Churches and Christian Reformed theologians, with the express purpose of negotiating the return of the Protestant Reformed ministers and their congregations to the Christian Reformed Church, were being made while the controversy over the Declaration was still going on in the Protestant Reformed Churches. That would have been basest treachery.

Even if arrangements were made after the schism had taken place, they would have had to have been instigated by the schismatic ministers at once upon the schism's having occurred. That would have betrayed the purpose of the schismatic ministers to return to the Christian Reformed Church while they were opposing the (Protestant Reformed) theology of the Declaration and dividing the Protestant Reformed Churches—and also while they were publicly assuring the members of their congregations that they intended to remain Protestant Reformed. That too would have been dishonorable.

DISREPUTABLE ECUMENICITY

Why those who separated from the Protestant Reformed Churches in 1953 joined the Christian Reformed Church rather than the Canadian Reformed Churches is, at first glance, puzzling.

Throughout the controversy over the covenant, the ministers who eventually broke with the Protestant Reformed Churches defended the covenant theology of Schilder and his Reformed Churches in the Netherlands (liberated). The Canadian Reformed Churches are daughters of these Dutch churches and ardent proponents of the conditional covenant theology of Schilder and the liberated churches. During the controversy, schismatic ministers met with leading ministers of the liberated churches, getting advice on perpetuating the conflict in the Protestant Reformed Churches.

Immediately after the schism, the Canadian Reformed Churches made overtures to the schismatic denomination. On the agenda of the 1955 synod of the schismatic "Protestant Reformed Churches" was a request from the synod of the Canadian Reformed Churches for official contact. The request specified that it was addressed to "those Churches which no longer are bound by the Declaration of Principles." The request stated that "sister church" relations was the goal.[19]

The two denominations carried on correspondence concerning the possibility of union. It soon became evident that the desire of the schismatic churches was for the Christian Reformed Church, not for the Canadian Reformed Churches. In fact, the determination of the schismatic churches to seek ecumenical relations with the Christian Reformed Church at once interfered with what little contact they did have with the Canadian Reformed Churches. The Canadian Reformed Churches informed the schismatic churches in no uncertain terms that, because of the Christian Reformed relationship with the Reformed Churches in the Netherlands (synodical), they—the Canadian Reformed Churches—could have no ecumenical relationship with a denomination that insisted on seeking fellowship with the Christian Reformed Church. The Canadian Reformed Churches judged the Reformed Churches in the Netherlands (synodical) to be false churches.[20]

Also, the Canadian Reformed Churches were fearful that there remained in the schismatic churches some residue of sympathy for the contention of the Declaration of Principles that its doctrine of the covenant was that of the three forms of unity. The schismatic churches gave occasion to this suspicion by their decision declaring the Declaration null and void in their communion. At their synod of 1954, these churches decided that the "Declaration of Principles is without force" in their fellowship. But they then added this observation, which caught the covenantally keen eyes of the Canadian Reformed: "These doctrinal points [about the covenant in the Declaration] are explained more fully and better in the Three Forms of Unity."[21]

The Canadian Reformed Churches pressed the schismatic synod

---

19 *Acts of Synod, Protestant Reformed Churches of America [schismatic], 1955,* 25–26.

20 *Acts of Synod, Protestant Reformed Churches of America [schismatic], 1957,* 51.

21 *Acts of Synod [schismatic], 1954,* 41.

for an answer to their question whether the churches that had renounced Hoeksema still harbored some commitment to the unconditional covenant as the teaching of the creeds. And the schismatic synod, oddly, refused to give an answer![22]

As it became obvious that the schismatic churches were going to cast in their lot with the Christian Reformed Church, the Canadian Reformed Churches went so far as to warn the erstwhile Protestant Reformed Churches of the prevailing evils in the Christian Reformed Church. Rev. Lambert Doezema informed the readership of the *Reformed Guardian* that the editor of the "Canadian Reformed Magazine" had challenged the "direction" in which the schismatic churches were going, namely, into the Christian Reformed Church. The Canadian Reformed minister suggested that the schismatics were "bow[ing] to the hierarchy of the Christian Reformed Church."[23] Doezema dismissed the warning: "Unless the Canadian Reformed people can show that the Three Points [of common grace] are contrary to Scripture, their criticism misses the mark."[24]

Nevertheless, in the end, despite their apparent theological oneness with the Canadian Reformed, despite the obviously ardent desire for close relations with them on the part of the Canadian Reformed, and despite the warning against the Christian Reformed Church

---

22 *Acts of Synod [schismatic], 1957*, 45–58. "We put to you a question in connection with the content of 'the Declaration'...Is our impression correct that [for you] the content of 'the Declaration' is more fully and better expressed in the three forms of unity, and if so, is that today still the conviction in which your churches live?...And do you therefore read in the three forms of unity, be it then more completely and better, what was expressed in 'the Declaration of Principles'?" The translation of the Dutch is mine. The schismatic synod of 1957 refused to answer this question: "We have no interest nor see the need of discussing said Declaration." No doubt, one of the reasons the schismatic synod evaded the question of the Canadian Reformed was that many of the schismatic ministers had repeatedly—and *recently*—qualified their objection to the Declaration with some form of the statement that they were in agreement with the doctrinal content of the Declaration, or at least that their objection did not express opposition to the doctrinal content of the Declaration.

23 L. Doezema, "Our Protestant Reformed Church," *Reformed Guardian* 6, no. 16 (January 25, 1961): 235.

24 Ibid.

from the Canadian Reformed, the formerly Protestant Reformed Churches rudely rejected the Canadian Reformed Churches, as they also turned their back on the Orthodox Presbyterian Church, which also had expressed interest in contact with the churches that had split from the Protestant Reformed Churches.[25]

Already in 1957, within four years of their break with the Protestant Reformed Churches, the schismatic churches initiated contact with the Christian Reformed Church with a view to their being received into the Christian Reformed Church. Committees of the two denominations began meeting in the fall of 1957.[26]

The simple explanation of the decision of the schismatic denomination to rejoin the Christian Reformed Church is that, in the decision regarding its future and the future of its members, the denomination was completely unprincipled. The issues deciding union and membership were not doctrinal orthodoxy, the right administration of the sacraments, discipline, and the holy, antithetical life that flows from orthodoxy and is preserved by discipline—the marks of the true church. The decisive question was not even, "With whom are we the closest theologically?"

The decisive issues were thoroughly practical and self-serving. Where would the ministers find churches of which they could be pastors, especially large churches? Where would the people find congregations close at hand (the Canadian Reformed Churches had few congregations in the United States)? Where would the people feel most comfortable—with friends and relatives already members of the churches they would join? To which church had

---

25 For the request for contact from the Orthodox Presbyterian Church and the response of the schismatic churches, see *Acts of Synod, Protestant Reformed Churches of America [schismatic], 1959*, 38–41. This synod received a "fraternal delegate" from the Orthodox Presbyterian Church, whose speech to the synod recognized the synod as the legitimate "Protestant Reformed Church" and gratuitously insulted the genuine Protestant Reformed Churches by praising the schismatic denomination for "a new vitality in your Gospel witness and to see you sailing down the main stream of the historic Christian faith" (40–41). The synod also appointed one of its own as a "fraternal delegate" to the general assembly of the Orthodox Presbyterian Church in 1960 (40).

26 Marvin Gritters, "Contact," *Reformed Guardian* 4, no 15 (December 25, 1958): 230–31.

many of the schismatics, ministers as well as members, already gone on their own?

One important reason for seeking admission into the Christian Reformed Church was openly acknowledged on the pages of the *Reformed Guardian* in the last days of the separate existence of the schismatic churches. Their children and young people were at home in the Christian Reformed Church by virtue of their attending the Christian Reformed grade schools and high schools. On behalf of his churches' uniting with the Christian Reformed Church, Rev. De Jong wrote, "Our people are cooperating with the Christian Reformed people in the matter of training our covenant youth."[27]

Not only did the schismatics immediately withdraw their children from the Protestant Reformed Christian schools as soon as the split occurred (which meant hardship for such schools as Adams Street and Hope), sending them instead to Christian Reformed schools, but also many of them had opposed Protestant Reformed schools while they were still members of the Protestant Reformed Churches. In his recognition that the schooling of their children led his churches toward the Christian Reformed Church, De Jong added: "The matter of Prot. Reformed Schools is a dead issue among us."[28]

All the members were well aware of the implications of their reunion with the Christian Reformed Church, out of which God had led them, or their fathers and mothers, in 1924. Their church paper, the *Reformed Guardian*, informed the membership of the schismatic churches that joining the Christian Reformed Church would mean accepting the three points of common grace as biblical and confessional and submitting themselves to indoctrination in the theology of common grace, as well as opening themselves to the practical, ethical fruits of common grace. The *Reformed Guardian* published the "Resolution of Reunion Protestant Reformed and Christian Reformed." This basis of the reunion stipulated that the returning Protestant Reformed

> agree that the Three Points are neither Arminian nor Pelagian; that in the light of the official interpretation

---

27 John De Jong, "Our Coming Synod," *Reformed Guardian* 5, no. 3 (May 25, 1959): 38.

28 Ibid.

given by our [Christian Reformed] Synod of 1959, the objection that the Three Points are in conflict with the Scriptures and the Forms of Unity is not valid; and that you [the returning Protestant Reformed people] will agree not to agitate against official interpretations.[29]

Although attempting to minimize these evil consequences of joining the Christian Reformed Church, one of the schismatic ministers brought to the attention of the members of his churches that by joining the Christian Reformed Church they would, in addition to approving the three points of common grace, be yoking themselves with the revolution of the ungodly labor unions, to which the Christian Reformed Church was committed, and with the adultery of divorce and remarriage, rampant in the Christian Reformed Church already in 1961.

Andrew Cammenga, the Protestant Reformed minister whose request, as missionary, for a "form" to be used in organizing churches occasioned the Declaration of Principles. Nevertheless, he became one of the most resolute adversaries of the Declaration. He was especially active and effective in bringing about the schism in the PRC. It was therefore fitting that he was president of the synod of 1961 that delivered the schismatic churches over to the CRC.
Photograph from Calvin College archives.

Rev. A. Cammenga was concerned to defuse objections to the coming reunion with the Christian Reformed Church on the part of those who regarded labor unionism and divorce and remarriage as sinful (as they had been taught by all the ministers in the

---

29 "Resolution of Reunion Protestant Reformed and Christian Reformed," *Reformed Guardian* 7, no. 4 (July 25, 1961): 56.

Protestant Reformed Churches, including Rev. A. Cammenga, for twenty-five years). He acknowledged, as objections to joining the Christian Reformed Church, that "one may point to the Christian Reformed attitude in the matters of Labor Unions, their decision on divorce, possible worldliness within the church, etc."

Cammenga responded to the more than hypothetical objection concerning divorce and remarriage: "Who knows what we would do if a *truly* converted couple, one or both having been divorced at one time or other, would present themselves to one of our consistories to plead membership in Christ's Church?"[30]

This argument, of course, was no allaying of the members' fear that, by joining the Christian Reformed Church, they would make themselves guilty of adultery. Rather, it was an admission that the schismatic churches had themselves already become so spiritually weak that they were ready to approve adultery, under the right circumstances.

Significantly, at the height of the negotiations of the churches that had split from the Protestant Reformed Churches with the Christian Reformed Church, the *Reformed Guardian* was constrained to take note of the warning by a leading Christian Reformed minister, Rev. H. J. Kuiper, in the April 1959 issue of *Torch and Trumpet*, of the increasing apostasy of the Christian Reformed Church. Rev. Hofman was candid: "Since our Churches are engaged in conferences with the Christian Reformed Church, we are interested to know what is happening within that group." He then quoted Kuiper at length revealing to the reading Reformed public that the Christian Reformed Church was at that time openly advocating, or tolerating, theistic evolution; denial of the infallibility of Scripture; efforts for union with the notoriously liberal, that is, lawless, Reformed Church in America; and cooperation with Methodists and Baptists in missions.[31]

For all of this and much more the returning schismatics made themselves responsible. To all of this and more they opened up their children and grandchildren.

---

30 Andrew Cammenga, "Contact and Principle," *Reformed Guardian* 5, no. 2 (May 10, 1959): 19–20, 31. The emphasis is Cammenga's.

31 Walter Hofman, "Introspection," *Reformed Guardian* 5, no. 1 (April 25, 1959): 12–13.

John D. De Jong, Protestant Reformed minister who was outspoken and blunt in his opposition to the Declaration, as later also in his insistence that the schismatics join the CRC. His treacherous dealings, with Rev. B. Kok, with liberated theologians in the Netherlands, undermining the PRC, made him especially *persona non grata* to Protestant Reformed ministers and members.

And the ministers led the way!

One can only conclude that, as Moses and Aaron brought many out of Egypt without bringing Egypt out of them, so also Hoeksema and Ophoff brought many out of the Christian Reformed Church without having brought the Christian Reformed Church out of them.

Driving the push of the schismatic churches for hasty union with the Christian Reformed Church was the disintegration of the churches. An overture from the Edgerton, Minnesota, congregation for quick reunion with the Christian Reformed Church honestly spoke of "losses and splinterings and people here and there are leaving our fellowship for sundry reasons."[32]

Rev. De Jong pleaded that the synod of 1959 decide on reunion with the Christian Reformed Church and not "drag it [the process] out and prolong the present situation" because "too many of our people and even congregations may fall by the wayside if it takes years before a final union can be effectuated."[33] In a later article, urging that reunion with the Christian Reformed Church be put on the fast track, De Jong appealed to the loss of members of his denomination: "We are not holding our own...We lose [members] instead of gain." He concluded, "The future of our churches does not look very bright."[34]

---

32 *Reformed Guardian* 4, no. 21 (March 25, 1959): 334.

33 J. De Jong, "Our Coming Synod," *Reformed Guardian* 5, no. 2 (May 10, 1959): 23.

34 J. De Jong, "Our Coming Synod: Facing the Facts," *Reformed Guardian* 5,

In January 1961 the schismatic denomination was reduced to ten congregations and eight ministers from an earlier high count of seventeen congregations and fifteen ministers.[35] One after another individual congregations had been disbanding, with the membership joining Christian Reformed congregations, and one after another individual ministers had been defecting from their own denomination to the Christian Reformed Church.

Reunion with the Christian Reformed Church on the part of a dissident faction of the Protestant Reformed Churches was desirable to the Christian Reformed Church, not only because this meant numerical growth consisting of solid, reliable members and the acquisition of considerable financial assets, both of money and of property (most of which was once devoted to the witness to the gospel of the Protestant Reformed Churches), but also because this was another opportunity to stab Herman Hoeksema in the back and to kick the Protestant Reformed Churches when they were down.

And this ecclesiastical skullduggery paraded as the Holy Spirit's lovely work of ecumenicity—the manifestation and realization of the unity of the church.

Genuine church unity is motivated by, and takes place on the basis of, oneness in confession of the truth of the gospel of grace—the good news of unconditional salvation. It certainly does not occur by the action of a denomination only eight years removed from its own unconfessed sin against the unity of the church—schism—in a true church of Jesus Christ.

"FINISHING OF THE STOCKING"

Another effect of the adoption of the Declaration was that Schilder and the liberated Reformed churches broke off relations with the Protestant Reformed Churches. Within a few months of the adoption of the Declaration in 1951, Schilder wrote in his *Reformatie* magazine that "The Stocking is Finished."[36] By this pic-

---

no. 3 (May 25, 1959): 39.

35 W. Hofman, "Inventory," *Reformed Guardian* 6, no. 16 (January 25, 1961): 244–45.

36 Schilder wrote the article in the November 17, 1951 issue of *De Reformatie*. The Dutch title was *"De Kous is Af."* Hoeksema summarized the

turesque statement, Schilder meant that the relationship between the Reformed Churches in the Netherlands (liberated) and the Protestant Reformed Churches was definitely and finally severed.

Thus ended, unpleasantly, a contact that was important to the Protestant Reformed Churches and to Herman Hoeksema personally. Both the churches and Hoeksema had endured isolation with regard to the community of Reformed churches on account of their uncompromising confession of the Reformed faith and their insistence on the antithetical walk of holiness. This isolation made the relationship with Schilder and the liberated churches especially dear to them.

SALVATION

Hurtful as these effects of the adoption of the Declaration were to the Protestant Reformed Churches, the effect of the Declaration on the churches was mainly beneficial, nothing less than the salvation of the Protestant Reformed Churches, in several senses of the word. As a synodical decision, adoption of the Declaration settled a controversy that was disturbing the peace of the denomination, indeed dividing the churches and thus in the process of destroying them. The synod of 1951 did what major assemblies are called to do in circumstances of doctrinal controversy: decide the doctrinal dispute by a clear, firm judgment on the issue. And the judgment must express the teaching of the creeds regarding the issue. Within two years the Protestant Reformed Churches were again at peace, on the basis of their unity in the confession of the doctrine of the covenant of grace.

No less beneficial was the effect of the Declaration of preserving the truth of the unconditional covenant in the churches. This

---

article and responded in his editorial, "The Stocking is Finished," in the *Standard Bearer* 28, no 7 (January 1, 1952): 148–53. After all that had transpired and in spite of Schilder's severing of relations with the Protestant Reformed Churches, Hoeksema urged that the two denominations "unravel that tangle" they had made of their relationship "and start from the beginning" to knit the stocking of the relationship. This indicated the strength of Hoeksema's personal desire for relations with Schilder and the liberated Reformed churches, something remarkable in view of his detestation of the doctrine of a conditional covenant.

truth had been fundamental to the confession, indeed to the very existence, of the Protestant Reformed Churches from the beginning of their history as a denomination of churches. All the ministers in the denomination knew this. As early as 1927, a mere three years after the founding of the denomination, Hoeksema wrote a series of articles in the *Standard Bearer* setting forth the distinctive doctrine of the covenant that is the confession of the Protestant Reformed Churches.[37]

In these articles, Hoeksema criticized the covenant doctrine of Professor Heyns. According to Heyns, wrote Hoeksema,

> this essence of the covenant indeed concerns all who are born in the sphere of the covenant in the historical sense. Hence, he also does not conceive of the promise of God as absolute and unconditional, but as relative and conditional. The essence of the covenant is the promise in the sense of a conditional offer…That conditional relationship in which God places Himself to the seed of the covenant, the realization of which depends on the consent and acceptance of the covenant member—that is for Heyns the essence of the covenant.[38]

Hoeksema charged, rightly, that this doctrine of a conditional covenant with all the children alike is "nothing but Pelagianism applied to the historical sphere of the covenant."[39] The title of the chapter in which Hoeksema subjected Heyns' doctrine of a conditional covenant to critique is "Arminianism Injected Into the Covenant."[40]

Hoeksema concluded his treatment of Heyns' doctrine of the covenant with these words:

> God does not promise salvation in Christ to every child of believers. No more than there is a general offer in the preaching to everyone who hears, no more is there such a general promise in God's covenant. This presentation must be totally

---

37 These articles, originally written in Dutch, were later translated and published as *Believers and Their Seed*.

38 Herman Hoeksema, *Believers and Their Seed*, 16–17.

39 Ibid., 18.

40 Ibid., 14–28.

rooted out. It lies wholly in the line of Pelagius and Arminius.[41]

Indicating that rejection of the doctrine of a conditional covenant promise to all the baptized children alike is fundamental to the very existence of the Protestant Reformed Churches, Hoeksema attributed the openness of Christian Reformed ministers and elders to the false doctrine of the well-meant offer of the gospel to their instruction by Heyns concerning a gracious, conditional covenant promise to all.

> Heyns' presentation [of the covenant of grace] has for years been imbibed by many who now serve as ministers in the Christian Reformed denomination. If we keep this in mind, it is no longer surprising that the doctrine of a general offer of grace on God's part in the preaching of the gospel to all who hear that gospel not only could find a reception but also could be so readily officially adopted by the Synod of 1924 as the only pure Reformed presentation.[42]

The well-meant offer—the most objectionable element of the doctrine of common grace that the Christian Reformed Church made official church doctrine in 1924—was a form of, and was due to, the doctrine of a gracious, conditional covenant promise to all the baptized children alike. Rejection of the well-meant offer therefore, which was basic to the separate existence of the Protestant Reformed Churches, by the admission of all, involves also the rejection of a conditional covenant.

Against the doctrine of a conditional covenant, Hoeksema, from the earliest years of the churches that God used him to found, declared, explained, proved, and defended the doctrine of the unconditional covenant.

The unconditional covenant flows out of and depends upon the eternal decree of election. This too Hoeksema demonstrated and taught as the Protestant Reformed confession of the covenant of grace, as early as the 1920s. Considering the question, "Are, then, all children who are born in the generations of the covenant also essentially *in* God's covenant?"[43] in a chapter titled "A Twofold

---

41 Ibid., 28.
42 Ibid., 14.
43 Ibid., 100.

Seed," Hoeksema proved from Scripture and the creeds that "the Word of [covenant] promise did not pertain to all the children of Abraham, but only to the seed of election."[44] "There is an elect kernel, and there is a reprobate shell. And God will be merciful to whom He will be merciful also within the sphere of the historical covenant in the world."[45] "The [covenant] promises of God are not for all [the baptized children of godly parents], head for head."[46]

In a chapter titled "The Reprobate in the Sphere of the Covenant," Hoeksema declared, "It is simply not true that God in holy baptism promises and seals something to all who are baptized."[47] "The reprobate shell in the sphere of God's covenant never receives anything else than cursing and wrath."[48]

These articles in the *Standard Bearer* were published as a booklet (in Dutch) prior to 1932.[49]

A second edition of the booklet was published in 1946. The reason for this second edition was mainly to address a controversy in the Netherlands over the covenant in the Reformed Churches in the Netherlands (GKN). That controversy concerned the same issues that Hoeksema addressed in the booklet. That was the controversy that resulted in the separation of Schilder and his liberated followers from the Reformed Churches in the Netherlands. Republishing and sending the booklet to the Netherlands in 1946 were premised on the fact that Hoeksema's repudiation of the Heynsian doctrine of a gracious, conditional covenant promise to all the baptized children alike as unreformed applies as well to the covenant doctrine of Schilder and the liberated Reformed.

In his foreword to the second edition of the booklet, Hoeksema

---

44 Ibid., 108.
45 Ibid., 114.
46 Ibid.
47 Ibid., 145.
48 Ibid., 148.
49 Herman Hoeksema, *De Geloovigen en Hun Zaad* [Believers and their seed] (Grand Rapids, MI: Doorn Printer, n. d.). That the booklet was published before or in 1932 is established by Hoeksema's comments on the reception of the booklet in the Netherlands, to which hundreds of copies had been sent, in his editorial "*De Geloovigen en Hun Zaad,*" *Standard Bearer* 9, no. 6 (December 15, 1932): 124–26.

was at pains to inform the reader that the issues troubling the Reformed Churches in the Netherlands were the very issues concerning the covenant that he had treated in the *Standard Bearer* in 1927 and that were now the content of the booklet. "It seemed useful to the mission committee of our churches to have this treatise republished, especially in connection with the present differences in the Netherlands." Hoeksema added that sending copies of the treatise on the covenant to the Netherlands was not motivated by the "desire to take a dog by the ears, but by the desire to serve the truth concerning God's everlasting covenant."[50]

Therefore, when the Protestant Reformed ministers who found themselves attracted to the covenant doctrine of the liberated Reformed opposed the Declaration, they were opposing the doctrine of the covenant that was fundamental to the very existence of the Protestant Reformed Churches—and to the maintenance of the sound Reformed faith—and they knew it.

When these same ministers argued that the Protestant Reformed Churches had no binding doctrine of the covenant, they were being disingenuous. The churches had not officially adopted a doctrine of the covenant, to be sure. This would not be the case until they adopted the Declaration of Principles. But the churches had accepted, preached, taught, and confessed the doctrine of an unconditional covenant, rooted in election, as the doctrine of the Protestant Reformed Churches from the beginning of their history. And not only as the doctrine of the Protestant Reformed Churches! They had received this doctrine as the truth of the covenant that alone harmonizes with the gospel of sovereign, particular grace that is taught by the Reformed confessions. The churches had also, with one consent, rejected the conditional covenant theology of Heyns as Arminianism in the realm of covenant theology.

In addition, inasmuch as the covenant doctrine of Heyns and Schilder is a form of the teaching of resistible (saving) grace, cut loose from election, which the Protestant Reformed Churches had definitely repudiated in their rejection of the first point of common grace (the well-meant offer), one can make a case, as Hoeksema

50 Herman Hoeksema, "Foreword to the Second Edition," in *De Geloovigen en Hun Zaad* (Grand Rapids, MI: Protestant Reformed Mission Committee, 1946), 4. The translation of the Dutch is mine.

indeed made it, that the Protestant Reformed Churches *had* a binding doctrine of the covenant.

These Protestant Reformed ministers, now attracted to the conditional covenant theology of Heyns and Schilder, seized on the earlier, incautious, occasional use of the word "condition" by Hoeksema in his voluminous writings, in order to convince the membership of the Protestant Reformed Churches that Hoeksema himself had once taught a conditional covenant. In this case his defense of the unconditional covenant, as confessed by the Declaration, would represent a change in his theology of the covenant. These ministers lied.

Hoeksema had repudiated the doctrine of a conditional covenant with all the baptized children alike, as unreformed, from his student days in Calvin Seminary. As Hoeksema himself related to me in my seminary days, he had told Heyns to his face on one occasion, when the two met by accident on some public transportation, "I do not yet know what the sound Reformed doctrine of the covenant is, but I know it is not what you teach."[51] Early in his ministry, he had worked out the sound, Reformed doctrine of God's unconditional covenant of grace with the elect. He explained this doctrine in articles in the *Standard Bearer* in 1927. He taught it to all his seminary students. He preached it to his congregation. He lectured on it throughout North America. He published it to the world. He defended it consistently throughout his ministry, especially in the treacherous, difficult times of the adoption of the Declaration.

Hoeksema regarded their doctrine of the covenant, in its fullness, as the most unique and most precious treasure of the Protestant Reformed Churches, as he himself announced. On the occasion of the twenty-fifth anniversary of the denomination, in the circumstances of the struggle over the doctrine of the unconditional covenant, Hoeksema wrote:

> If you ask me what is the most peculiar treasure of the Protestant Reformed Churches, I answer without any hesitation: their peculiar view of the covenant.

51 See the account, in slightly different words, in Gertrude Hoeksema, *Therefore Have I Spoken: A Biography of Herman Hoeksema* (Grand Rapids, MI: Reformed Free Publishing Association, 1969), 109–10.

And what is their particular conception?

It stands closely connected with their denial of common grace, and with their emphasis on the doctrine of election and reprobation...

Briefly stated it teaches that God realizes His eternal covenant of friendship, in Christ, the Firstborn of every creature and the Firstbegotten of the dead, organically, and antithetically along the lines of election and reprobation, and in connection with the organic development of all things.[52]

He added the warning, "He that has been captivated by this beautiful Reformed truth must have nothing of anything that smacks like Heynsian theology, nor will he ever retrogress into a traditional conditional theology."[53]

The Declaration did not merely preserve in the Protestant Reformed Churches a doctrine of the covenant that was fundamental to the churches. It preserved that doctrine of the covenant that maintains the gospel of salvation by grace. The doctrine of the unconditional covenant is, in truth, the expression of the Reformed confessions. The Declaration applied especially the doctrines of the Canons of Dordt to the doctrine of the covenant.

Salvation is no more conditional in the covenant than it is on the mission field. Grace is no more universal and resistible in the covenant than it is anywhere else. What Canons 1.9 says of "every saving good," namely, that it flows out of election as its "fountain" and that election is its cause, applies to the covenant and its saving good.[54] Canons 2.8 explicitly teaches that the limited atonement of the cross of Christ "confirmed the new covenant," which therefore is not established, or intended by God to be established, with others than "all those, and those only, who were from eternity chosen to salvation and given to him [Jesus Christ] by the Father," and whom

---

52 Herman Hoeksema, "Protestant Reformed," *Standard Bearer* 26, no. 12 (March 15, 1950): 259.

53 Ibid.

54 Canons of Dordt 1.9, in Schaff, *Creeds of Christendom*, 3:583.

alone Christ effectually redeemed.[55] As much as the promise of the gospel is addressed by God to and concerns only those who believe, according to Canons 2.5, or as Canons 3–4.8 identifies them, "as many as shall come to him, and believe on him," so also is the covenant promise addressed to believing children.[56] And faith, according to the Canons, is the gift of God to the elect, flowing out of election as its fountain and earned by Christ for the elect.[57]

As ought to have been obvious to all during the time of the struggle over the Declaration, and as the heresy of the federal vision makes undeniably clear today, the conditional covenant theology of Heyns and Schilder is Arminianism introduced into the doctrine of the covenant.

Because the Declaration, once decisively adopted, would save the churches *from* the influence of the conditional covenant theology of Heyns and Schilder and would save the churches *in* the unconditional covenant theology of the confessions, Hoeksema wrote as he did just before the gathering of the synod of 1951: "If our next synod should dare to reject it [the Declaration], I see no longer any hope for the future of our Protestant Reformed Churches as remaining distinctively Reformed." He added: "Hence, 'with malice toward none,' I shall fight for it."[58]

One aspect of the Declaration's preservation of the truth of salvation by grace in the covenant in the Protestant Reformed Churches was its blocking entrance into the churches on the part of the Dutch immigrants who were committed to the liberated doctrine of the covenant and who were intent on making propaganda for their covenant doctrine in the Protestant Reformed Churches. The Declaration originated in a request to the Protestant Reformed Churches' mission committee from one of these immigrants, asking whether the Protestant Reformed doctrine of the covenant was binding in the churches.

---

55 Canons of Dordt 2.8, in ibid., 3:587.

56 Canons of Dordt 2.5, in ibid., 3:586; Canons of Dordt 3–4.8, in ibid., 3:589.

57 Canons of Dordt 3–4.14, in ibid., 3:591; Canons of Dordt 1.9, in ibid., 3:583; Canons of Dordt 2.8, in ibid., 3:587.

58 Herman Hoeksema, "The Declaration of Principles," *Standard Bearer* 27, no. 14 (April 15, 1951): 318.

I would be pleased, and as one of the most important points, to receive from you enlightenment whether the former Liberated Reformed members when they are accepted as confessing members into your Protestant Reformed Churches, will hold them to your views concerning Covenant and Baptism, or that they need not to expect any binding with regard to those doctrines from you.[59]

The liberated immigrants did not intend to join the Protestant Reformed Churches in order to enjoy and be edified by the doctrine of the covenant of the churches. They did not even intend to join in order to learn the doctrine of the Protestant Reformed Churches. Rather, they were instructed by the liberated theologians in the Netherlands to join the Protestant Reformed Churches in order to disseminate the liberated covenant theology in the Protestant Reformed Churches. This was made plain by the letter to the immigrants in Canada from Professor Holwerda, which surfaced during the conflict over the Declaration.

In this situation I believe that joining the Prot. Ref. church is [the liberated immigrants'] calling. And let them then as Liberated preserve their contact with Holland by all means, and also spread our literature...If Rev. Hoeksema's conception [of the covenant] was binding, I would say, Never join. Now I believe, however, that accession is calling; and then so that the Liberated also help to disseminate the dogmatical wealth of Holland [that is, the liberated doctrine of the covenant] in the Prot. Ref. Churches.[60]

Of the beneficial effect of the Declaration in preventing the influx of liberated men and women into the Protestant Reformed Churches, who would then have evangelized the membership of the churches with their doctrine of the covenant, Hoeksema took note in one of his recorded speeches at the synod of 1953. "And this [the adoption of the Declaration] was absolutely necessary in order to prevent the Liberated from streaming into our communion of

59 *Acts of Synod, 1953*, 165. This is the translation of the request, which was originally in Dutch.

60 Letter by Holwerda, in G. M. Ophoff, "Revs. De Jong and Kok in The Netherlands," *Standard Bearer* 25, no. 20 (August 1, 1949): 470.

Churches and corrupting it with their doctrinal errors regarding the PROMISE and the COVENANT and related matters."[61]

Certainly, a benefit of the Declaration has been the use of it according to the expressed purpose of the document, namely, that it be used "for the organization of prospective Churches."[62] In this usage of the Declaration, the document is not the basis of the organization of churches. The Reformed creeds are the basis. But the Declaration serves, and must serve, as an instrument that prepares groups to be organized as Protestant Reformed congregations. Intended is that these congregations know and are in agreement with the doctrine of the unconditional covenant as confessed by the Protestant Reformed Churches. As the covenant theology of the Reformed confessions, the doctrine of the covenant that is outlined in the Declaration is binding in the Protestant Reformed Churches. It is an essential aspect of the oneness of doctrine that is fundamental to the unity of the federation of churches.

Use of the Declaration in the organizing of new churches benefits the new congregations by instructing them in the truth of the covenant of grace. It also benefits the Protestant Reformed Churches by safeguarding them from intimate fellowship with congregations that hold and propagate a false doctrine of the covenant.

This use of the Declaration implies that the Declaration also be used in all the ecumenical work of the Protestant Reformed Churches. The same principle that underlies use of the Declaration in organizing churches applies to ecumenical relationships. No ecumenical alliance may be forged apart from discussion concerning the doctrine of the covenant and regardless of disagreement over this doctrine. No church or denomination of churches may be received as a sister church without understanding of and agreement with the doctrine of the unconditional covenant as set forth in the Declaration.

As both a synodical decision and the avowed expression of the Reformed creeds, the Declaration is binding on the Protestant Reformed Churches themselves and on every member of the denomination. No member may agitate for the doctrine of a

61 Herman Hoeksema, in *Acts of Synod, 1953*, 264.
62 Preamble of the Declaration of Principles, in *Confessions and Church Order*, 412.

conditional covenant. No minister may teach a doctrine of the covenant that is in conflict with the Declaration, for example, the doctrine of the covenant presently being proposed in the community of Reformed churches by the men of the federal vision. To do so would be schismatic.

Obviously, if the Protestant Reformed Churches require confession of the unconditional covenant from others, this confession is and must be their own.

Although it is not a fourth creed, as a document expressing what the Protestant Reformed Churches are convinced is the teaching of the creeds concerning the covenant of grace, the Declaration serves as an important witness to other churches and to members of other churches. Hoeksema extolled this use of the Declaration:

> The Declaration of Principles will serve as a clear proclamation to all that are without of the faithful adherence of the Protestant Reformed Churches to the Reformed faith as expressed in the Three Forms of Unity, over against all that deviate from these Confessions. This is true particularly in the first place over against the errors of the Three Points, which teach that there is a grace of God to all men...And secondly, this is true over against the Heynsian view of the promise and the covenant, which according to the conviction of the Protestant Reformed Churches is certainly Arminian.[63]

It is a witness with some force. For it claims to be the expression of the Reformed creeds concerning the covenant, not merely the expression of Protestant Reformed thinking about the covenant. In keeping with this claim, the content of the Declaration is mainly quotations of the creeds bearing on the fundamental issues regarding covenant doctrine.

If the Declaration is, as it claims to be and as it shows itself to be, just the expression of the creeds, all those who subscribe to the three forms of unity are as bound to confess the truth of the covenant as outlined in the Declaration as are members of the Protestant Reformed Churches. Those Reformed theologians

---

63 Herman Hoeksema, "The Proposed Declaration," *Standard Bearer* 27, no. 8 (January 15, 1951): 173.

and churches that vehemently oppose the doctrine of an unconditional covenant, flowing from and governed by election, must consider whether in fact they are opposing the Reformed creeds and therefore the Reformed faith, which they profess to love and confess.

The Declaration is a public charge by the Protestant Reformed Churches that all those who repudiate the doctrine of an unconditional covenant are guilty of opposition to, and departure from, the creeds in the great matter of the covenant of grace.

One beneficial effect of the adoption of the Declaration could not have been foreseen by the Protestant Reformed synod of 1951. The Declaration would stand the Protestant Reformed Churches in good stead and would be a beacon of light to the Reformed community of churches some fifty years after its adoption with regard to the heresy of the federal vision.

By its own self-description, the theology of the federal vision is the development of the conditional covenant doctrine of Schilder, Holwerda, Veenhof, and the Reformed Churches in the Netherlands (liberated). It is the development of the doctrine of a conditional covenant, cut loose from election, that teaches justification by works and, with this cardinal heresy, conditional, resistible grace at every stage of covenant salvation, to the overthrow of the five points of Calvinism as confessed by the Canons, *with specific regard to the covenant*.[64]

---

64 See Engelsma, *Federal Vision*. See also the acknowledgment by Ralph F. Boersema, avowed defender of Norman Shepherd and his theology, that the federal vision theology of Norman Shepherd is the conscious development of the covenant theology of Schilder and the liberated Reformed. "Many ministers, including men like...K. Schilder, provided a different solution to this problem [of the relation of covenant and election]...The covenant is to be understood in terms of God's revelation. He has revealed to us that he has a covenant with believers *and all their children. It is not only with the elect. The covenant is not unconditional.* In it God gives his promises and also his people have their obligations and must make their commitments. *The promises are addressed to all* and all are called to repentance and faith, lest they be cut off. *It is this solution that Shepherd has adopted and which he brings to expression when he says that we should look at God's decrees from the perspective of the covenant*" (Ralph F. Boersema, *Not of Works: Norman Shepherd and His Critics* [Minneapolis, MN: Next-Step Resources, 2012], 85; emphasis added). Shepherd himself approves

Whether or not this development was foreseen, it was inevitable, because as Hoeksema charged against the covenant doctrine of Heyns and the covenant doctrine of Schilder and the liberated, which is essentially the same as the doctrine of Heyns, the doctrine of a conditional covenant is "Arminianism in the covenant."

Arminianism is the perversion of the gospel consisting of the teaching of universal, resistible grace; of the teaching of a saving grace of God that does not have its source in, nor is governed by, the eternal, unconditional decree of election; of the teaching of a saving grace that begins the work of salvation in one but fails to maintain and perfect the work—resistible grace; of the teaching of a general grace that depends, finally, on some work of the sinner—a *condition*.

Precisely this is the theology of the federal vision—*with regard to the covenant and covenant salvation.*

That the fundamental doctrine of the theology of the federal vision is its teaching that salvation (in the covenant) depends on the (covenant) sinner and that this is the sense of his, and the federal vision's, insistence that the covenant is "conditional," Norman Shepherd, leading spokesman for the federal vision, has recently declared in unambiguous language: "The New Testament as well as the Old makes our eternal welfare contingent in some way and to some extent on what we do."[65]

This was the issue in the struggle, schism, and salvation of the Protestant Reformed Churches in the early 1950s. To the heresy that overturns Dordt's confession that our eternal welfare depends wholly and exclusively on what God has done, does, and will do by grace in Jesus Christ, by proclaiming that "our eternal welfare [is] contingent...on what we do [in the covenant]," the Declaration of Principles said, and still says, no.

Many of the reputedly conservative Presbyterian and Reformed churches in North America have had the federal vision appear in their midst. A number of them have not only refused to condemn the heresy and the heretics, but have also exonerated the heretics and approved the heresy. None of their assemblies or theologians,

---

this defense of his theology in a foreword to the book. Boersema is a liberated Reformed theologian.

65   Norman Shepherd, foreword in Boersema, *Not of Works,* ix.

Protestant Reformed theological conference on the covenant held in 1947, featuring Dr. Klaas Schilder. This conference, as well as lecture and sermons by him throughout the PRC, introduced the liberated theology of a conditional covenant into the PRC and led to both the adoption of the Declaration in 1951 and the schism of 1953.

with the sole exception of the Protestant Reformed Churches, have exposed and condemned the root of the heresy, namely, the doctrine of a conditional covenant divorced from eternal election.

Through the fierce struggle over the covenant in the early 1950s, resulting in the painful schism, and by the adoption of the Declaration, God immunized the Protestant Reformed Churches against the heresy of the federal vision. He also put them in the position to witness concerning the covenant to the churches troubled by this gross covenant heresy.

SALUTARY WARNING TO THE PRC

There is one other salutary effect that the Declaration and the history of its adoption ought to have upon the Protestant Reformed Churches. The history of the Declaration, including its occasioning a schism, is a warning against the danger of an unsound zeal for

Schilder

THEOLOGICAL CONFERENCE
NOVEMBER 6-1947

ecumenicity, of an unhealthy emphasis on missions, and of allowing personal friendships to motivate ecumenicity. These were the follies of the leaders in the Protestant Reformed Churches in the late 1940s and early 1950s, including Herman Hoeksema, that made the Declaration necessary and that resulted in grievous schism.

Protestant Reformed ministers were overly enthusiastic to get the large numbers of Dutch immigrants into the Protestant Reformed Churches and in this way swell the rolls of the membership of the denomination. At the same time they were zealous to have ecumenical relationship with the Reformed Churches in the Netherlands (liberated), with a zeal that was not according to knowledge. And Hoeksema allowed his personal friendship with Klaas Schilder to influence the ecumenical relations of the Protestant Reformed Churches.

The denominational committee for foreign correspondence gave expression to this enthusiasm to receive the Dutch immigrants. A letter to the Reformed Churches in the Netherlands (liberated) in 1948 stated that the Protestant Reformed Churches "would gladly take them [the Dutch, liberated immigrants] into our Churches or organize them as autonomous congregations, where this is possible." This mission work with the Dutch immigrants, the letter continued, made "very desirable" that there be "closer fellowship between our Churches."[66]

That the thinking among the ministers was a notion to soften the doctrinal witness of the Protestant Reformed Churches for the sake of more effective missions is evident in the report of the denominational mission committee to the synod of 1948. The committee suggested that "much of our literature, due to the controversial nature, is outmoded and would have to be revised."[67] Then, with regard specifically to the "Holland immigration into Canada," the mission committee recommended sending the immigrants "*positive* Protestant Reformed literature."[68]

The leaders of the Protestant Reformed Churches opened up the churches to the conditional covenant theology of Schilder and the liberated by their invitation of Schilder to theological conferences with Protestant Reformed ministers and especially by their opening of the pulpits of the churches to Schilder in the fall of 1947. He preached throughout the denomination. Thus the denomination indicated to the members of the churches that Schilder and the liberated Reformed, on the one hand, and the Protestant Reformed Churches, on the other hand, were one in the Reformed faith. Thus the denomination also opened up the congregations and especially many of the ministers to Schilder's persuasive influence.

In the letter to the Reformed Churches in the Netherlands (liberated) referred to earlier, which of course was public knowledge in the Protestant Reformed Churches, the synodical Committee for Foreign Correspondence declared that the liberated churches were "a Reformational holding fast and return to the old, Reformed, tested paths." The letter added this fatal sentence: "Dogmatical differences which possibly exist between you and us are no confessional differences."[69]

The 1948 synod of the Protestant Reformed Churches approved this letter "in general."[70]

---

66 *Acts of Synod, Protestant Reformed Churches, 1948*, 38–39. The translation of the Dutch in this and following quotations is mine.

67 Ibid., 27.

68 Ibid., 27–28. I italicize the word that tells the story.

69 Ibid., 38.

70 Ibid., 53. In another letter to the Reformed Churches in the Netherlands

The three members of the committee who signed this letter included Hoeksema and Ophoff. Both later recanted their signing and sending the letter. But the damage had been done.

Fueling the later fire over the synodical decision adopting the Declaration was this line in the letter, which deliberately tried to find favor with the liberated: "Both your denomination and ours, then, do not countenance any binding synodical decrees which are expressions of or supplements to the confession."[71] And then a few years later comes the Declaration, as an "expression" of the confessions, directed specifically against the liberated doctrine and people!

In an editorial in the *Standard Bearer*, after the theological conferences with Schilder about the covenant in 1947, Hoeksema announced to the membership of the Protestant Reformed Churches that Schilder and the Protestant Reformed Churches were one in the fundamentals of the Reformed faith and differed only in the incidentals: "We agreed upon fundamentals, and for the rest we agreed to differ...A true brotherly feeling was maintained to the very last."[72]

The Protestant Reformed Churches themselves lighted the conflagration that nearly consumed the denomination. They brought the schism upon themselves. And the reasons were exaggerated zeal for ecumenicity and untoward enthusiasm for missions.

Against these serious errors, the Protestant Reformed Churches must guard. They have been warned by severe strokes—the conflict in the churches in the late 1940s and early 1950s and schism

---

(liberated), the synod of 1948 said this about the earlier letter from its committee for foreign correspondence: "*Onze Synode het in het algemeen met de strekking van voornoemden brief eens is*" ("Our synod is in general in agreement with the sentiments of the letter mentioned before"). Hoeksema was the author of this second letter, expressing general agreement with the sentiments of the first letter.

71   Ibid., 38.

72   Herman Hoeksema, "Our Conference with Dr. Schilder," *Standard Bearer* 24, no. 5 (December 1, 1947): 103. This was Hoeksema's analysis of the agreement of the two theologies of the covenant immediately after his noting that "according to the Liberated Churches the promise is for all that are born in the covenant line."

in 1953. Ecumenicity may not be pursued at the expense of the truth. Missions may not be conducted by minimizing or ignoring the cardinal doctrines of the word of God. All ecumenicity and missions must proceed on the basis of oneness in and faithfulness to the truth. For a Reformed denomination, this means oneness in and faithfulness to the Reformed creeds.

The churches may not carelessly expose the members to false teachings, underestimating the influence these teachings may have, or recklessly endanger the unity of the denomination by contact with churches that are not one with the denomination doctrinally.

The church of Jesus Christ is one and catholic. This calls her to manifest oneness and catholicity. But the true oneness of the church is a oneness that is in harmony with the church's also being apostolic, that is, founded on the doctrines of the apostles.

The history of the Declaration calls to mind the ancient proverb, "*confusione homine, providentia Dei*," that is, "by the confusion of man, the providence of God."

With the Protestant Reformed men, there was confusion—the confusion of foolishness and error. But in and by that confusion, God worked with his special providence in true churches of Jesus Christ to produce a statement of the gospel of grace with regard to the covenant and to establish a denomination of Reformed churches in the truth of the unconditional, that is, gracious, covenant.

This was the history of the Declaration of Principles, in the light of eternity.

Chapter Seven

Response to Criticism of the Declaration

Basically, there have been two overt, prominent attacks on the Declaration. One was the attack leveled by the schismatic faction in the Protestant Reformed Churches in the early 1950s. They made their attack in the pages of *Concordia* and the *Reformed Guardian* and in their protests to and speeches at the synods of the Protestant Reformed Churches that considered the Declaration.

The other attack was made by Schilder. He published his criticism of the Declaration first in a series of articles in his magazine, *De Reformatie*. These articles were later published in a booklet titled *Bovenschriftuurlijke Binding—Een Nieuw Gevaar* [Extra-scriptural binding—a new danger].[1] Schilder's criticism has recently been published in English translation as "Extra-Scriptural Binding—A New Danger" in the book by Canadian Reformed theologian Jelle Faber, *American Secession Theologians on Covenant and Baptism*.[2]

CRITICISM BY THE SCHISMATICS

The attack on the Declaration by the Protestant Reformed ministers who opposed its adoption in the early 1950s was twofold. They identified their twofold attack in their rejection of the Declaration after they had separated from the Protestant Reformed Churches. Their synod adopted a report of a committee that judged the

1   Klaas Schilder, "*Bovenschriftuurlijke Binding—Een Nieuw Gevaar*," in *Woord en Wereld: Een Brochurereeks* (Goes, the Netherlands: Comite tot Verspreiding van Goedkoope Geref. Lectuur, n.d.).

2   Klaas Schilder, "Extra-Scriptural Binding," in Faber, *American Secession Theologians*, 55–167.

objections against the Declaration as dividing "into two parts: 1) that dealing with the legal aspect; 2) that dealing with the material aspect [the content] of the Declaration of Principles."[3]

The objection concerning legality argued that the matter of a Declaration of Principles, including its adoption, arose at synod and was decided by synod, whereas it ought to have come to synod, if at all, by an overture from a consistory. The charge was repeatedly couched in the phrase, "The Declaration did not arise *out of the bosom of the churches*": "Such material cannot be initiated by Synod, but…must arise out of the bosom of the Churches."[4]

To this objection concerning legality, the Protestant Reformed men defending the Declaration responded by noting that the original request for a "form" to be used in organizing new churches came to synod from synod's denominational mission committee. Article 30 of the Church Order permits, indeed requires, that a synod treat "matters…[that] pertain to the churches of the major assembly in common."[5] A form (which the Declaration is) that is needed and requested by the denominational mission committee is properly the business of a synod. No consistory could be expected to initiate a request for a form that the mission committee of the denomination needs.

Article 51 of the Church Order states that "the missionary work of the churches is regulated by the general synod in a mission order."[6]

To the related objection that the Declaration is not exactly the form that the mission committee had in mind, or wanted, the response is that this objection does not concern legality but content. The question is not exactly what kind of form did the mission committee desire, but what kind of form did the synod deem appropriate and necessary.

The objections by the Protestant Reformed ministers against the content of the Declaration in 1951 and 1953 were carefully phrased. As has already been noted, in the words of the objectors themselves, "all the Protestants expressed their general agreement with

---

3   *Acts of Synod [schismatic], 1954*, 67.

4   *Acts of Synod, 1953*, 349.

5   Church Order Article 30, in *Confessions and Church Order*, 389.

6   Church Order Article 51, in ibid., 396.

the basic thrust and general doctrinal content of the Declaration of Principles."[7] Agreement with "the basic thrust and general doctrinal content of the Declaration" would seem to preclude strong objection to the content, or at least to weaken the objection.

Nevertheless, those opposing the Declaration expressed strong, determined objections to especially two aspects of the doctrinal content of the Declaration. One was the Declaration's definition of the promise of the covenant as "an oath of God that He will infallibly lead all the elect unto salvation and eternal glory through faith."[8] The second aspect of the content of the Declaration with which the adversaries found fault was the Declaration's denial that the covenant and its promise are conditional: "Objections concerning the element of conditionality."[9]

The weaknesses of the Declaration concerning the definition of the promise and concerning conditionality, it was charged, result in a loss of the "experiential" nature of preaching. By its definition of the covenant promise and by its repudiation of a conditional covenant, as taught by the liberated Reformed, the Declaration "creates a shift in the emphasis of our Confessions," that is, the Declaration conflicts with the "experiential approach" of the confessions.[10]

The response to these objections concerning the content of the Declaration is, first, that the covenant promise of God to Abraham is explicitly affirmed by Scripture to have been confirmed by an oath.

> For when God made promise to Abraham, because he could swear by no greater, he sware by himself, Saying, Surely blessing I will bless thee, and multiplying I will multiply thee. And so, after he had patiently endured, he obtained the promise. For men verily swear by the greater: and an oath for confirmation is to them an end of all strife. Wherein God, willing more abundantly to shew unto the heirs of promise the immutability of his counsel, confirmed it by an oath: That by two immutable things, in which it was impossible for God to lie, we might have

---

7   *Acts of Synod [schismatic], 1954*, 72.

8   Ibid.

9   Ibid., 73.

10 Ibid.

a strong consolation, who have fled for refuge to lay hold upon the hope set before us (Heb. 6:13–18).

According to verse 17 of Hebrews 6, this oath of God confirms the promise down the ages, whenever and wherever it is given to the "heirs of promise."

Objection to the oath-bound character of the covenant promise seems foolish on its face, because God's promise is absolutely certain—certain regarding its *fulfillment*—whether an oath is attached or not. The oath was not necessary in order to assure God's keeping, that is, *fulfilling*, the promise, but in order to assure Abraham—and us—of his fulfillment of the promise.

The real issue concerning the covenant promise in the conflict in the Protestant Reformed Churches in the early 1950s was the objects of the covenant promise, whether all the baptized children conditionally or the elect children unconditionally. This remains the real issue in the covenant controversy in the Reformed churches still today. Scripture and the Reformed creeds identify the object of the promise as Jesus Christ himself, as representative head of the covenant of grace. "Now to Abraham and his seed were the [covenant] promises made. He saith not, And to seeds, as of many; but as of one, And to thy seed, which is Christ" (Gal. 3:16). Galatians 3:19 adds: "The law...was added because of transgressions, till the seed [that is, Jesus the Christ] should come *to whom the promise was made*" (emphasis added). The covenant promise was not made in the first instance either to all the physical offspring of father Abraham without exception, or to the elect descendants of the patriarch. But the promise was made to the Christ, who was in God's decree of the covenant and in Abraham's loins.

Galatians 3:29 expands on the identity of the object of the covenant promise by noting that "if ye be Christ's, then are ye Abraham's seed, and heirs according to the promise." Jesus Christ is the object of the covenant promise, not by himself alone, but with all those humans out of all nations who belong to him in the union of true faith according to eternal election. This implies Jesus Christ's headship of the covenant. The heirs, and therefore objects, of the covenant promise are not all the baptized offspring of godly parents without exception, but only those who "are Christ's," that is, the elect descendants of Abraham and the elect children of believing parents, whom Jesus Christ represents as head of the covenant.

The biblical teaching that election governs the covenant and its establishment by divine promise is faithfully reflected in the Reformed confessions. The Westminster Larger Catechism is explicit. "With whom was the covenant of grace made? The covenant of grace was made with Christ as the second Adam, and in him with all the elect as his seed."[11]

The Canons of Dordt are no less clear in 2.8: "Christ by the blood of the cross...confirmed the new covenant." By his death, which was the confirming of the covenant, Christ redeemed "all those, and those only, who were from eternity chosen to salvation, and given to him by the Father."[12] Christ Jesus is the head of the covenant of grace, representing, particularly in his redeeming death, those, and those only, who are his by virtue of their having been given to him in election. This answers the question, still being raised by Reformed theologians, "Who are included in the covenant of grace by divine promise?"

If the three forms of unity often describe the objects of the promise as "believers," this in no wise negates the truth that the objects of the promise are particular, definite persons, rather than all men or all the physical offspring of godly parents generally. For believers are those humans, or more specifically those children of godly parents, to whom God has given faith, according to his election of them. "Believers" are the elect in Jesus Christ.

In the early 1950s those Protestant Reformed preachers who objected to the Declaration's confession that the covenant promise is the (unconditional) oath of God that he will save the elect children, because they favored a general, conditional promise to all the children, often appealed to Canons 2.5 against the Declaration's teaching. Their assumption was that this article of the Canons teaches a general, conditional promise. The article reads as follows:

Moreover the promise of the gospel is, that whosoever

---

11 Westminster Larger Catechism Q&A 31, in *The Subordinate Standards and Other Authoritative Documents of the Free Church of Scotland* (Edinburgh: repr., William Blackwood & Sons, 1973), 57.

12 Canons of Dordt 2.8, in Schaff, *Creeds of Christendom*, 3:587.

believeth in Christ crucified shall not perish, but have everlasting life. This promise, together with the command to repent and believe, ought to be declared and published to all nations, and to all persons promiscuously and without distinction, to whom God out of his good pleasure sends the gospel.[13]

But Canons 2.5 does not, in fact, teach that God promises salvation to all humans, regardless of predestination. The article does not teach that God promises salvation to all humans to whom the preaching of the gospel is sent. On the contrary, Canons 2.5 restricts the promise to those who believe: "The promise of the gospel is that *whosoever believeth* in Christ crucified shall not perish, but have everlasting life." The promise of the gospel is to and for "whosoever believeth." It is not to or for anyone else. It is not to or for the unbeliever. To the unbeliever, God does not promise everlasting life. Rather, in the preaching of the gospel God warns the unbeliever of condemnation: "He that believeth not is condemned already, because he hath not believed in the name of the only begotten Son of God" (John 3:18).

Canons 2.5 does teach that this promise of everlasting life through faith must be "*declared and published* to all persons promiscuously and without distinction." The preacher may, and "ought," to declare to all in his audience, "God promises to save every one who repents of his sins and believes in Christ crucified."

But the article in the creed does not authorize the preacher to promise salvation to all hearers, on condition that they will believe.

When God promises salvation to a person, the promise is sure. It is sure *with regard to the fulfillment of the promise, namely, the everlasting life of the person.* A divine promise, indeed even a human promise, not only involves the expression of the good intention of the one who promises. But it involves the realizing of that which is promised. If a promise is of any worth, it assures one that the promise will be fulfilled.

The charge that the dogmatical statement of truth concerning the promise, that is, that the promise of the covenant is the solemn oath of God that he will infallibly bring the elect to glory, somehow

---

13 Canons of Dordt 2.5, in ibid., 3:586.

adversely affects the experiential nature of preaching and believing is false. The dogmatical statement in Canons 1.7 that there is an eternal decree of election and that this decree assures the everlasting salvation of all whom God has chosen does not at all hinder the activity of promiscuous preaching, the urgency of the call (or command) to repent and believe, and the necessity of believing as the only way of salvation.

Canons 2.5 is in perfect harmony with Canons 1.7. Indeed, to use the language of the charge against the Declaration by its enemies, the "experiential" Canons 2.5 is *based on* the dogmatical Canons 1.7.

The second objection to the content of the Declaration by its foes within the Protestant Reformed Churches in the early 1950s concerned the Declaration's denial that the covenant promise and the covenant itself are conditional. A major section of the report on the content of the Declaration adopted by the schismatic synod of 1954 was headed, "Objections concerning the element of conditionality."[14]

In proof of their contention that the covenant is conditional, the objectors to the Declaration quoted a number of Reformed theologians using the term "condition." They also called attention to what they called "the conditional form" of expression in the confessions and to "conditional speech in the Bible."[15]

That in the Declaration against which the objectors were contending was the Declaration's statement that "faith is not a prerequisite or condition unto salvation, but a gift of God, and a God-given instrument whereby we appropriate the salvation in Christ."[16] They were also opposing the Declaration's statement that "the preaching of the gospel is not a gracious offer of salvation on the part of God to all men, nor a conditional offer to all that are born in the historical dispensation of the covenant, that is, to all that are baptized."[17]

As an expression of the creeds, the Declaration's repudiation of the teaching that faith is a condition unto salvation, in the covenant or anywhere else, is explicit creedal doctrine.

---

14   *Acts of Synod [schismatic], 1954*, 353.

15   *Acts of Synod, 1953*, 353–62.

16   Declaration of Principles, in *Confessions and Church Order*, 423.

17   Ibid., 413.

Canons 1, Error 3 condemns as Arminian heresy the teaching that "God chose...the act of faith...as a condition of salvation."[18]

Similarly, Canons 1, Error 5 condemns as Arminian heresy the teaching that "faith...[is] not fruit of the unchangeable election unto glory, but [is a] condition which, being required beforehand [a prerequisite], [was] foreseen as being met by those who will be fully elected, and [is] cause without which the unchangeable election to glory does not occur."[19]

The Declaration cites a number of passages from the three forms of unity that teach that faith is the fruit of election, that faith was earned for the elect by the death of Christ, and that faith is the gift to the elect by the work of the Holy Spirit. These creedal passages include Canons 1.7; Canons 1.9; Canons 2.8; Canons 3–4.10, 14; Belgic Confession, Article 22; and more.

These passages in the Reformed creeds are the primary response of the Protestant Reformed Churches to the attack on the Declaration's repudiation of a conditional covenant and covenant promise. The Reformed creeds explicitly deny that faith is a condition unto salvation. This denial applies to salvation in the covenant. Covenant grace and covenant salvation are not conditional. That is, they do not depend upon anything that the saved sinner must do. It is heresy to teach that faith is a condition, or prerequisite, unto salvation in the covenant, regardless whether one refers to the beginning of covenant salvation or to the continuation and perfection of covenant salvation.

On the contrary, as the very opposite of the teaching that faith is a condition, the creeds describe faith as God's gift to some sinners, whether adults or children. God purposed their faith in the eternal decree of election: "Men are chosen to faith...Election is the fountain of every saving good; from which proceed[s] faith...as its fruit."[20] God merited faith for them by the death of Jesus: "that he [Jesus Christ] should confer upon them [the elect] faith, which... he purchased for them by his death."[21] And God the Holy Spirit

---

18 Canons of Dordt 1, Error 3, in ibid., 160.

19 Canons of Dordt 1, Error 5, in ibid., 161.

20 Canons of Dordt 1.9, in Schaff, *Creeds of Christendom*, 3:583.

21 Canons of Dordt 2.8, in ibid., 3:587.

works faith in the elect, not only the spiritual ability to believe, but also the activity of believing: "Faith is therefore to be considered as the gift of God...because he...produces both the will to believe and the act of believing also."[22] Further, God the Holy Spirit preserves faith in all those to whom he gives it: "It is...of God's free mercy, that they do not totally fall from faith and grace...Of this preservation of the elect to salvation, and of their perseverance in the faith, true believers for themselves may and do obtain assurance."[23]

All of this creedal doctrine now is, and must be, applied to the actual teaching on behalf of which the schismatic Protestant Reformed ministers were contending for conditionality. In their opposition to the Declaration's (and the Reformed confessions') repudiation of conditions, those ministers were defending a certain theology of the covenant and of covenant salvation. Their concern was not merely to justify the use of the term "condition" by orthodox Reformed theologians in the past, who meant by the term "a necessary means of the covenant and its salvation," that is, that faith is the necessary means or way of salvation in the covenant of grace.

The doctrinal issue in the Protestant Reformed Churches in the late 1940s and early 1950s, as every minister knew and as every church member should have known, was that of the covenant theology of Schilder and his colleagues. That is, the issue was the covenant theology of the Reformed Churches in the Netherlands (liberated) and of the two nineteenth-century Dutch ministers, K. J. Pieters and J. R. Kreulen, after which the liberated theologians patterned their covenant doctrine.[24]

---

22 Canons of Dordt 3–4.14, in ibid., 3:591.

23 Canons of Dordt 5.8–9, in ibid., 3:594.

24 For a detailed analysis of the origin and nature of the liberated doctrine of the covenant, particularly the novel and controversial doctrine of Pieters and Kreulen, see David J. Engelsma, *Covenant and Election in the Reformed Tradition* (Jenison, MI: Reformed Free Publishing Association, 2011), 1–32, 120–21. That the liberated Reformed deliberately patterned their doctrine of the covenant after that proposed by Pieters and Kreulen is acknowledged by Jelle Faber: In their "positive exposition of their insights on covenant and baptism," the liberated theologians "did so in conscious harmony with the teachings of...Pieters and Kreulen" (Faber, *American Secession Theologians*, 38).

According to the covenant theology of the liberated Reformed, election is not the source of the covenant, nor does it govern the covenant and its grace. Rather, God is gracious to all the physical offspring of believing parents without exception.

In this universal grace regarding all the baptized children, God on his part promises every child that he will save that child, on condition that the child on his or her part will believe and then live in obedience all his or her life.

Indeed, by this gracious, general promise regarding all the baptized children, God on his part establishes his covenant with all the children alike. The saving effect of this covenant includes that God begins to bestow upon all the children certain covenant blessings, including justification.

But none of this—gracious disposition of God, gracious promise, and gracious establishment of the covenant—assures the final, everlasting salvation of any of the children. For the covenant is conditional. The main condition, contrary to the Reformed confessions (and to the Declaration, expressing the truth of the confessions), is faith, although lifelong obedience is also a condition. Whether the covenant promise is fulfilled in a child (in that child's everlasting salvation), whether the covenant continues with a child (after the initial establishment of the covenant), and whether a child enjoys all the blessings of the covenant (which include the resurrection of the body in the day of Christ) depend on the child's performing the conditions of the covenant.

The implication of this doctrine of the covenant is that the covenant promise to many children is frustrated and fails. The implication is also that one can fall out of the covenant and lose covenant blessings that he has begun to enjoy. There is a real falling away of covenant saints. Therefore, another implication is that every baptized believer, to the end of his days, must live in the fear that he may fall away and go lost forever, for salvation in the covenant depends on the performance of the conditions as long as he lives.

The theology of the covenant that the Protestant Reformed ministers who affirmed conditionality were defending views the covenant as promise and demand. The promise (to all the baptized children) is divine grace; the demand is the human condition. And the gracious promise depends squarely on the condition of the demand.

Like the liberated Reformed, from whom the Protestant Reformed ministers who opposed the Declaration learned this theology of the covenant, the Protestant Reformed critics of the Declaration in the early 1950s attempted to ward off the charge of Arminianism by pleading that God himself fulfills the conditions of the covenant. The committee of three ministers, all of whom were determined foes of the Declaration, that reported concerning protests against the Declaration to the 1953 synod of the Protestant Reformed Churches used this defense on behalf of their advocacy of a conditional covenant.

> We must never say that the speech of God in the conditional, as it points to the conditions...ever implies that man can fulfill these...Rather when God comes in the conditional to His people He works the very demand in them...It is God in action.[25]

This defense of a conditional covenant and a conditional covenant salvation is an utter failure. When the apostle writes in Romans 9:16 that salvation "is not of him that willeth, nor of him that runneth, but of God that sheweth mercy," he is referring concretely to salvation in the covenant of grace, as the context makes plain. That this salvation is not *of* him that willeth nor *of* him that runneth means, among other things, that covenant salvation does not *depend* upon the willing or working of covenant children. To explain the text as teaching that salvation does not depend upon the one who wills, *apart from the help of God working this willing in him,* and that salvation does not depend upon the one who works, *apart from the help of God working this working in him,* so that the apostle teaches in Romans 9:16 that salvation is, in reality, of him that willeth *with the help of God* and of him that runneth *with the help of God,* is to contradict the plain sense of the words of the text and to destroy the gospel of grace, which the text teaches.

One who reads the first part of Romans 9:16 as allowing for salvation's depending on the willing and running sinner, as long as his willing and running are the work of God in him, must read the second part of Romans 9:16 similarly: Covenant salvation is

---

25 *Acts of Synod, 1953,* 362.

"of God that sheweth mercy, *and of the sinner who wills and works with the help of grace*, that is, salvation *depends* both upon God who shows mercy and upon the sinner who wills and runs, if only he wills and runs with the help of God."

It is this covenant theology that the federal vision is developing at the end of the twentieth century and the beginning of the twenty-first century. This development openly denies the great gospel-truth of justification by faith alone and the doctrines of grace confessed by the Canons of Dordt. The federal vision denies the gospel of grace *with regard to the covenant and covenant salvation.*

The federal vision's development of the covenant theology rejected by the Protestant Reformed Churches in the early 1950s by their Declaration of Principles is natural and necessary. A conditional covenant implies, indeed *means*, a conditional salvation from beginning to end. And a conditional salvation is the Arminian and, ultimately, the Pelagian heresy.

Hoeksema's prophecy, therefore, has been realized. In the midst of the controversy over the Declaration, when a majority of his own students and colleagues, a majority of his own congregation, and a majority of Protestant Reformed people opposed the doctrine of the covenant that he was defending and opted for a conditional covenant, Hoeksema exclaimed, "History will justify, not them, but us."[26] What he meant was that history would justify the Protestant Reformed stand that the creeds teach an unconditional covenant as part and parcel of their theology of salvation by sovereign, particular grace alone.

By the heresy of the federal vision, the battle of the Protestant Reformed Churches for the unconditional covenant has been justified by God in history.

Inasmuch as the objections against the Declaration's condemnation of conditionality intended to defend the theology of a conditional covenant and conditional covenant salvation, the response to those objections was, and is, that the covenant is truly a covenant of grace. And grace is without condition.

This, essentially, was the doctrinal controversy at Dordt in the early seventeenth century. Arminianism was, and is, a doctrine of

---

26 Herman Hoeksema, "The Heart of the Matter," *Standard Bearer* 31, no. 5 (December 1, 1954): 100.

conditional salvation, according to which (saving) grace is universal and resistible, depending for its saving effect upon the will and work of the sinner. Dordt rejected this theology as the overthrow of the gospel of grace. And the Declaration does nothing else than apply Dordt's doctrinal affirmations and rejections to the theology of the covenant.

That the Synod of Dordt combated and condemned a theology of conditional grace and salvation, indeed a *covenant* theology of conditional grace and salvation, is evident throughout the Canons, but especially in Canons 2, Errors 2–4. In this section, the Canons reject the errors of those

> Who teach that it was not the purpose of the death of Christ that He should confirm the new covenant of grace through His blood, but only that He should acquire for the Father the mere right to establish with man such a covenant as He might please, whether of grace or of works.

> Who teach that Christ, by His satisfaction, merited neither salvation itself for anyone, nor faith, whereby this satisfaction of Christ unto salvation is effectually appropriated; but that He merited for the Father only the authority or the perfect will to deal again with man, and to prescribe new conditions as He might desire, obedience to which, however, depended on the free will of man, so that it therefore might have come to pass that either none or all should fulfill these conditions.

> Who teach that the new covenant of grace, which God the Father, through the mediation of the death of Christ, made with man, does not herein consist that we by faith, inasmuch as it accepts the merits of Christ, are justified before God and saved, but in the fact that God, having revoked the demand of perfect obedience of the law, regards faith itself and the obedience of faith, although imperfect, as the perfect obedience of the law, and does esteem it worthy of the reward of eternal life though grace.[27]

In a long speech at the synod of 1953, where the Declaration and

---

27 Canons of Dordt 2, Errors 2–4, in *Confessions and Church Order*, 164–65.

its confession of creedal unconditionality were under fierce attack, having demonstrated that he had taught an unconditional covenant from the beginning of his public ministry, Hoeksema declared:

> This...is Protestant Reformed. Conditional theology is not Protestant Reformed, and has never been...Conditional theology and Liberated theology is certainly quite different, fundamentally different, from our Protestant Reformed truth.[28]

Hoeksema was constrained to emphasize that unconditionality had always been the hallmark of the theology preached and confessed by the Protestant Reformed Churches because of the charge by the foes of the Declaration that in the past leaders in the denomination, including Hoeksema and Ophoff, had taught a conditional covenant.

What the Declaration emphasizes is that unconditional theology is the hallmark not only of the Protestant Reformed Churches but also of the Reformed confessions, that is, of the Reformed faith.

CRITICISM BY SCHILDER

The other main attack on the Declaration was lodged by the Dutch Reformed theologian Klaas Schilder. Schilder made his attack in a series of articles in the Dutch religious periodical *De Reformatie* in 1950 and 1951, at the time when the Protestant Reformed Churches were adopting the Declaration of Principles. These articles were later translated into English and published with the title "Extra-Scriptural Binding—A New Danger."[29] Schilder's attack was at the same time a defense of his doctrine of a conditional covenant.

The Dutch theologian's attack on the Declaration was two-pronged. The first prong was expressed in the title of his attack: the Declaration is "extra-scriptural binding." Supporters of Schilder have emphasized this element of Schilder's attack on the

---

28   Herman Hoeksema's speech at the synod of 1953, in *Acts of Synod, 1953*, 277.

29   Klaas Schilder, "Extra-Scriptural Binding—A New Danger," in Faber, *American Secession Theologians*, 55–167. My critique of Schilder's attack on the Declaration works with this English translation and publication. Schilder wrote the original articles in Dutch.

Declaration, although Schilder himself made very little of it in his brochure, other than giving the brochure the title he did and alluding to it occasionally.

Implied in the title is that a church may not settle a doctrinal controversy by a binding synodical decision that does anything but quote Scripture. Because the Declaration is a synodical decision that settles a doctrinal controversy by quoting the creeds rather than quoting Scripture, the Declaration is "extra-scriptural" and therefore illegitimate.

But this criticism of the Declaration is mistaken in every respect. First, a Reformed denomination of churches not only *may* but also *must* settle doctrinal controversies by judging them according to the standard of the Reformed confessions. This is the significance of the Reformed Formula of Subscription. Every Reformed officebearer promises

> diligently to teach and faithfully to defend...all the articles and points of doctrine contained in the [Belgic] Confession and [Heidelberg] Catechism of the Reformed Churches, together with the explanation of some points of the aforesaid doctrine made by the National Synod of Dordrecht, 1618-19.[33]

The Formula of Subscription calls consistories, classes, and synods to judge the teaching of officebearers and doctrinal controversies on the basis of the creeds.

When a synod condemns a teaching by appeal to the creeds and at the same time confesses the truth by quotations from the creeds, thus binding its members, it is not guilty of "extra-scriptural binding," for the creeds "do fully agree with the Word of God."[31] Binding by the creeds *is* scriptural binding.

If Schilder's point in the title of his attack on the Declaration is that the Declaration is a binding synodical decision that goes beyond the creeds, the Declaration itself proves him mistaken. It claims to be only the "expression" of the creeds regarding a truth that is basic to missions and regarding the doctrinal controversy in the Protestant Reformed Churches at the time the Declaration was

---

30   Formula of Subscription, in *Confessions and Church Order*, 326.
31   Ibid.

drawn up and adopted. The content of the Declaration confirms the claim. The content is almost wholly quotations of the creeds, including the Reformed baptism form. There is hardly any further explanation of the passages quoted, much less theological argumentation. The content of the Declaration is the Reformed creeds as they apply to the doctrine of the covenant of grace.

Since all Reformed people agree that the creeds are scriptural, the Declaration can only be regarded by them as scriptural binding.

If Schilder or a likeminded critic of the Declaration objects that the quotations of the creeds are carefully selected and arranged, so that in this way the Declaration is a synodical decision that is "extra-confessional," the response is that it is certainly true that the synod carefully selected and arranged the creedal citations. But this does not make the Declaration "extra-confessional" and therefore "extra-scriptural." Rather, it indicates that the Declaration pointedly addresses important issues in the controversy that was raging in the Protestant Reformed Churches.

What do the creeds say about the denial by the doctrine of a conditional covenant that election is the fountain and cause of grace, faith, justification, holiness, and final salvation in the covenant?

What do the creeds say about the teaching of the doctrine of a conditional covenant that the faith of a baptized child is a condition that he must perform unto his remaining in the covenant and unto his everlasting salvation?

What do the creeds say about the teaching of a gracious but conditional promise of God to all the baptized children alike?

A Reformed synod would be derelict in its duty if it did not quote the creedal passages that bear on the controversy that the synod is called to judge.

Indeed, the Declaration would have been perfectly within its rights had it added much more explanation and argumentation based on the creeds than is actually found in the document.

Article 31 of the Reformed Church Order of Dordt declares that "whatever may be agreed upon by a majority vote" by a major ecclesiastical assembly is rightly "settled and binding, unless it be proved to conflict with the Word of God or with the articles of the Church Order."[32] Major assemblies may settle issues with good reasonings and sound argumentation, based on the Reformed confessions.

The charge against the Declaration, which is still current in the mind and circles of the liberated Reformed, that the Declaration is "extra-scriptural binding," with the suggestion of synodical hierarchy, is utterly false.[33] It is remarkable that the charge has acquired such wide currency and has had such a long life. It has not even a semblance of truth.

The second prong of Schilder's attack was what he himself stressed in his brochure. This aspect of the attack was criticism of the content of the Declaration.

But also this attack was unsuccessful. Schilder did not forthrightly respond to the Declaration's weighty objections, derived from the creeds, against his and the liberated Reformed's doctrine of a conditional covenant. Nor did the liberated theologian, having opposed his covenant doctrine to that confessed in the Declaration, defend the covenant doctrine that the Declaration condemns.

Rather, Schilder contented himself with undermining certain statements and positions in the Declaration. He argued that the word "condition" can have several meanings, so that the Declaration's condemnation of the specific conditionality of the covenant in liberated theology is dubious. He quoted from various Reformed sources, showing that they used the word "condition," leaving the impression that by adopting the Declaration the Protestant Reformed Churches excommunicated the likes of Beza and the translators of the Dutch version of the Bible that appeared soon after Dordt. Schilder also suggested that a dogmatical statement of the truth of the covenant promise precludes lively, personal address in the preaching.

All of these observations, and more, were beside the point. The question was not how many senses can the word "condition" have

---

32 Church Order Article 31, in *Confessions and Church Order*, 390.

33 Canadian Reformed (liberated) theologian Jelle Faber has recently perpetuated the charge in the book in which he publishes Schilder's attack on the Declaration. Faber speaks of the "infamous *Declaration of Principles*" and quickly praises Schilder for his maintenance of the "struggle against extra-Scriptural binding" (Faber, *American Secession Theologians*, 51).

in general discourse, or even in theological discourse, but what sense does "condition" necessarily have in a doctrine of the covenant that extends covenant grace more widely than election.

The issue in the covenant controversy in the Protestant Reformed Churches in the early 1950s (and in the Reformed community of churches in North America today) was (and is) not that Calvin, Beza, and others used the word "condition" when they were not confronted by, or themselves teaching, a doctrine that denied particular, sovereign grace in connection with the covenant and salvation in the covenant. The issue was the use of the word "condition" in the covenant theology of the liberated Reformed, as it surfaced in the Protestant Reformed Churches in the late 1940s and early 1950s.

There is no dispute between the Protestant Reformed Churches and the Reformed Churches in the Netherlands (liberated) that there must be a lively, personal address in the preaching of the gospel. The dispute is whether that address is based on solid, Reformed theology and whether the lively address itself is sound and true. The Arminian preacher faults Reformed theology for forbidding the lively, personal address to all men, "God loves you, Christ died for you, and the Holy Spirit now sincerely, graciously offers you salvation on condition that you accept the offer." The Reformed church will not, for the sake of this lively address in the preaching, give up the dogma of election, the dogma of limited atonement, and the dogma of sovereign, particular grace in the preaching of the gospel.

Despite Schilder's inexcusable failure clearly to lay out the liberated doctrine of the covenant and then forthrightly to defend it against the condemnation by the Declaration, his attack on the Declaration does indicate the "principles" of the liberated doctrine of the covenant. Thus his attack also demonstrates that the condemnation of these principles by the Declaration is solid and sound.

Schilder's first attempt to blunt the force of the Declaration against the liberated doctrine of a conditional covenant was to confuse the meaning of the term "condition." Schilder proposed four possible meanings of the word "condition." Three of these possible meanings he rejected as erroneous in connection with the covenant. He affirmed the fourth meaning as sound, suggesting that this is the meaning of "condition" in the confession of a conditional covenant by himself and the liberated Reformed churches.

> Do you mean by *condition* something which God has *joined to something else*, to make clear to us that the *one* cannot come *without the other* and that we cannot be *sure* of the one, unless we are at the same time *assured* of the other? Then we say unconditionally: "conditional is the password!"[34]

This meaning of "condition," which Schilder claims for his theology of a conditional covenant, is merely "the necessary way," or "order," in which God saves the sinner.

Later, Schilder becomes more specific. "Condition" in liberated theology is merely "means for the execution of the decree of ELECTION."[35] A "condition" is merely "the *way* by which the elect *come to* and are *assured* of salvation…God…does not give B without A, C without B, and D without C."[36]

Of course, if this is what "condition" means in the covenant theology of the liberated Reformed, the Declaration is confused and mistaken in its opposition to conditional covenant theology. What Reformed church or theologian denies that faith is the "way" to forgiveness and salvation, or that God follows a certain "order" in his salvation of his people in the covenant?

The fatal weakness of Schilder's explanation of "condition" is simply that this is not the meaning of "condition" in liberated covenant theology. For one thing, the covenant doctrine of the liberated Reformed has deliberately cut the covenant and its salvation loose from election. Schilder may not dodge the Declaration's condemnation of his covenant doctrine by defining "condition" as merely the "way" in which God executes his counsel of election. For as liberated theologian Cornelis Veenhof has informed the Reformed community of churches, the founding fathers of the

---

34 Schilder, "Extra-Scriptural Binding," in Faber, *American Secession Theologians*, 78. The emphasis is Schilder's.

35 Ibid., 118. Schilder here is explaining "condition" as it occurs in Beza, but he intends to apply this explanation also to the covenant doctrine of the liberated.

36 Ibid., 132.

Reformed Churches in the Netherlands (liberated) decided that "with regard to what was taught concerning covenant, the promise of the covenant, and baptism, very consciously [this] was *not* placed under the government of election."[37]

Schilder admitted that the covenant in his theology does not have its source in election. He criticized the Declaration for calling election "the sole cause and fountain of all our salvation."

> When the declaration states that *election* is the *cause* and *fountain* is it using theoretically precise, accurate, scholarly terminology? I don't believe it! To be accurate it should say: "Election is the *ground*." A decree of God is never the *cause* of its execution, nor its *fountain*.[38]

Schilder insisted that the cause and fountain of (covenant) salvation are rather "something which comes in time": "Election is not the cause...That which causes anything in us and which is thus *cause* and *fountain* of *all salvation,* is something which comes in time...The doctrine of election is not a doctrine of causes or fountains. Causes and fountains only occur in history...Consequently, we do not make people rely upon election, as ground and fountain, but upon *the Word.*"[39]

Contrary to Schilder's criticism of the Declaration, as also to his statements about cause and fountain, the Canons of Dordt teach that "election is the *fountain* of every saving good," specifically,

---

37 C. Veenhof, *Prediking en Uitverkiezing* [Preaching and election] (Kampen: Kok, 1959), 299. The translation of the Dutch is mine. In the sentence that immediately precedes, Veenhof acknowledges that the liberated doctrine of the covenant was deliberately patterned after the covenant doctrine of "Pieters en Kreulen." These two Dutch ministers introduced into the Secession Reformed Churches in the middle of the nineteenth century a doctrine of the covenant about which they themselves said, "Let us then regarding Baptism forget about eternal election and establish that the promise of the covenant is bestowed and offered as the revealed counsel of God and refers to every baptized [child] in the visible church without any exception" (translated and quoted in David J. Engelsma, "The Covenant Doctrine of the Fathers of the Secession," in *Always Reforming: Continuation of the Sixteenth-Century Reformation* [Jenison, MI: Reformed Free Publishing Association, 2009], 109).

38 Schilder, "Extra-Scriptural Binding," in Faber, *American Secession Theologians,* 82–83. The emphasis is Schilder's.

39 Ibid., 85–86. The emphasis is Schilder's.

"faith."[40] When the Canons go on to describe faith as the "effect" of election, they are clearly viewing election as the "cause" of faith.[41]

In calling election the fountain and cause of faith, as of all the other gifts of (covenant) salvation, the Declaration was only faithfully and accurately expressing the teaching of the Reformed creeds.

In challenging this statement of the Declaration, Schilder erred, badly. The error was more than only a factual mistake, ignoring a teaching of the creed. But the significance of the challenge was that it indicated that in liberated covenant theology, election is not the source of, nor does it govern, the covenant, contrary to the plain teaching of the Canons of Dordt.

A theology that cuts the covenant loose from election cannot defend its use of conditions in the covenant by explaining "condition" in terms of the order in which God executes the decree of election. Such a theology denies that the covenant is the execution of the decree of election.

A covenant theology that divorces covenant and covenant grace from election, thus extending grace more widely than only the elect, and then speaks of faith as a "condition" does not and *cannot* mean by "condition" merely the way in which God executes his counsel of election. What such a covenant theology means by "condition" is a work of the child upon which God depends for his further work of saving the child. And this is the meaning of "condition" in every language.

What such a covenant theology means by "condition" is also, therefore, the work of a child by which he distinguishes himself from other children, similarly graced by the covenant promise and certain covenant blessings, as worthy of remaining in the covenant and finally of obtaining eternal life.

That Schilder and the liberated deny that such conditions are "meritorious," as they do, is of no importance, although they emphasize this, as though the non-meritoriousness of their conditions somehow rescues their theology from the Arminian

---

40 Canons of Dordt 1.9, in Schaff, *Creeds of Christendom*, 3:583. The emphasis is added.

41 Ibid. The complete sentence reads: "Therefore election is the fountain of every saving good; from which proceed faith, holiness, and the other gifts of salvation, and finally eternal life itself, as its fruits and effects."

heresy. Regardless whether a condition is meritorious or simply a non-meritorious work upon which the saving grace of God depends, a condition is the denial of the grace of salvation. In the language of Romans 9:16, both the Roman Catholic theology of merit and the liberated theology of conditions teach that salvation is "of him that willeth and of him that runneth, and not of God who shows mercy."

To such conditions as obtain in liberated covenant theology, the Canons of Dordt refer when they deny that any "possible qualities of human actions" are "a condition of salvation."[42] To such conditions, whether meritorious or non-meritorious, the Canons refer when they deny that "the act of faith...[is] a condition of salvation."[43]

As he misfired when he attacked the Declaration's condemnation of the liberated Reformed's making faith a condition of covenant salvation, so did Schilder egregiously err when he dealt with the Declaration's insistence that the promise of God is always particular, ultimately only to and for the elect.

Schilder vehemently opposed this teaching of the Declaration. He took issue with the Declaration's denial that "the preaching of the gospel is...a conditional offer to all who are born in the historical dispensation of the covenant, that is, to all that are baptized." For Schilder, the covenant promise is for all the offspring of Abraham and of godly parents without exception. According to the liberated theologian, God makes his covenant promise to every baptized child, *conditionally.* "The promise does not come to unknown *elect,* but to those *called* by name and surname, who *are included* in the *covenant community.*"[44] In further explanation of this general, conditional promise to every baptized person in the visible church, particularly every baptized child of believers, Schilder wrote:

> The promise of the gospel is not an *oath* that God will lead all the elect to a destination (although this is all true) but

---

42 Canons of Dordt 1.10, in Schaff, *Creeds of Christendom*, 3:583.

43 Canons of Dordt 1, Error 3, in *Confessions and Church Order*, 160.

44 Schilder, "Extra-Scriptural Binding," in Faber, *American Secession Theologians*, 145.

an oath *to* a specific person, that He wants to lead this specific person, *called by* name, to the final salvation.[45]

Schilder's assertion that the general promise expresses God's desire to save every one who is baptized, those who ultimately perish as well as those who ultimately are saved, only makes explicit what is implied by the teaching that the covenant promise is general. God's grace in the covenant is wider than election. In promising salvation to all the baptized children, God is gracious to all, if not by an internal saving work, then with regard to his attitude of favor and sincere desire to save: his desire "to lead this specific person [that is, every baptized child]...to the final salvation."

Schilder himself must have felt that at this point his covenant theology plainly sails on the foul waters of the Arminian heresy, for he immediately added, "If someone calls this Arminian, I would quietly say, 'It is not, and you do not understand the situation.'"[46] Mere denial, however, does not suffice to refute the charge. And a Reformed believer understands the situation very well, indeed. Extending the favorable attitude of God toward sinners—grace!—and a desire of God to save humans—grace!—more widely than election is due to cutting the covenant and its salvation loose from election. And then to teach that this general covenant grace, with its salvation, is conditional is sheer Arminianism, with specific application to the covenant.

Schilder is clear enough that he opposes the restriction of the covenant promise to the elect. He is also clear in affirming that God extends the gracious covenant promise to all who are baptized. He states that this general promise expresses the desire of God to save all who are baptized without exception.

But Schilder completely fails to prove a general promise from Scripture and the Reformed confessions. First, he takes no notice of Paul's restriction of the covenant promise to Jesus Christ as head of the covenant in Galatians 3:16 and to those who are Christ's (by divine election) in Galatians 3:29. Any discussion of the object of the covenant promise that wants to be taken seriously must take Galatians 3:16 and 29 into account.

45 Ibid., 146.
46 Ibid.

Second, Schilder fails to recognize that the two passages from the confessions that he appeals to in support of a general promise, a promise to many others than the elect, in fact contradict the position for which he is fighting. The two creedal passages are Canons 2.5 and Canons 3–4.8.

Concerning Canons 2.5, Schilder wrote:

> When I read of the promise of the gospel then I stick to this leading thought...I want to read this term *promise of the gospel* as it is used in the Canons of Dort, especially in II, 5, where we can read that the promise of the gospel ought to be announced...The Canons also say that this promise-with-command has to be declared and published...to all nations, without distinction, to whom God out of His good pleasure...*sends* the gospel...Added is *promicue*, communally, collectively; without discrimination.[47]

Evidently, Schilder's remarks about Canons 2.5 are supposed to elucidate the teaching of the article that the promise is addressed to all who hear the preaching of the gospel.

But Canons 2.5 does not teach that the promise of the gospel is addressed by God to all who come under the preaching. Rather, this article of the creed addresses the promise to "whosoever believeth in Christ crucified." The promise is particular and limited: to and for those who believe, and them only. This particular promise must be "declared and published to all nations, and to all persons promiscuously and without distinction," but the promise that is promiscuously published is particular. The preaching of the promise is promiscuous and general, although even this preaching of the promise is limited by the "good pleasure" of God. The promise itself, however, is not promiscuous and general. To all, promiscuously and without distinction, the church must preach that God promises salvation to *every believer in Jesus Christ*.

Rather than promise salvation to unbelievers, the same preaching warns the unbelievers that the wrath of God abides on them (John 3:36).

Although in our preaching we will use the language of Canons 2.8, namely, "whosoever believes," the truth is that believers are the

---

47   Ibid., 136–37. The emphasis is Schilder's.

elect. The article, therefore, is in reality confessional proof of the teaching of the Declaration that the promise is God's sure word of grace and salvation to and for the elect.

Schilder also wanted his readers to think that Canons 3–4.8 supported his theology of a general promise, against the teaching of the Declaration.

> The *Brief Declaration* says that the promise of the gospel is an oath *about the elect*, but the Canons of Dort say that the promise of the gospel is an oath *to the called* (III/IV, 8).... But that which God announces as a promise, that which He promises, is not unconditional, but is...a conditional promise to the ones who are called.[48]

But also this article restricts the promise. Who are they to whom God himself "seriously promises eternal life and rest" in the gospel? The answer of Canons 3–4.8 is "as many as shall come to him and believe on him."[49] These are not all humans who hear the preaching. They are not those men and women whom God unfeignedly calls, or commands, to come to him by believing the gospel. These are not all the children of believers who are baptized. These are those humans, whether adults on the mission field or children in the sphere of the covenant, whom the Spirit of Jesus Christ irresistibly draws to Jesus Christ in true faith.

And this is determined by election, as the Canons teach in the following articles, especially Canons 3–4.11:

> But when God accomplishes his good pleasure in the elect, or works in them true conversion [so that they come to him and believe on him], he not only causes the gospel to be externally preached to them, and powerfully illuminates their minds by his Holy Spirit...but by the efficacy of the same regenerating Spirit he pervades the inmost recesses of the man.[50]

At the end of "Extra-Scriptural Binding," the reader awaits, in vain, for some creedal rebuttal of the Declaration and some creedal

---

48 Ibid., 140–41. The emphasis is Schilder's.
49 Canons of Dordt 3–4.8, in Schaff, *Creeds of Christendom*, 3:589.
50 Canons of Dordt 3–4.11, in ibid., 3:590.

support for the principles of the doctrine of a conditional covenant of the liberated Reformed. Schilder does not provide such support. He does not provide such support because it does not exist.

Schilder's challenge was: What does the Reformed preacher say, by way of direct address, to all hearers, if he may not promise all of them salvation conditionally? The answer is: He does not say to all, "God loves you and desires your salvation," or "Christ died for you," or "the Spirit is patiently waiting for you to choose Christ so that he may enter your heart." Neither does he say, "God graciously promises every one of you salvation, on condition that you believe."

But the Reformed preacher, whose preaching is governed by Scripture as Scripture is faithfully summarized by the creeds, says this: "You are guilty, depraved, and damnable before the just and holy God. God has graciously provided a way of escape from sin and death into his fellowship by his Son Jesus Christ for every one who repents of his sins and believes on Jesus Christ crucified and risen. Believe on this Jesus Christ. God promises to every one who repents and believes that you will be forgiven and saved everlastingly. And if you repent and believe, that is because God has graciously drawn you to himself according to his eternal choice of you in Christ."

Such an address is lively and direct.

Such an address does not compromise the grace of salvation or the truth that election is the cause and fountain of all salvation.

Such an address is biblical, grounded on the creeds, and an address that magnifies the sovereign grace of God, to his glory.

And this is the testimony of the Declaration of Principles.

Appendices

Appendix One

Time Line of the History of the Declaration of Principles and of the Schism in the Protestant Reformed Churches

Fall 1947: Dr. K. Schilder, theologian in the Reformed Churches in the Netherlands (liberated), visits the Protestant Reformed Churches (PRC) at their invitation. Schilder speaks at ministers' conferences, lectures to large audiences, mostly of Protestant Reformed people, and preaches in congregations throughout the denomination. Schilder promotes his distinctive doctrine of a conditional covenant.

Protestant Reformed minister Rev. A. Petter begins a series of articles in the Protestant Reformed periodical *Concordia*, defending Schilder's and the liberated churches' doctrine of a conditional covenant against the established Protestant Reformed doctrine of an unconditional covenant. Thus Petter launches the controversy over the covenant in the PRC that will culminate in the adoption of the Declaration of Principles and in schism.

1948: The PRC begin working in missions with mostly liberated, Dutch immigrants in Ontario, Canada, with a view to organizing them as Protestant Reformed congregations.

May 1, 1949: Prof. G. M. Ophoff, professor of theology at the Protestant Reformed Seminary, begins his public response to Petter's defense of a conditional covenant. Ophoff's response in the *Standard Bearer* is titled "Open Letter to Rev. Andrew Petter." In the fifth installment of his response to Petter in the July 1, 1949 issue of the *Standard Bearer*, Ophoff writes that the truth of the unconditional covenant is established doctrine in the PRC. He writes also that the difference regarding the covenant "between the Protestant Reformed and the Liberated...is fundamental." And he calls the conditional covenant doctrine of Christian Reformed theologian Prof. W. Heyns and of the liberated "heretical." Thus the controversy over the covenant heats up.

June 1950: The synod of the Protestant Reformed Churches adopts, provisionally, a document called "A Brief Declaration of Principles of the PRC." Synod composes and adopts the document in response to the request of the denominational mission committee for a "form" to be used in organizing a "Protestant Reformed congregation." The occasion of the request is the work of the mission committee with liberated immigrants in Canada. The Declaration establishes from the creeds the basic truths of the covenant doctrine of the PRC, a covenant doctrine that the PRC have confessed and preached from their founding. All churches organized by the PRC or affiliating with the PRC must be in heartfelt agreement with this doctrine of the covenant. Synod decides that, after being examined by the churches for a year, the Declaration will be adopted, decisively, by the synod of 1951.

January 1951: The recently organized Protestant Reformed church in Hamilton, Ontario, Canada, whose members are almost entirely former members of the Reformed Churches in the Netherlands (liberated), summarily deposes its pastor, Rev. H. Veldman, and Elder S. Reitsma and severs relations with the PRC. The reason is the commitment of the consistory and congregation to the liberated doctrine of the covenant and their detestation of the Protestant Reformed doctrine of the covenant.

April 1951: Rev. H. De Wolf, one of the three pastors of the large and influential First Protestant Reformed Church in Grand Rapids, Michigan, preaches a sermon promoting the doctrine of a conditional promise of the gospel, thus taking up the cudgels on behalf of the liberated covenant doctrine in the controversy that is ongoing in the PRC and contradicting the covenant doctrine of the Declaration of Principles. Members of the congregation protest the sermon, but a bitterly divided consistory cannot render a verdict on the protests.

June, September, and October 1951: A lengthy and recessed synod of the PRC adopts the Declaration of Principles, decisively, as had been envisioned by the synod of 1950. Synod revises the

Declaration somewhat, without changing the doctrinal content of the document as provisionally adopted by the synod of 1950. As a synodical decision, the Declaration is official, binding confession by the PRC that the covenant of God, having its source in God's eternal election, is governed by election and is therefore established unconditionally with Jesus Christ as head of the covenant people and with the elect in him. It condemns the doctrine of a conditional covenant as heretical.

November 1951: Schilder writes an article in the paper of the liberated Reformed in the Netherlands stating that the relations between the PRC and the liberated churches are now at an end, because of the adoption by the PRC of the Declaration of Principles.

September 1952: De Wolf preaches another sermon teaching conditional salvation, in support of the liberated doctrine of the covenant and in opposition to the doctrine of the Declaration of Principles, which the synod of the PRC had decisively adopted in 1951. This sermon causes still more strife in First Church and in the denomination. Also this sermon is protested by members of the congregation, but a divided consistory is unable to pass judgment. Half of the elders support De Wolf.

April and May 1953: Classis East of the PRC judges appeals against the refusal of the consistory of First Church to condemn the statements and doctrine of De Wolf in his sermons in April 1951 and in September 1952. Classis condemns the offensive statements and the doctrine of De Wolf as heretical. Classis advises the consistory to demand a public apology from De Wolf for the statements on penalty, for refusal, of suspension from office. Classis also advises that the elders who support De Wolf in his false teaching are to concur in his apology.

June 1, 1953: A committee of Classis East meets with the consistory of First Church to deliver, explain, and urge adoption of the decisions of Classis East concerning the heretical statements of De Wolf and concerning the action to be taken by the consistory, including requiring their pastor to make a public apology. The consistory takes a decision acquiescing to the decisions of classis.

June 21, 1953: In a worship service of First Church, De Wolf gives what he presents as the public apology advised by Classis East and required by his consistory. In fact, his statement from the pulpit of First Church is not an apology. De Wolf does not read the apology that had been drawn up for him by the consistory of First Church. Against De Wolf's pseudoapology, there are objections by members of the congregation.

June 22, 1953: The consistory of First Church fails on a tie vote to reject De Wolf's purported apology.

June 23, 1953: The consistory of First Church (consisting of Rev. H. Hoeksema and Rev. C. Hanko and of the elders who, having voted to carry out the advice of Classis East, also voted to reject De Wolf's pseudoapology) suspends De Wolf from office and deposes the elders who support De Wolf, rejecting the advice of Classis East. Because De Wolf and the elders who support him are not informed of this consistory meeting and are not present at it, this meeting and the actions taken at it come under severe criticism both in First Church and throughout the denomination. Present at this meeting of the consistory are the committee of Classis East that had been appointed to help First Church with its difficulties and a neighboring consistory, which approves the suspension of De Wolf and the deposition of the elders who supported him.

June 28, 1953: The now-divided congregation of First Church holds separate worship services. The smaller part of the congregation worships under the auspices of the consistory whose ministers are Hoeksema and Hanko. The larger part worships under the auspices of a consistory whose minister is the suspended De Wolf. This congregation does not recognize the suspension of De Wolf. The group meeting with De Wolf temporarily retains the church building. This is fully developed schism in First Church.

June 1953: The annual synod of the PRC meets in the charged atmosphere of the developments in First Church, which are common knowledge. On the agenda of synod are a number of protests against the adoption of the Declaration. Classis West, one of the two classes of the denomination, informs synod that it supports the protests against the Declaration and that it "considers the Declaration to be illegal." In view of the fact that the Declaration was adopted by majority vote at the broadest assembly of the denomination, the statement by Classis West is revolutionary. Synod is deadlocked. Every vote concerning the Declaration is a tie. For this reason and in order, if possible, to avert the impending schism in the denomination, synod recesses until March 1954. It puts the matter of the protests against the Declaration into the hands of a study committee, which is to give advice to the reconvened synod in March 1954. The study committee consists of three ministers who are avowed foes of the Declaration.

September 1953: Classis West of the PRC decides that it will not recognize the suspension of De Wolf and the deposition of the elders who support him. Thus the churches and members of Classis West, with a few exceptions, separate from the PRC, making themselves guilty of schism in the body of Christ. Classis West, of course, has no jurisdiction over a church in Classis East. Interfering in the disciplinary work of a church in Classis East, the churches of Classis West make themselves guilty of hierarchy. Article 84 of the Church Order of Dordt reads: "No church shall in any way lord it over other churches, no minister over other ministers, no elder or deacon over other elders or deacons."

October 1953: Two delegations appear at the meeting of Classis East, both presenting themselves as the lawful delegation of First Church in Grand Rapids. Classis East recognizes and seats the delegation from the consistory whose pastors are Hoeksema and Hanko. Classis rejects the delegation from the consistory whose pastor is De Wolf. Upon this decision of Classis East, a number of pastors and elders, supporters of De Wolf and foes of the Declaration, withdraw from the classis. Thus schism now occurs also throughout Classis East. The schism is denomination wide.

January 1954: Ministers of the schismatic churches hold secret meetings with leading ministers and theologians of the Christian Reformed Church (CRC) negotiating agreement over the doctrines that historically have divided the PRC and the CRC, undoubtedly with a view to the eventual return of the schismatic churches to the CRC. One of these meetings, perhaps but not definitely the first, took place January 15, 1954. This is barely three months after the schism in the PRC became a reality throughout the denomination (by the actions of some at the October 1953 meeting of Classis East).

March 1954: The schismatic faction, still claiming to be the legitimate PRC, holds a synodical meeting, as though their synod were the continued session of the synod that had recessed in June 1953. This synod of the schismatics postpones repudiating the Declaration to their synod of June 1954.

The reconvened synod of the PRC meets. Synod appoints a committee to advise synod on the report of the study committee appointed by synod at its meeting in June 1953. The report advises synod to accede to the protests against the Declaration, thus declaring the Declaration null and void in the PRC. The committee appointed by the reconvened synod of March 1954 will fail to carry out its mandate and will eventually be discharged. The synod of the PRC, therefore, never judges the protests against the Declaration that were on the agenda of the synod of 1953.

June 1954: The synod of the schismatic churches declares the Declaration to be "without force" in their churches.

1957: The synod of the schismatic churches, still calling themselves the PRC, addresses the CRC asking for "ecumenical contact" with the CRC.

1960: The synod of the schismatic churches meets in special session to decide on a proposal to return to the CRC. The proposal fails on a tie vote.

1961: The schismatic churches return to the CRC, expressing that they do not object to the three points of common grace and that they will not agitate against them. Thus these churches come to an ignominious end, a mere eight years after their separation from the PRC. Thus also their noisy claim at the time of the schism and for some years thereafter that they were, and intended to remain, Protestant Reformed is exposed.

1954-2000: The Declaration fades into the background in the PRC. There is little reference to it. Little use is made of it. Few study it. It is not impossible that some members of the PRC wrongly dislike the document as the cause of admittedly very painful strife and division—strife and division that affected families. "Wrongly," because the Declaration was not the cause of the schism. The cause of the schism, as is so often the case in the history of Christ's church in the world, was the introduction of false doctrine into the churches—false doctrine concerning the covenant of grace.

2000: With the surfacing in almost all the reputedly conservative Presbyterian and Reformed churches in North America of the heresy of the federal vision, occasioned by the publication of the book by Norman Shepherd, *The Call of Grace: How the Covenant Illuminates Salvation and Evangelism* (Phillipsburg, NJ: P&R, 2000), the Declaration becomes a vitally important document both for the PRC and for the wider Reformed community. For the Declaration exposes and condemns the covenant doctrine that is the root of the federal vision. The federal vision openly denies justification by faith alone and the five doctrines of grace that are confessed by the Canons of Dordt. Where the federal vision reigns, or is tolerated, the Reformed faith goes under. But the Reformed faith is Holy Scripture's gospel of salvation by sovereign grace as confessed by the Reformed creeds.

Appendix Two

Declaration of Principles of the Protestant Reformed Churches

PREAMBLE

DECLARATION OF PRINCIPLES, to be used only by the Mission Committee and the missionaries for the organization of prospective churches on the basis of Scripture and the confessions as these have always been maintained in the Protestant Reformed Churches and as these are now further explained in regard to certain principles.

The Protestant Reformed Churches stand on the basis of Scripture as the infallible Word of God and of the Three Forms of Unity. Moreover, they accept the liturgical forms used in the public worship of our churches, such as: Form for the Administration of Baptism, Form for the Administration of the Lord's Supper, Form of Excommunication, Form of Readmitting Excommunicated Persons, Form of Ordination of the Ministers of God's Word, Form of Ordination of Elders and Deacons, Form for the Installation of Professors of Theology, Form of Ordination of Missionaries, Form for the Confirmation of Marriage Before the Church, and the Formula of Subscription.

On the basis of this Word of God and these confessions:

I. They repudiate the errors of the Three Points adopted by the Synod of the Christian Reformed Church of Kalamazoo, 1924, which maintain:

A. That there is a grace of God to all men, including the reprobate, manifest in the common gifts to all men.

B. That the preaching of the gospel is a gracious offer of salvation on the part of God to all that externally hear the gospel.

C. That the natural man through the influence of common grace can do good in this world.

D. Over against this they maintain:

1. That the grace of God is always particular, i.e., only for the elect, never for the reprobate.

2. That the preaching of the gospel is not a gracious offer of salvation on the part of God to all men, nor a conditional offer to all that are born in the historical dispensation of the covenant, that is, to all that are baptized, but an oath of God that He will infallibly lead all the elect unto salvation and eternal glory through faith.

3. That the unregenerate man is totally incapable of doing any good, wholly depraved, and therefore can only sin.

For proof we refer to

Canons 1, Articles 6–8:

Article 6. That some receive the gift of faith from God and others do not receive it proceeds from God's eternal decree, "For known unto God are all his works from the beginning of the world" (Acts 15:18). "Who worketh all things after the counsel of his will" (Eph. 1:11). According to which decree He graciously softens the hearts of the elect, however obstinate, and inclines them to believe, while He leaves the nonelect in His just judgment to their own wickedness and obduracy. And herein is especially displayed the profound, the merciful, and at the same time the righteous discrimination between men equally involved in ruin; or that decree of election and reprobation, revealed in the Word of God, which, though men of perverse, impure, and unstable minds wrest to their own destruction, yet to holy and pious souls affords unspeakable consolation.

Article 7. Election is the unchangeable purpose of God whereby, before the foundation of the world, He hath out of mere grace, according to the sovereign good pleasure of His own will, chosen, from the whole human race, which had fallen through their own fault from their primitive state of rectitude into sin and destruction, a certain number of persons to redemption in Christ, whom He from eternity appointed the Mediator and Head of the elect, and the foundation of salvation. This elect number, though by nature neither better nor more deserving than others, but with them involved in one common misery, God hath decreed to give to Christ, to be saved by Him, and effectually to call and draw them to His communion by His Word and Spirit, to bestow upon them true faith, justification, and sanctification; and having powerfully preserved them in the fellowship of His Son, finally to glorify them for the demonstration of His mercy and for the praise of His glorious grace; as it is written: "According as he hath chosen us in him before the foundation of the world, that we should be holy and without blame before him in love; having predestinated us unto the adoption of children by Jesus Christ to himself, according to the good pleasure of his will, to the praise of the glory of his grace, wherein he hath made us accepted in the beloved" (Eph.1:4–6). And elsewhere: "Whom he did predestinate, them he also called, and whom he called, them he also justified, and whom he justified, them he also glorified" (Rom. 8:30).

Article 8. There are not various decrees of election, but one and the same decree respecting all those who shall be saved, both under the Old and New Testament; since the Scripture declares the good pleasure, purpose, and counsel of the divine will to be one, according to which He hath chosen us from eternity, both to grace and glory, to salvation and the way of salvation, which He hath ordained that we should walk therein.

Canons 2, Article 5:

Article 5. Moreover, the promise of the gospel is that whosoever believeth in Christ crucified shall not perish, but have everlasting life. This promise, together with the command to repent and believe, ought to be declared and published to all nations, and to all persons promiscuously and without distinction, to whom God out of His good pleasure sends the gospel.

The Canons in 2.5 speak of the preaching of the promise. It presents the promise not as general, but as particular, i.e., as for believers, and, therefore, for

> *the elect. This preaching of the particular promise is promiscuous to all that hear the gospel, with the command, not a condition, to repent and believe.*

Canons 2, ...Error 6:

[Error] 6. Who use the difference between meriting and appropriating, To the end that they may instill into the minds of the imprudent and inexperienced this teaching, that God, as far as He is concerned, has been minded of applying to all equally the benefits gained by the death of Christ; but that, while some obtain the pardon of sin and eternal life and others do not, this difference depends on their own free will, which joins itself to the grace that is offered without exception, and that it is not dependent on the special gift of mercy, which powerfully works in them, that they rather than others should appropriate unto themselves this grace.

Rejection: For these, while they feign that they present this distinction in a sound sense, seek to instill into the people the destructive poison of the Pelagian errors.

For further proof we refer to Heidelberg Catechism, Lord's Day 3, Question and Answer 8:

Q. 8. Are we then so corrupt that we are wholly incapable of doing any good, and inclined to all wickedness?

A. Indeed we are, except we are regenerated by the Spirit of God.

Lord's Day 33, Question and Answer 91:

Q. 91. But what are good works?

A. Only those which proceed from a true faith, are performed according to the law of God, and to His glory; and not such as are founded on our imaginations or the institutions of men.

And also to the Belgic Confession, Article 14:

Article 14. We believe that God created man out of the dust of the earth, and made and formed him after His own image and likeness, good, righteous, and holy, capable in all things to will agreeably to the will of God. But being in honor he understood it not, neither knew his excellency, but willfully subjected himself to sin, and consequently to death and the curse, giving ear to the words of the devil. For the commandment of life which he had received he transgressed; and by sin separated himself from God, who was his true life; having corrupted his whole nature; whereby he made himself liable to corporal and spiritual death. And being thus become wicked, perverse, and corrupt in all his ways, he hath lost all his excellent gifts which he had received from God, and retained only a few remains thereof, which, however, are sufficient to leave man without excuse; for all the light which is in us is changed into darkness, as the Scriptures teach us, saying: The light shineth in darkness, and the darkness comprehendeth it not: where St. John calleth men darkness.

Therefore we reject all that is taught repugnant to this concerning the free will of man, since man is but a slave to sin, and has nothing of himself, unless it is given from heaven. For who may presume to boast that he of himself can do any good, since Christ saith, No man can come to Me except the Father, which hath sent Me, draw him? Who will glory in his own will, who understands that to be carnally minded is enmity against God? Who can speak of his knowledge, since the natural man receiveth not the things of the Spirit of God? In short, who dare suggest any thought, since he knows that we are not sufficient of ourselves to think anything as of ourselves, but that our sufficiency is of God? And therefore what the apostle saith ought justly to be held sure and firm, that God worketh in us both to will and to do of His good pleasure. For there is no will nor understanding conformable to the divine will and understanding but what Christ hath wrought in man, which He teaches us when He saith, Without Me ye can do nothing.

Once more we refer to [the] Canons

Canons 3–4, Articles 1–4:

Article 1. Man was originally formed after the image of God. His understanding was adorned with a true and saving knowledge of his Creator and of spiritual things; his heart and will were upright; all his affections pure; and the whole man was holy. But, revolting from God by the instigation of the devil and abusing the freedom of his own will, he forfeited these excellent gifts, and on the contrary entailed on himself blindness of mind, horrible darkness, vanity, and perverseness of judgment, became wicked, rebellious, and obdurate in heart and will, and impure in his affections.

Article 2. Man after the fall begat children in his own likeness. A corrupt stock produced a corrupt offspring. Hence all the posterity of Adam, Christ only excepted, have derived corruption from their original parent, not by imitation, as the Pelagians of old asserted, but by the propagation of a vicious nature.

Article 3. Therefore all men are conceived in sin, and by nature children of wrath, incapable of saving good, prone to evil, dead in sin, and in bondage thereto, and without the regenerating grace of the Holy Spirit they are neither able nor willing to return to God, to reform the depravity of their nature, nor to dispose themselves to reformation.

Article 4. There remain, however, in man since the fall the glimmerings of natural light, whereby he retains some knowledge of God, of natural things, and of the differences between good and evil, and discovers some regard for virtue, good order in society, and for maintaining an orderly external deportment. But so far is this light of nature from being sufficient to bring him to a saving knowledge of God and to true conversion, that he is incapable of using it aright even in things natural and civil. Nay further, this light, such as it is, man in various ways renders wholly polluted, and holds it in unrighteousness, by doing which he becomes inexcusable before God.

II. They teach on the basis of the same confessions:

A. That election, which is the unconditional and unchangeable decree of God to redeem in Christ a certain number of persons, is the sole cause and fountain of all our salvation, whence flow all the gifts of grace, including faith.

This is the plain teaching of our confessions in the Canons of Dordrecht 1, Articles 6–7. See above.

And in the Heidelberg Catechism, Lord's Day 21, Question and Answer 54, we read:

> Q. 54. What believest thou concerning the "holy catholic church" of Christ?
>
> A. That the Son of God, from the beginning to the end of the world, gathers, defends, and preserves to Himself by His Spirit and Word, out of the whole human race, a church chosen to everlasting life, agreeing in true faith; and that I am, and forever shall remain, a living member thereof.

This is also evident from the doctrinal part of the Form for the Administration of Baptism, where we read:

> For when we are baptized in the name of the Father, God the Father witnesseth and sealeth unto us that He doth make an eternal covenant of grace with us, and adopts us for His children and heirs, and therefore will provide us with every good thing, and avert all evil or turn it to our profit. And when we are baptized in the name of the Son, the Son sealeth unto us that He doth wash us in His blood from all our sins, incorporating us into the fellowship of His death and resurrection, so that we are freed from all our sins and accounted righteous before God. In like manner, when we are baptized in the name of the Holy Ghost, the Holy Ghost assures us, by this holy sacrament, that He will dwell in us and sanctify us to be members of Christ, applying unto us that which we have in Christ, namely, the washing away of our sins and the daily renewing of our lives, till we shall finally be presented without spot or wrinkle among the assembly of the elect in life eternal.

> B. That Christ died only for the elect and that the saving efficacy of the death of Christ extends to them only.

This is evident from Canons 2, Article 8:

> Article 8. For this was the sovereign counsel and most gracious will and purpose of God the Father, that the quickening and saving efficacy of the most precious death of His Son should extend to all the elect, for bestowing upon them alone the gift of justifying faith, thereby to bring them infallibly to salvation; that is, it was the will of God that Christ by the

blood of the cross, whereby He confirmed the new covenant, should effectually redeem out of every people, tribe, nation, and language all those, and those only, who were from eternity chosen to salvation and given to Him by the Father; that He should confer upon them faith, which, together with all the other saving gifts of the Holy Spirit, He purchased for them by His death; should purge them from all sin, both original and actual, whether committed before or after believing; and, having faithfully preserved them even to the end, should at last bring them free from every spot and blemish to the enjoyment of glory in His own presence forever.

> *This article very clearly teaches:*
>
> *1. That all the covenant blessings are for the elect alone.*
>
> *2. That God's promise is unconditionally for them only: for God cannot promise what was not objectively merited by Christ.*
>
> *3. That the promise of God bestows the objective right of salvation not upon all the children that are born under the historical dispensation of the covenant, that is, not upon all that are baptized, but only upon the spiritual seed.*

This is also evident from other parts of our confessions, as, for instance:

Heidelberg Catechism, Lord's Day 25, Questions and Answers 65–66:

Q. 65. Since then we are made partakers of Christ and all His benefits by faith only, whence doth this faith proceed?

A. From the Holy Ghost, who works faith in our hearts by the preaching of the gospel, and confirms it by the use of the sacraments.

Q. 66. What are the sacraments?

A. The sacraments are holy, visible signs and seals, appointed of God for this end, that by the use thereof He may the more fully declare and seal to us the promise of the gospel, namely, that He grants us freely the remission of sin and life eternal, for the sake of that one sacrifice of Christ accomplished on the cross.

> *If we compare with these statements from the Heidelberger what was taught concerning the saving efficacy of the death of Christ in Canons 2, Article 8, it is evident that the promise of the gospel which is sealed by the sacraments concerns only the believers, that is, the elect.*

This is also evident from Heidelberg Catechism, Lord's Day 27, Question and Answer 74:

Q. 74. Are infants also to be baptized?

A. Yes; for since they, as well as the adult, are included in the covenant and church of God; and since redemption from sin by the blood of Christ, and the Holy Ghost, the author of faith, is promised to them no less than to the adult; they must therefore by baptism, as a sign of the covenant, be also admitted into the Christian church, and be distinguished from the children of unbelievers as was done in the old covenant or testament by circumcision, instead of which baptism is instituted in the new covenant.

> *That in this question and answer of the Heidelberger not all the children that are baptized, but only the spiritual children, that is, the elect, are meant is evident. For:*
>
> *a. Little infants surely cannot fulfill any conditions. And if the promise of God is for them, the promise is infallible and unconditional, and therefore only for the elect.*
>
> *b. According to Canons 2, Article 8, which we quoted above, the saving efficacy of the death of Christ is for the elect alone.*
>
> *c. According to this answer of the Heidelberg Catechism, the Holy Ghost, the author of faith, is promised to the little children no less than to the adult. And God surely fulfills His promise. Hence, that promise is surely only for the elect.*

The same is taught in the Belgic Confession, Articles 33–35.

In Article 33 we read:

> Article 33. We believe that our gracious God, on account of our weakness and infirmities, hath ordained the sacraments for us, thereby to seal unto us His promises, and to be pledges of the good will and grace of God toward us, and also to nourish and strengthen our faith, which He hath joined to the Word of the gospel, the better to present to our senses both that which He signifies to us by His Word and that which He works inwardly in our hearts, thereby assuring and confirming in us the salvation which He imparts to us. For they are visible signs and seals of an inward and invisible thing, by means whereof God worketh in us by the power of the Holy Ghost. Therefore the signs are not in vain or insignificant, so as to deceive us. For Jesus Christ is the true object presented by them, without whom they would be of no moment.

And from Article 34, which speaks of holy baptism, we quote:

> Article 34. We believe and confess that Jesus Christ, who is the end of the law, hath made an end, by the shedding of His blood, of all other sheddings of blood which men could or would make as a propitiation or satisfaction for sin; and that He, having abolished circumcision, which was done with blood, hath instituted the sacrament of baptism instead thereof, by which we are received into the church of God and separated from all other people and strange religions, that we may wholly belong to Him whose ensign and banner we bear, and which serves as a testimony to us that He will forever be our gracious God and Father.
>
> Therefore He has commanded all those who are His to be baptized with pure water, "in the name of the Father, and of the Son, and of the Holy Ghost," thereby signifying to us that, as water washeth away the filth of the body when poured upon it, and is seen on the body of the baptized when sprinkled upon him, so doth the blood of Christ, by the power of the Holy Ghost, internally sprinkle the soul, cleanse it from its sins, and regenerate us from children of wrath unto children of God. Not that this is effected by the external water, but by the

sprinkling of the precious blood of the Son of God, who is our Red Sea, through which we must pass to escape the tyranny of Pharaoh, that is, the devil, and to enter into the spiritual land of Canaan.

Therefore the ministers, on their part, administer the sacrament and that which is visible, but our Lord giveth that which is signified by the sacrament, namely, the gifts and invisible grace; washing, cleansing, and purging our souls of all filth and unrighteousness; renewing our hearts and filling them with all comfort; giving unto us a true assurance of His fatherly goodness; putting on us the new man, and putting off the old man with all his deeds...

> *Article 34 speaks of holy baptism. That all this, washing and cleansing and purging our souls of all filth and unrighteousness, the renewal of our hearts, is only the fruit of the saving efficacy of the death of Christ and therefore is only for the elect is very evident. The same is true of what we read in the same article concerning the baptism of infants:*

Article 34 [continued]. And indeed Christ shed His blood no less for the washing of the children of the faithful than for adult persons; and therefore they ought to receive the sign and sacrament of that which Christ hath done for them; as the Lord commanded in the law that they should be made partakers of the sacrament of Christ's suffering and death shortly after they were born, by offering for them a lamb, which was a sacrament of Jesus Christ. Moreover, what circumcision was to the Jews, that baptism is to our children. And for this reason Paul calls baptism the "circumcision of Christ."

> *If, according to Article 8 of Canons 2, the saving efficacy of the death of Christ extends only to the elect, it follows that when in this article of the Belgic Confession it is stated that "Christ shed his blood no less for the washing of the children of the faithful than for the adult persons," also here the reference is only to the elect children.*

Moreover, that the promise of the gospel which God signifies and seals in the sacraments is not for all is also abundantly evident from Article 35 of the same Belgic Confession, which speaks of the holy supper of our Lord Jesus Christ. For there we read:

> Article 35. We believe and confess that our Savior Jesus Christ did ordain and institute the sacrament of the holy supper to nourish and support those whom He hath already regenerated and incorporated into His family, which is His church.

In the same article we read:

> Further, though the sacraments are connected with the thing signified, nevertheless both are not received by all men. The ungodly indeed receives the sacrament to his condemnation, but he doth not receive the truth of the sacrament—as Judas and Simon the sorcerer both indeed received the sacrament but not Christ who was signified by it, of whom believers only are made partakers.
>
> *It follows from this that both the sacraments, as well as the preaching of the gospel, are a savor of death unto death for the reprobate, as well as a savor of life unto life for the elect. Hence, the promise of God, preached by the gospel, signified and sealed in both the sacraments, is not for all but for the elect only.*

And that the election of God, and consequently the efficacy of the death of Christ and the promise of the gospel, is not conditional is abundantly evident from the following articles of the Canons.

Canons 1, Article 10:

> Article 10. The good pleasure of God is the sole cause of this gracious election, which doth not consist herein, that out of all possible qualities and actions of men God has chosen some as a condition of salvation; but that He was pleased out of the common mass of sinners to adopt some certain persons as a peculiar people to Himself, as it is written, "For the children being not yet born, neither having done any good or evil," etc., it was said (namely to Rebecca): "the elder shall serve the younger; as it is written, Jacob have I loved, but Esau have I hated" (Rom. 9:11-13). "And as many as were ordained to eternal life believed" (Acts 13:48).

In Canons 1...Error 2, the errors are repudiated of those who teach:

[Error] 2. That there are various kinds of election of God unto eternal life: the one general and indefinite, the other particular and definite; and that the latter in turn is either incomplete, revocable, non-decisive, and conditional, or complete, irrevocable, decisive, and absolute....

And in the same chapter of Canons 1...Error 3, the errors are repudiated of those who teach:

[Error] 3. That the good pleasure and purpose of God, of which Scripture makes mention in the doctrine of election, does not consist in this, that God chose certain persons rather than others, but in this, that He chose out of all possible conditions (among which are also the works of the law), or out of the whole order of things, the act of faith, which from its very nature is undeserving, as well as its incomplete obedience, as a condition of salvation, and that He would graciously consider this in itself as a complete obedience and count it worthy of the reward of eternal life....

Again...in Canons 1...Error 5, the errors are rejected of those who teach:

Article 5. That...faith, the obedience of faith, holiness, godliness, and perseverance are not fruits of the unchangeable election unto glory, but are conditions which, being required beforehand, were foreseen as being met by those who will be fully elected, and are causes without which the unchangeable election to glory does not occur.

Finally, we refer to the statement of the Baptism Form:

And although our young children do not understand these things, we may not therefore exclude them from baptism, for as they are without their knowledge partakers of the condemnation in Adam, so are they again received unto grace in Christ...

That here none other than the elect children of the Covenant are meant and that they are unconditionally, without their knowledge, received unto

> *grace in Christ, in the same way as they are under*
> *the condemnation of Adam, is very evident.*

C. That faith is not a prerequisite or condition unto salvation, but a gift of God, and a God-given instrument whereby we appropriate the salvation in Christ.

This is plainly taught in the following parts of our confessions:

Heidelberg Catechism, Lord's Day 7, Question and Answer 20:

> Q. 20. Are all men then, as they perished in Adam, saved by Christ?
>
> A. No, only those who are ingrafted into Him, and receive all His benefits, by a true faith.

Belgic Confession, Article 22:

> Article 22. We believe that, to attain the true knowledge of this great mystery, the Holy Ghost kindleth in our hearts an upright faith, which embraces Jesus Christ with all His merits, appropriates Him, and seeks nothing more besides Him. For it must needs follow, either that all things which are requisite to our salvation are not in Jesus Christ, or, if all things are in Him, that then those who possess Jesus Christ through faith have complete salvation in Him. Therefore, for any to assert that Christ is not sufficient, but that something more is required besides Him, would be too gross a blasphemy; for hence it would follow that Christ was but half a Savior. Therefore we justly say with Paul, that we are justified by faith alone, or by faith without works. However, to speak more clearly, we do not mean that faith itself justifies us, for it is only an instrument with which we embrace Christ our righteousness. But Jesus Christ, imputing to us all His merits and so many holy works which He has done for us and in our stead, is our righteousness. And faith is an instrument that keeps us in communion with Him in all His benefits, which, when become ours, are more than sufficient to acquit us of our sins.

Confer also Belgic Confession, Articles 33–35 quoted above.

In Canons 3–4, Article 10... we read:

> Article 10. But that others who are called by the gospel obey

the call and are converted is not to be ascribed to the proper exercise of free will, whereby one distinguishes himself above others equally furnished with grace sufficient for faith and conversion, as the proud heresy of Pelagius maintains; but it must be wholly ascribed to God, who as He has chosen His own from eternity in Christ, so He confers upon them faith and repentance, rescues them from the power of darkness, and translates them into the kingdom of His own Son, that they may show forth the praises of Him who hath called them out of darkness into His marvelous light, and may glory, not in themselves, but in the Lord, according to the testimony of the apostles in various places.

Again, in the same chapter of [the] Canons, Article 14, we read:

Article 14. Faith is therefore to be considered as the gift of God, not on account of its being offered by God to man, to be accepted or rejected at his pleasure, but because it is in reality conferred, breathed, and infused into him; or even because God bestows the power or ability to believe, and then expects that man should by the exercise of his own free will consent to the terms of salvation and actually believe in Christ, but because He who works in man both to will and to do, and indeed all things in all, produces both the will to believe and the act of believing also.

III. Seeing then that this is the clear teaching of our confession,

A. We repudiate

1. The teaching that the promise of the covenant is conditional and for all that are baptized.

2. The teaching that we may presuppose that all the children that are baptized are regenerated, for we know on the basis of Scripture, as well as in the light of all history and experience, that the contrary is true.

For proof we refer to

Canons 1, Articles 6–8 (quoted above)

The doctrinal part of the Baptism Form:

The principal parts of the doctrine of holy baptism are these three:

First. That we with our children are conceived and born in sin, and therefore are children of wrath, in so much that we cannot enter into the kingdom of God except we are born again. This the dipping in or sprinkling with water teaches us, whereby the impurity of our souls is signified, and we admonished to loathe and humble ourselves before God, and seek for our purification and salvation without ourselves.

Secondly. Holy baptism witnesseth and sealeth unto us the washing away of our sins through Jesus Christ. Therefore we are baptized in the name of the Father, and of the Son, and of the Holy Ghost. For when we are baptized in the name of the Father, God the Father witnesseth and sealeth unto us that He doth make an eternal covenant of grace with us, and adopts us for His children and heirs, and therefore will provide us with every good thing, and avert all evil or turn it to our profit. And when we are baptized in the name of the Son, the Son sealeth unto us that He doth wash us in His blood from all our sins, incorporating us into the fellowship of His death and resurrection, so that we are freed from all our sins and accounted righteous before God. In like manner, when we are baptized in the name of the Holy Ghost, the Holy Ghost assures us, by this holy sacrament, that He will dwell in us and sanctify us to be members of Christ, applying unto us that which we have in Christ, namely, the washing away of our sins and the daily renewing of our lives, till we shall finally be presented without spot or wrinkle among the assembly of the elect in life eternal.

Thirdly. Whereas in all covenants there are contained two parts, therefore are we by God, through baptism, admonished of and obliged unto new obedience, namely, that we cleave to this one God, Father, Son, and Holy Ghost; that we trust in Him, and love Him with all our hearts, with all our souls, with all our mind, and with all our strength; that we forsake the world, crucify our old nature, and walk in a new and holy life.

And if we sometimes through weakness fall into sin, we must not therefore despair of God's mercy, nor continue in sin, since baptism is a seal and undoubted testimony that we have an eternal covenant of grace with God.

The Thanksgiving after baptism:

Almighty God and merciful Father, we thank and praise Thee that Thou hast forgiven us and our children all our sins through the blood of Thy beloved Son Jesus Christ, and received us through Thy Holy Spirit as members of Thine only begotten Son, and adopted us to be Thy children, and sealed and confirmed the same unto us by holy baptism. We beseech Thee, through the same Son of Thy love, that Thou wilt be pleased always to govern these baptized children by Thy Holy Spirit, that they may be piously and religiously educated, increase and grow up in the Lord Jesus Christ, that they then may acknowledge Thy fatherly goodness and mercy, which Thou hast shown to them and us, and live in all righteousness under our only Teacher, King, and High Priest, Jesus Christ; and manfully fight against and overcome sin, the devil, and his whole dominion, to the end that they may eternally praise and magnify Thee, and Thy Son Jesus Christ, together with the Holy Ghost, the one only true God. Amen.

The prayer refers only to the elect; we cannot pre-suppose that it is for all.

3. [We also repudiate] the teaching that the promise of the covenant is an objective bequest on the part of God, giving to every baptized child the right to Christ and all the blessings of salvation.

B. And we maintain:

1. That God surely and infallibly fulfills His promise to the elect.

2. The sure promise of God which He realizes in us as rational and moral creatures not only makes it impossible that we should not bring forth fruits of thankfulness but also confronts us with the obligation of love, to walk in a new and holy life, and constantly to watch unto prayer.

All those who are not thus disposed, who do not repent but walk in sin, are the objects of His just wrath and excluded from the kingdom of heaven.

That the preaching comes to all; and that God

seriously commands to faith and repentance; and that to all those who come and believe He promises life and peace.

Grounds:

The Baptism Form, part 3.

The Form for the Lord's Supper, under "thirdly":

All those, then, who are thus disposed, God will certainly receive in mercy and count them worthy partakers of the table of His Son Jesus Christ. On the contrary, those who do not feel this testimony in their hearts eat and drink judgment to themselves.

Therefore, we also, according to the command of Christ and the apostle Paul, admonish all those who are defiled with the following sins to keep themselves from the table of the Lord, and declare to them that they have no part in the kingdom of Christ; such as all idolaters, all those who invoke deceased saints, angels, or other creatures; all those who worship images; all enchanters, diviners, charmers, and those who confide in such enchantments; all despisers of God, and of His Word, and of the holy sacraments; all blasphemers; all those who are given to raise discord, sects, and mutiny in church or state; all perjured persons; all those who are disobedient to their parents and superiors; all murderers, contentious persons, and those who live in hatred and envy against their neighbors; all adulterers, whoremongers, drunkards, thieves, usurers, robbers, gamesters, covetous, and all who lead offensive lives.

All these, while they continue in such sins, shall abstain from this meat (which Christ hath ordained only for the faithful), lest their judgment and condemnation be made the heavier.

The Heidelberg Catechism, Lord's Day 24, Question and Answer 64:

Q. 64. But doth not this doctrine make men careless and profane?

A. By no means; for it is impossible that those who are implanted into Christ by a true faith should not bring forth fruits of thankfulness.

The Heidelberg Catechism, Lord's Day 31, Question and Answer 84:

Q. 84. How is the kingdom of heaven opened and shut by the preaching of the holy gospel?

A. Thus: when according to the command of Christ it is declared and publicly testified to all and every believer, that, whenever they receive the promise of the gospel by a true faith, all their sins are really forgiven them of God, for the sake of Christ's merits; and on the contrary, when it is declared and testified to all unbelievers, and such as do not sincerely repent, that they stand exposed to the wrath of God and eternal condemnation, so long as they are unconverted; according to which testimony of the gospel God will judge them, both in this and in the life to come.

The Heidelberg Catechism, Lord's Day 44, Question and Answer 116:

Q. 116. Why is prayer necessary for Christians?

A. Because it is the chief part of thankfulness which God requires of us; and also, because God will give His grace and Holy Spirit to those only who with sincere desires continually ask them of Him, and are thankful for them.

Canons 3–4, Articles 12, 16–17:

Article 12. And this is the regeneration so highly celebrated in Scripture and denominated a new creation: a resurrection from the dead, a making alive, which God works in us without our aid. But this is in no wise effected merely by the external preaching of the gospel, by moral suasion, or such a mode of operation that after God has performed His part it still remains in the power of man to be regenerated or not, to be converted or to continue unconverted; but it is evidently a supernatural work, most powerful, and at the same time most delightful, astonishing, mysterious, and ineffable; not inferior in efficacy to creation or the resurrection from the dead, as the Scripture inspired by the Author of this work declares; so that all in whose heart God works in this marvelous manner are certainly, infallibly, and effectually regenerated and do actually believe. Whereupon the will thus renewed is not only actuated and influenced by God, but in consequence of this influence becomes itself active. Wherefore also, man is himself rightly said to believe and repent by virtue of that grace received.

Article 16. But as man by the fall did not cease to be a creature endowed with understanding and will, nor did sin which pervaded the whole race of mankind deprive him of the human nature, but brought upon him depravity and spiritual death; so also this grace of regeneration does not treat men as senseless stocks and blocks, nor takes away their will and its properties, neither does violence thereto; but spiritually quickens, heals, corrects, and at the same time sweetly and powerfully bends it; that where carnal rebellion and resistance formerly prevailed, a ready and sincere spiritual obedience begins to reign, in which the true and spiritual restoration and freedom of our will consist. Wherefore, unless the admirable Author of every good work wrought in us, man could have no hope of recovering from his fall by his own free will, by the abuse of which, in a state of innocence, he plunged himself into ruin.

Article 17. As the almighty operation of God whereby He prolongs and supports this our natural life does not exclude, but requires, the use of means, by which God of His infinite mercy and goodness hath chosen to exert His influence, so also the before mentioned supernatural operation of God by which we are regenerated in no wise excludes or subverts the use of the gospel, which the most wise God has ordained to be the seed of regeneration and food of the soul. Wherefore, as the apostles and teachers who succeeded them piously instructed the people concerning this grace of God, to His glory, and the abasement of all pride, and in the meantime, however, neglected not to keep them by the sacred precepts of the gospel in the exercise of the Word, sacraments, and discipline; so, even to this day, be it far from either instructors or instructed to presume to tempt God in the church by separating what He of His good pleasure hath most intimately joined together. For grace is conferred by means of admonitions; and the more readily we perform our duty, the more eminent usually is this blessing of God working in us, and the more directly is His work advanced; to whom alone all the glory, both of means and of their saving fruit and efficacy, is forever due. Amen.

Canons 3–4…Error 9

Article 9. Who teach: that grace and free will are partial causes, which together work the beginning of conversion, and that grace, in order of working, does not precede the working of the will; that is, that God does not efficiently help the will of man unto conversion until the will of man moves and determines to do this.

Rejection: For the ancient church has long ago condemned this doctrine of the Pelagians, according to the words of the apostle: "So then it is not of him that willeth, nor of him that runneth, but of God that hath mercy" (Rom. 9:16). Likewise: "For who maketh thee to differ? and what hast thou that thou didst not receive?" (1 Cor. 4:7). And: "For it is God who worketh in you both to will and to work for his good pleasure" (Phil. 2:13).

Canons 5, Article 14:

Article 14. And as it hath pleased God, by the preaching of the gospel, to begin this work of grace in us, so He preserves, continues, and perfects it by the hearing and reading of His Word, by meditation thereon, and by the exhortations, threatenings, and promises thereof, as well as by the use of the sacraments.

Belgic Confession, Article 24:

Article 24. We believe that this true faith, being wrought in man by the hearing of the Word of God and the operation of the Holy Ghost, doth regenerate and make him a new man, causing him to live a new life, and freeing him from the bondage of sin. Therefore it is so far from being true that this justifying faith makes men remiss in a pious and holy life, that, on the contrary, without it they would never do anything out of love to God, but only out of self-love or fear of damnation. Therefore it is impossible that this holy faith can be unfruitful in man; for we do not speak of a vain faith, but of such a faith which is called in Scripture a faith that worketh by love, which excites man to the practice of those works which God has commanded in His Word.

These works, as they proceed from the good root of faith, are good and acceptable in the sight of God, forasmuch as they are all sanctified by His grace; howbeit they are of no account towards our justification. For it is by faith in Christ that we are justified, even before we do good works; otherwise they could not be good works, any more than the fruit of a tree can be good before the tree itself is good.

Therefore we do good works, but not to merit by them (for what can we merit?), nay, we are beholden to God for the good works we do, and not He to us, since it is He that worketh in us both to will and to do of His good pleasure. Let us therefore attend to what is written: When ye shall have done all those things which are commanded you, say, we are unprofitable servants; we have done that which was our duty to do. In the meantime, we do not deny that God rewards our good works, but it is through His grace that He crowns His gifts.

Moreover, though we do good works, we do not found our salvation upon them; for we do no work but what is polluted by our flesh, and also punishable; and although we could perform such works, still the remembrance of one sin is sufficient to make God reject them. Thus, then, we would always be in doubt, tossed to and fro without any certainty, and our poor consciences continually vexed, if they relied not on the merits of the suffering and death of our Savior.

> 3. [We also maintain] that the ground of infant baptism is the command of God and the fact that according to Scripture He established His covenant in the line of continued generations.

IV. Besides, the Protestant Reformed Churches believe and maintain the autonomy of the local church.

For proof we refer to the Belgic Confession, Article 31:

Article 31. We believe that the ministers of God's Word, and the elders and deacons, ought to be chosen to their respective offices by a lawful election by the church, with calling upon the name of the Lord, and in that order which the Word of God teacheth. Therefore every one must take heed not to intrude himself by indecent means, but is bound to wait till it shall please God to call him, that he may have testimony of his calling and be certain and assured that it is of the Lord.

As for the ministers of God's Word, they have equally the same power and authority wheresoever they are, as they are all ministers of Christ, the only universal Bishop and the only Head of the church. Moreover, that this holy ordinance of God may not be violated or slighted, we say that every one ought to esteem the ministers of God's Word and the elders of the church very highly for their work's sake, and be at peace with them without murmuring, strife, or contention, as much as possible.

Church Order, Article 36:

The classis has the same jurisdiction over the consistory as the general synod has over the classis.

Only the consistory has authority over the local congregation. Church Order, Article 84:

No church shall in any way lord it over other churches, no minister over other ministers, no elder or deacon over other elders or deacons.

The Form for the Installation of Elders and Deacons:

...called of God's church, and consequently of God Himself....

Appendix Three

Brief Commentary on the Declaration of Principles of the Protestant Reformed Churches

A. What the Declaration is.

1. The Declaration of Principles is a brief statement of the basic truths (principles) of the Reformed confessions concerning God's covenant that was adopted provisionally by the synod of the Protestant Reformed Churches (PRC) in 1950 and decisively by the synod of the PRC in 1951.

2. It is not a fourth confession alongside the three forms of unity, but only an expression of the teaching of the three forms of unity regarding certain fundamental aspects of the truth of the covenant of grace. The PRC synod of 1953, treating protests against the adoption of the Declaration, spoke of the Declaration as an "interpretation" and "application" of the confessions.

3. The Declaration consists of four main sections, headed by a preamble. The four sections are:

   a. A declaration of the confessions' and therefore the PRC's repudiation of the three points of common grace, which were adopted by the Christian Reformed Church (CRC) in 1924 and became the occasion of the separate existence of the PRC. Of special importance is the repudiation of the teaching that the preaching of the gospel is a gracious, or well-meant, offer to all hearers.

   b. A declaration of the confessions' and therefore the PRC's teaching that the covenant promise of God is unconditional and for the elect only. This section denies that faith is a condition unto salvation.

   c. A declaration of the confessions' and therefore the PRC's repudiation of the teaching of a conditional covenant promise to all baptized children alike and affirmation of the doctrine that God infallibly fulfills the covenant promise to the elect. This section also guards against the false doctrines of antinomianism and hyper-Calvinism.

d. A declaration of the confessions' doctrine and therefore the PRC's doctrine and practice of the autonomy of the local church.

4. Essentially, the Declaration states that the confessions teach an unconditional covenant promise only to God's elect, particularly among the physical children of believing parents, and that the confessions deny that faith is a condition upon which a general, gracious promise to all the children depends for its fulfillment in everlasting, covenant salvation.

5. Because the Declaration is intended to be only the expression of the doctrine of the Reformed confessions, specifically the three forms of unity, regarding certain aspects of the covenant:

a. The Declaration is mostly quotations of the confessions.

b. There is no quotation or interpretation of Scripture. The only references to Scripture are those included in the quotations of the confessions. Because the confessions are binding on all Reformed people, a document expressing the doctrine of the confessions need only quote the confessions, not Scripture. All Reformed people accept the doctrine of the confessions as scriptural.

c. There is almost no theological argument, only affirmations and repudiations (based on the confessions). Here and there, at least the hint of theological argument surfaces, for example: "Little infants surely cannot fulfill any conditions…"

6. The name Declaration of Principles of the Protestant Reformed Churches is significant in all its aspects.

a. The document consists only of principles, that is, basic truths, concerning the covenant; it is not a thorough doctrinal explanation of the covenant—much about the covenant is lacking. One basic truth of the covenant set forth in the Declaration is that the covenant promise proclaimed by the gospel and sealed by baptism is to and for the elect children alone, unconditionally, and that therefore the covenant itself is unconditional. The other basic truth is that faith is not a condition unto the covenant and its salvation, particularly with regard to baptized children of believers, but is a gift of God to his elect.[1]

b. As a declaration, the document does not propose any new doctrine but only states, or declares, what has always been the confession of the PRC concerning the covenant. The Declaration directs its statement of the belief of the PRC concerning the covenant especially to groups intending to organize as Protestant Reformed churches, to congregations desirous to affiliate with the PRC, and to churches considering sister-church relations with the PRC.

c. Inclusion of the name of the denomination that adopted the document points out both that the principles concerning the covenant declared by the document are those distinctive of the PRC and that it is the PRC that make the witness concerning the covenant contained in the document.

7. The author of the Declaration was Rev. Herman Hoeksema, at the time pastor of First Protestant Reformed Church in Grand Rapids, Michigan, and professor of theology at the Theological School of the Protestant Reformed Churches in Grand Rapids. Hoeksema himself mentioned that he drew up the first draft of the Declaration, as requested by a committee of synod of which he was member.[2] The faction in the PRC opposed to the Declaration later acknowledged that Hoeksema was "author of the Declaration."[3] The synod of 1951, which adopted the Declaration in its final form, made some relatively minor revisions of the draft prepared by Hoeksema.[4]

---

1   For a thorough treatment of the truth of the covenant with special reference to the place of children in the covenant, see Herman Hoeksema, *Believers and Their Seed: Children in the Covenant* (Grandville, MI: Reformed Free Publishing Association, 1997).

2   Herman Hoeksema, "Reply to Rev. Blankespoor," *Standard Bearer* 27, no. 1 (October 1, 1950): 4.

3   *Acts of Synod, Protestant Reformed Churches of America, 1953*, 353.

4   The first draft of the Declaration, provisionally adopted by the PRC synod of 1950, is found in the *Acts of Synod, Protestant Reformed Churches of America, 1950*, 83–90.

8. The historical occasion of the adoption of the Declaration is of great importance for understanding the document. The Declaration was not adopted in a vacuum. Without the knowledge of the historical circumstances of the PRC at the time the Declaration was adopted, one cannot understand the Declaration—its meaning and significance, as well as why it was adopted in the face of strong opposition in the PRC, indeed in the knowledge that the result of adoption would be a split in the denomination.

9. The immediate and obvious occasion of the Declaration was a request from the denominational mission committee to the Protestant Reformed synod of 1950 that synod "draw up a form that may be used by those families requesting organization into a Prot. Ref. congregation."[5] This request by the mission committee was occasioned by the question of Dutch immigrants in Canada with whom Protestant Reformed missionaries were working whether the distinctive Protestant Reformed beliefs concerning "covenant and baptism" would be binding on them, should they affiliate with the PRC.[6] These immigrants had been members in the Netherlands of the Reformed Churches in the Netherlands (liberated), the denomination in which Klaas Schilder, Benne Holwerda, and Cornelis Veenhof were leading theologians. The immigrants held, and intended to hold and propagate in the PRC, the distinctive covenant doctrine of the liberated.

10. The deeper and more comprehensive occasion was the controversy that was already raging in the PRC over the doctrine of the covenant, whether the covenant is with the elect only and unconditional, or conditionally with all the baptized children of believers alike. The controversy was being carried out in the pulpits of the churches; in two of the periodicals that circulated among the membership of the PRC, the *Standard Bearer*, which defended the doctrine of an unconditional covenant with the elect (and condemned the doctrine of a conditional covenant with all the children as Arminianism in the covenant), and *Concordia*, which defended (and vigorously promoted) the doctrine of a conditional

---

5   See *Acts of Synod, 1950*, 54.
6   Ibid., 52–53.

covenant with all the baptized children alike; and in the heated conversations of the members of the churches.

By a visit of Schilder to the PRC in 1947 and through work with the immigrants in Canada, whom they hoped to bring into the PRC, many Protestant Reformed ministers had become enamored of, or at least open to, the liberated doctrine of the covenant.

The Declaration was therefore the clear, pointed expression of the distinctive Protestant Reformed doctrine of the covenant in contrast to the liberated doctrine of the covenant. It was also a clear, sharp repudiation of the doctrine of a conditional covenant with all the children alike as held (unofficially) by the liberated.

The entire Declaration must be read, and can only be rightly understood, in light of this controversy and with reference to the issue of the radical difference between the doctrine of an unconditional covenant and the doctrine of a conditional covenant. For instance, the declaration in the opening section of the Protestant Reformed repudiation of the three points of common grace adopted by the CRC in 1924 is not so much a reminder that the PRC reject the false doctrine of common grace, although the declaration does also serve this purpose with regard to the organizing of new churches. But the repudiation of the three points of common grace, especially the doctrine in the first point that the preaching is a gracious, well-meant offer to all hearers, is basic to a repudiation of the doctrine of a conditional covenant. According to the doctrine of a conditional covenant, the preaching of the gospel in the church is a gracious, conditional offer to all the baptized children alike. That is, the doctrine of a conditional covenant is essentially the same as the first point of common grace, which the PRC rejected in 1924 and in all their history.

Similarly, the affirmation of the second section, that election is the sole cause and fountain of all our salvation, is not simply an orthodox doctrinal proposition, not even simply a fundamentally important doctrinal proposition. In fact, the affirmation strikes, and is intended to strike, a mortal blow to the heart of the doctrine of a conditional covenant. The doctrine of a conditional covenant *denies* that election is the cause and fountain of *covenant grace and covenant salvation.*

At the same time, the affirmation is the foundation of the doctrine of the unconditional covenant. *Election governs the covenant.* God's saving will with the covenant, the gracious covenant promise, covenant grace, all the blessings of the covenant, and covenant salvation—all proceed and flow from God's eternal decree of gracious election in Jesus Christ. One of these blessings of covenant grace and salvation is faith. Faith is not a condition upon which the covenant and its salvation depend (as is the teaching of the doctrine of a conditional covenant), but the gift of God to the elect.

11. Since the Declaration rose out of and addresses this controversy over the covenant, it is necessary to know the doctrine of a conditional covenant that the Declaration repudiates as contrary to the Reformed confessions and as heresy. The principles of the doctrine of a conditional covenant, taught particularly (but by no means exclusively) by the liberated, are the following:

a. God graciously establishes his covenant with all the baptized infants of believers alike, those who eventually perish as well as those who are everlastingly saved.

b. God establishes the covenant with all the infants alike by his gracious covenant promise addressed to all alike, "I will be your God and save you in Jesus Christ, and you will be my child." This means, for the defenders of the conditional covenant, that what the Reformed baptism form confesses concerning the covenant grace of God toward the children of believers *refers to all the physical children alike, those who eventually perish* as well as those who are everlastingly saved. For example, that God the Father makes an eternal covenant of grace with the baptized children; that the Son washes the baptized children with his blood; that the Holy Spirit assures the baptized children that he will dwell in them; that the children are "received unto grace in Christ"; and especially that (as the first question put to the parents teaches) the children are "sanctified in Christ"—all refer to all the baptized children alike.

c. Since the covenant is established with all the children alike, all the children possess the blessings of covenant salvation, "objectively." This includes the benefit of justification; all the children are put in possession of justification, "objectively."

d. But the covenant is conditional, that is, the continuation of the covenant with a child and the realization of the covenant in a particular child's everlasting salvation *depend upon a work, or upon works, that the child must perform,* especially faith. Faith is the condition of the covenant. Likewise, the covenant promise (made to every child alike at baptism) is conditional: For its fulfillment in the child's salvation, the promise depends upon something the child must do, namely, believe. To the obvious charge that this doctrine makes grace and salvation dependent upon the will and work of the child, contrary to the gospel of grace in the confessions and in Scripture (which it does), the response usually is that God helps some children perform the condition by his grace. (It will be noted that this response, although it has a superficial appearance of confessing grace, still leaves the decisive act of covenant salvation in the hands of the child and teaches resistible grace in the case of many children, who, although they too are the objects of covenant grace, are not saved by this grace.)

e. Fundamental to the doctrine of a conditional covenant is the denial that the covenant is governed by election. This denial is usually deceptively phrased thus: "Covenant and election are not identical." (No Reformed theologian has ever identified covenant and election; what the denial means is that election does not *govern* the covenant, covenant grace, covenant blessing, and everlasting covenant salvation; covenant grace and the gracious covenant are wider in extent than election).

f. Against this doctrine of the covenant of grace, especially regarding the baptized infants of believers, the Declaration is directed.

B. Legitimacy of the Declaration.

1. The legitimacy of the Declaration was challenged by many Protestant Reformed ministers and people in 1951 and thereafter. Basically, the challenge was twofold: that the Declaration was composed and imposed upon the churches by synod, rather than arising out of a congregation, and that adoption of the Declaration was the creation of a fourth confession (alongside the three forms of unity).

The response by the PRC was (and is) that the composing and adoption of the Declaration by synod was proper because such a form was requested of synod by the synodical mission committee. Also, the PRC deny that the Declaration is a fourth confession; it is the expression of the teaching of the existing Reformed confessions, especially the three forms of unity, concerning the covenant.

2. The legitimacy of the Declaration was also challenged by the leading liberated theologian, Klaas Schilder. This challenge is perpetuated today by theologians in the Reformed Churches in the Netherlands (liberated), by theologians in their daughter denominations, particularly the Canadian Reformed Churches, and by theologians who promote the conditional covenant doctrine of the liberated.

Schilder denounced the Declaration as "extra-Scriptural binding."[7] The response of the PRC was (and is), first, that the Declaration is only the explanation and application of the teaching of the confessions regarding the covenant, not an additional creed. Second, a Reformed church has the perfect right, indeed the solemn calling from Christ the king of the church, to settle doctrinal controversy with a binding synodical decision, *based on the Reformed confessions,* and to assure that new churches are organized on the basis of the confessions, as the organizing denomination (rightly) understands the confessions.

C. Significance of the Declaration.

1. The Declaration expresses the distinctive doctrine of the covenant of the PRC, demonstrating that this covenant doctrine is that of the three forms of unity.

2. The Declaration was the occasion not of the schism in the PRC in 1953, but of bringing to light and of bringing to a head the existing difference of doctrine in the PRC concerning the covenant. In 1953 more than half the ministers and members

---

7   For Schilder's published attack on the Declaration, see Klaas Schilder, "Extra-Scriptural Binding—a New Danger," in Jelle Faber, *American Secession Theologians on Covenant and Baptism* (Neerlandia, Alberta, Canada: Inheritance Publications, 1996), 55–167.

of the PRC separated from the PRC over the covenant doctrine affirmed by the Declaration. The schismatic faction vehemently renounced the Declaration. Within a few years this faction returned to the CRC.

3. In the past few years, since about the year 2000, the Declaration has taken on new, weighty significance with the emergence in conservative Reformed and Presbyterian churches in North America of the heretical theology and movement that call themselves the federal vision.

a. The men of the federal vision deny justification by faith alone and, with this fundamental gospel-truth, all the doctrines of grace as confessed in the three forms of unity and in the Westminster standards.

b. The men of the federal vision teach that at baptism every baptized child is truly united to Christ so that the new life of Christ becomes his or hers, and with this life of Christ, the blessings of salvation, including justification. For the continuing of the covenant with a child, however, and for the child's everlasting salvation in the covenant, the child's performance of conditions is necessary. The conditions are faith and life-long faithfulness. Failure to perform the conditions means for many children that their union with Christ is severed, that they fall away from grace and salvation (which they once possessed), and that they perish.

c. The root of the federal vision, by its own acknowledgment, is the doctrine of a conditional covenant that the PRC repudiates in the Declaration.

d. The orthodox alternative to the covenant doctrine of the federal vision is the doctrine of the unconditional covenant, the principles of which are stated in the Declaration.[8]

---

8   On the federal vision, its root in the doctrine of a conditional covenant, and the orthodox doctrine of the unconditional covenant, see David J. Engelsma, *Covenant of God and the Children of Believers: Sovereign Grace in the Covenant* (Jenison, MI: Reformed Free Publishing Association, 2005), 133–232; and David J. Engelsma, *Federal Vision: Heresy at the Root* (Jenison, MI: Reformed Free Publishing Association, 2012).

I. PREAMBLE

A. The preamble was not part of the draft of the Declaration adopted provisionally by the synod of 1950. As provisionally adopted by the synod of 1950, the Declaration began with the statement of the basis of the PRC: "The Protestant Reformed Churches stand on the basis…"

1. The preamble was added by the synod of 1951 in response to the overture of Classis East.[9]

2. In adopting the preamble, synod made changes in the wording of Classis East. Synod inserted the word "only": "to be used *only* by the Mission Committee." Synod also added all the words following the word "missionaries."[10]

B. Concerning the content of the preamble.

1. In keeping with the occasion of the drawing up of the Declaration—a request by the mission committee of the PRC—the preamble designates the use of the document: the organization of prospective churches.

a. All churches organized by the PRC as the result of missions must have been instructed concerning, and be in agreement with, the Declaration. That is, these churches must be one with the PRC regarding the doctrine of the unconditional covenant of grace with the elect in Jesus Christ.

b. Implied is that all churches with whom the PRC establish a sister-church relationship must also be one with the PRC on the doctrine of the unconditional covenant.

2. The significance of the word "only" in the preamble is that it wards off the charge by the enemies of the Declaration at the time of its adoption that it was, and would serve as, a fourth confession of the PRC. The Declaration is not and may not be used as a fourth confession.

For example, at one point in the heated debate leading up to the adoption of the Declaration it was agreed by the delegates

---

9 *Acts of Synod, Protestant Reformed Churches in America, 1951,* 107.

10 Ibid., 195–96.

at synod that the Declaration might not be used as a basis for deposing ministers in the PRC (as the confessions can be used).

3. Regardless that the Declaration is not a fourth confession, it authoritatively establishes the doctrine of the unconditional covenant as the position of the PRC, forbidding the teaching of an unconditional covenant.

a. If the PRC require confession of the doctrine of the unconditional covenant on the part of groups desiring to be organized as Protestant Reformed churches, the PRC are committed to the doctrine.

b. One immediate, urgent, practical purpose of the Declaration was to prevent the PRC from being flooded with members holding the conditional covenant doctrine of Schilder and the liberated, with the result that the doctrine of the unconditional covenant would be lost in the PRC.

c. The adoption of the Declaration by a majority vote of synod makes the Declaration and its doctrine of the covenant "settled and binding" for all the members of the PRC, according to Article 31 of the Church Order.

d. The fact that synod 1950 had adopted the Declaration provisionally, including in the decision that in the "meantime"—the time between synod 1950 and synod 1951 (which would adopt the Declaration decisively)—the Declaration would function as a "working hypothesis for our mission committee," makes doubly inexcusable the preaching of the conditional covenant by one of the ministers of First Protestant Reformed Church, Grand Rapids, Michigan, in April 1951. Flouting the decision of synod 1950 a few months earlier, the minister preached, "God promises every one of you that, if you believe, you shall be saved."[11] In September 1952, after synod 1951 had adopted the Declaration finally and decisively, the same minister preached the doctrine of a conditional covenant (which synod 1951 had condemned) in these words, "Our act of conversion is a prerequisite to enter the kingdom of God." It was these statements and the

---

11 *Acts of Synod, 1950*, 90.

subsequent discipline of the offending minister that directly resulted in a great schism in the PRC in 1953.

e. As a synodical decision of the PRC, the Declaration certainly is a witness to others, especially other Reformed and Presbyterian churches, of the distinctive doctrine of the covenant of the PRC. More precisely, the Declaration is a witness to the PRC's understanding of the teaching of the Reformed confessions concerning the covenant.

4. The words in the preamble, "on the basis of Scripture and the confessions as these have always been maintained in the PRC..." are also significant.

a. They insist that the doctrine of an unconditional promise, determined by election, is not something new to the PRC. Rather, the PRC have held this doctrine from the beginning of their history. It is an integral part of the confession of the PRC that the preaching of the gospel is not a general, conditional offer, but particular grace.

b. These words affirm that the basis of churches that may be organized by the PRC is "Scripture and the confessions"— as rightly understood by the PRC, specifically concerning the covenant.

c. The words identify the Declaration as only a "further explanation" of the confessions and not a new, fourth confession.

II. SECTION ONE

A. Fundamental not only to the first section of the Declaration but to all four sections is the preliminary statement concerning the basis, or foundation, of the PRC: "Scripture as the infallible Word of God and...the Three Forms of Unity," that is, the Belgic Confession of Faith, the Heidelberg Catechism, and the Canons of Dordt. This preliminary statement also declares the Reformed liturgical forms to be authoritative for the PRC. These forms are listed. Of special importance among them for the Declaration is the Form for the Administration of Baptism.

1. Although the recognition of Scripture as the infallible word of God is important, especially in light of the contemporary denial

both that Scripture *is* the word of God and that it is infallible, or inerrant, the more important element of the basis for the Declaration is the three forms of unity.

2. The purpose of the Declaration is to demonstrate and affirm that the doctrine of the unconditional covenant with the elect is confessional.

a. As a Reformed denomination, the PRC receive the three forms of unity and, among the liturgical forms, especially the baptism form as biblical and therefore authoritative. As the faithful summary and systematization of Scripture, these creeds are the basis of the PRC.

b. To establish a doctrine as sound and right, all that needs to be done is to demonstrate that the doctrine is the teaching of the confessions.

c. This explains why there is almost no reference to Scripture in the Declaration; reference to Scripture is unnecessary, since the PRC receive the confessions as expressing the truth of Scripture.

3. Mention particularly of the three forms of unity in the preliminary paragraphs of section one of the Declaration is also important because the Declaration is not, and is determined not to be, a fourth confession, but only an explanation of the three forms of unity with regard to the issue of the covenant.

4. The phrase "on the basis of Scripture…and of the Three Forms of Unity" must be understood thus: The Declaration briefly states the main truths, or principles, especially of the covenant of grace ("especially" because the Declaration also states something about the church in section four) as these truths are taught by the three forms of unity, which are received by the PRC as faithful expressions of Scripture.

B. The fundamental truths of the covenant declared in section one:

1. The preaching of the gospel at its heart is the proclamation of God's solemn promise ("an oath of God") to, for, and about the elect, and the elect only ("that He will infallibly lead all the elect unto salvation and eternal glory through faith").

2. The preaching of the gospel as this solemn promise concerning the elect has particular application to the baptized infants of believing parents: "[those] born in the historical dispensation of the covenant, that is,...[those] that are baptized."

3. That the preaching of the gospel regarding the baptized infants of believers is not a "conditional offer to all" the baptized infants. That the preaching of the gospel is a conditional offer to all baptized infants is the covenant doctrine of the liberated, which doctrine the Declaration repudiates.

4. In explanation of the declaration of these truths:

a. The great issue in the controversy between the doctrine of the unconditional covenant and the doctrine of a conditional covenant is the nature of the preaching of the gospel regarding baptized children: Is it the preaching of a gracious but conditional offer (that is, a conditional promise, which by virtue of being conditional is a mere offer) of salvation to all the children alike (dependent upon their performing the condition), or is it the preaching of the promise of God that he will "infallibly," that is, unconditionally, save the elect children?

b. On the basis of the Reformed confessions, it is the doctrine of the PRC that the covenant promise, "I will be your God and the God of your children," cannot fail, is always realized, and is realized by the promising God himself. That is, the covenant promise is unconditional.

c. Implied is that the objects of the promise are not all the baptized infants, but only the elect among them (although when the infants grow up, all will and must *hear* the promise).

d. Of special importance regarding the nature and address of the covenant promise is the reference to Canons 2.5, as is evident from the brief explanation of this article, such explanation of the confessions being rare in the Declaration.

At the time of the adoption of the Declaration, defenders of a conditional covenant promise to all the children alike appealed to this article in support of their position.

The explanation of the article by the Declaration points out that, although the preaching of the promise is "promiscuous," that is, goes out to all hearers, the promise itself is particular, that is, for and to some only (with special reference to baptized children of believers): "whosoever believeth in Christ crucified," or believers.

Against the teaching of the defenders of a general, conditional covenant promise that Canons 2.5 presents repentance and faith as conditions upon which a general promise depends for its realization and fulfillment in the everlasting salvation of the children, the explanation of the Declaration points out that Canons 2.5 describes the call to repent and believe as a "command," not a condition.

e. If the covenant promise, which establishes the covenant of grace with individuals, is God's oath-bound promise to the elect, and to the elect only, it follows that God makes his covenant with the elect, and the elect only.

C. The repudiation of the three points of common grace, with which repudiation section one begins, is not the rejection of a false doctrine distinct from that which is the concern of the Declaration, namely, the preaching of the covenant promise as a "conditional offer to all that are born in the historical dispensation of the covenant." Rather, the Declaration brings up the "errors" of the three points of common grace because the doctrine of common grace and the doctrine of a conditional offer of grace to all baptized infants alike are related: The doctrine of a gracious, conditional promise to all the children of believers alike simply applies the false doctrine of the preaching of the gospel as a gracious offer of salvation to all hearers to the sphere of the covenant.

1. The gist of each of the three points in order is stated in I, A–C of the Declaration.[12]

2. That element of the doctrine of common grace that bears most heavily and directly on the controversy over the covenant promise, as it is the most grievous error of the three points of common

---

12 For the complete statement of the three points of common grace as adopted by the CRC synod of 1914 and a thorough criticism of them, see Herman Hoeksema, *The Protestant Reformed Churches in America: Their Origin, Early History and Doctrine*, 2nd ed. (Grand Rapids: n.p., 1947), 291–410.

grace, is the teaching of the first point that "the preaching of the gospel is a gracious offer of salvation on the part of God to all that externally hear the gospel."

a. Just as the first point of common grace teaches a (saving but resistible) grace of God in the preaching for all hearers, so the conditional covenant teaches a (saving but resistible) grace of God in the preaching of a covenant promise for all baptized children.

As the first point of common grace views the preaching of the gospel as a gracious (well-meant) offer of salvation to all hearers, so the conditional covenant views the preaching of the gospel of the covenant promise as a gracious offer to all the baptized children.

b. There is yet another tight link between the doctrine of preaching as gracious offer to all and the doctrine of a gracious, conditional promise (offer) to all baptized children alike: The doctrine of preaching as gracious offer to all hearers, adopted by the CRC in 1924, rose out of the teaching of William Heyns, longtime professor of theology at Calvin Theological Seminary.

3. Heyns taught many Christian Reformed ministers that God graciously establishes his covenant with all baptized infants alike, even bestowing on them sufficient covenant grace to believe, if they would, and that God at baptism promises all the infants alike salvation on condition that they believe.

From this doctrine of a gracious, conditional covenant promise to all baptized infants came the first point of common grace in 1924.[13]

The Declaration refers to the three points of common grace in order to establish that the doctrine of a gracious, conditional promise to all baptized children is essentially the same false doctrine as the doctrine of the well-meant offer that the PRC rejected in 1924.

---

13 On the relation between Heyns' doctrine of a conditional covenant and covenant promise and the first point of common grace concerning the preaching as well-meant offer adopted by the CRC in 1924, see Hoeksema, *Believers and Their Seed*, 1–28.

Put simply, the doctrine of a conditional covenant promise to all infants of believers is the teaching of grace for reprobate unbelievers—common grace.

Against the doctrine of common grace in all its forms ("that there is a grace of God to all men, including the reprobate" [Declaration I, A]), the PRC maintain "that the grace of God is always particular, i.e., only for the elect, never for the reprobate" (Declaration, I, D, 1).

4. Establishing the connection, both theologically and historically, between the doctrine of a conditional covenant promise to all baptized children and the doctrine of the preaching as a gracious offer to all hearers, the Declaration makes plain that their rejection of the conditional covenant promise was implicit in the PRC's rejection of the doctrine of common grace in 1924, especially the first point concerning the preaching as a well-meant offer.

a. To introduce the doctrine of a conditional covenant promise into the PRC (as some Protestant Reformed ministers tried to do in the late 1940s and early 1950s) was to oppose the truth of the preaching of the gospel as particular grace to the elect only, which the PRC had confessed from the beginning of their history, and thus to threaten the destruction of the churches.

b. In repudiating the doctrine of a conditional covenant promise and in affirming the unconditional promise to the elect only, in 1951, the PRC were not only consistently developing the truth of particular, sovereign grace they had confessed from the beginning of their history. But they were also making explicit in a Declaration the truth about the covenant they had always held.

c. It was therefore nothing less than astounding that Protestant Reformed ministers attempted to introduce the doctrine of a conditional covenant promise into the PRC and still more astounding that they promoted the doctrine as perfectly in harmony with the faith and tradition of the PRC.

d. But the question still remains: Do the confessions speak of the issue of the covenant promise and covenant grace? Do they teach that the covenant promise is unconditionally for and to the elect only? Do they do so in such a way as to condemn the doctrine of a gracious, conditional promise to all the baptized children alike as false doctrine? Or, perhaps, do they allow for both doctrines in a Reformed church that has the three forms of unity as its creeds?

D. The confessions on the preaching of the covenant promise as the oath of God concerning elect infants.

1. Section one quotes, in this order, from Canons 1.6–8; Canons 2.5; Canons 2, Error 6; the Heidelberg Catechism, Questions 8 and 91; Belgic Confession, Article 14; and Canons 3–4.1–4.

2. With the exception of a short explanation of Canons 2.5, the Declaration does not give any explanation of the passages of the confessions it quotes. The significance of the quotations, therefore, must be deduced from the doctrines they are intended to prove, especially the doctrine that the preaching of the covenant promise is not a gracious, conditional offer to all the children, but the solemn promise about and to the elect, which God infallibly realizes in every one to whom the promise pertains and is addressed.

3. In this light the appeal to the confessions in section one is to be understood as follows.

a. Canons 1.6–8 proves that the preaching of the gospel is God's effectual call of the elect children, and them only; negatively, this section of the Canons proves that the preaching is not a gracious offer to all the children, reprobate as well as elect, dependent for its realization and fulfillment upon conditions the children must perform.

Especially pertinent to the main issue of the covenant addressed in section one of the Declaration is the statement in Canons 1.7: "This elect number...God hath decreed...effectually to call...to bestow upon them true faith." The preaching of the gospel is not a gracious, conditional promise, or offer, to all the baptized children alike. Rather, it is God's effectual call of the "elect number" of baptized children.

b. Canons 2.5 teaches that the promise of the gospel, *which includes the covenant promise to the children of believers*, is particular, concerning and to the one who believes, not general (to all the baptized children alike). There is, and must be, a promiscuous and indiscriminate publication and proclamation of the promise: The *preaching* of the promise that whosoever believes shall be saved must go out to "all nations, and to all persons." But the promise itself is always particular, *and always reveals itself as particular*: "whosoever believeth in Christ crucified."

In addition, the article presents repentance and faith as a "command" to all who hear the gospel, not as a condition upon which a general, gracious promise depends for its fulfillment.

The Declaration departs from its policy of not explaining its quotation of the confessions because the advocates of a general, conditional promise appeal to Canons 2.5 in support of their position, just as those who view the preaching as a well-meant offer have always done. They mistakenly seize upon the phrase "whosoever believeth," as the Arminians seize upon the biblical phrase "whosoever will." All these defenders of a form of the heresy of a universal, saving, but resistible grace ignore the truth that the only humans who believe and who will are the elect of God, in whom God works the willing and believing by sovereign, particular grace.

c. Canons 2, Error 6 is an especially powerful, pointed condemnation of the false teaching of a gracious, conditional offer of salvation to all the children alike. This article of the Canons repudiates the error of those who teach that God offers grace to all (the baptized children) without exception and that the difference between those who are saved and those who are not saved is that some (children) perform the condition upon which this general grace depends, whereas the others do not perform the condition. According to the error that the Canons condemn, some children "appropriate" the offered grace, whereas the others do not. Cleverly, the teachers of this heresy use the word "appropriate" to obscure their false doctrine in the minds of weak Reformed Christians.

Because the heresy refuted by this article is Arminianism, the appeal to the article by the Declaration condemns the teaching of a gracious, conditional covenant promise to all the children as Arminianism applied to the covenant and to covenant salvation. Because the article damns the Arminian heresy as a form of Pelagianism, the use of the article by the Declaration condemns the doctrine of a gracious, conditional promise to all the children as a modern form of the ancient heresy of Pelagianism. In essence Pelagianism is the false doctrine that in the end salvation depends upon and is accomplished by the sinner himself.

d. Heidelberg Catechism, Questions 8 and 91 prove, generally, that the unregenerated person is incapable of any good and, specifically regarding the covenant controversy, that unregenerated children cannot perform any condition upon which the fulfillment of a general promise is supposed to depend.

e. Belgic Confession, Article 14, in addition to proving that the salvation of infants—who are conceived and born with a totally depraved nature—cannot depend upon conditions they must perform, proves that the doctrine of a gracious, conditional offer to all the children alike is erroneous in that this doctrine teaches the error of free will. Covenant salvation by a grace that is offered to all alike implies covenant salvation by free will. The decision of the child makes the offer, or conditional promise, effectual in his salvation. In short, covenant grace depends on the will of the child.

The truth is that the salvation of the covenant child is his being drawn by the Father by the sovereign grace of a particular promise.

f. Canons 3–4.1–4 (a powerful, indeed conclusive, refutation of the three points of common grace) proves that the covenant promise of God cannot be a general, conditional offer of salvation to all the baptized children. By nature, all the children of believers are conceived and born "dead in sin, and in bondage thereto." A general, well-meant offer, or a general, gracious, conditional promise, does them absolutely no good. With a well-meant offer, or a conditional promise, they all perish. What they need is a gracious promise that is irresistibly powerful—effectual—by the Holy Spirit. This promise God makes with an oath to the elect children, and this promise God infallibly realizes and fulfills in the elect children.

III. SECTION TWO

A. Section two is undoubtedly the heart of the Declaration and is the longest section.

1. In section two, it becomes unmistakably plain that the controversy of the Declaration is with the doctrine of a conditional covenant.

2. Section two makes statements (based always on the confessions) that inflict a mortal blow to the doctrine of a conditional covenant ("faith is not a prerequisite or condition unto salvation, but a gift of God"); that establish the doctrine of the unconditional covenant ("God's promise is unconditionally for them [the elect] only"); and that make plain to every Reformed church and every member of a Reformed church how serious the issue of the unconditional covenant is (for example, "election…is the sole cause and fountain of all our salvation").

3. In section two occurs the only argument found in the Declaration. Significantly, this argument bases itself on Question 74 of the Heidelberg Catechism, concerning the baptism of the infants of believers. The controversy with the doctrine of a conditional covenant in the early 1950s had to do with the salvation of the infant children of believers and the meaning of infant baptism. Today the controversy of orthodox Reformed Christianity with the development of the doctrine of a conditional covenant by the men of the federal vision likewise has to do with the salvation of infants in the covenant and the meaning of infant baptism.

4. Basic to the controversy over the salvation of baptized infants of believers is the great issue of the relation of the covenant and election.

a. The advocates of a conditional covenant with all the children alike deny that election governs the covenant.

This is the position of the Reformed Churches in the Netherlands (liberated) and their daughters and theological allies.

This is also the position of those in the twenty-first century who are developing the covenant conception of the liberated in what calls itself the federal vision.

b. The PRC, carrying on a prominent element of the Reformed tradition going back to Calvin, confess that election governs the covenant.

c. Section two therefore begins with the Reformed confession concerning election.

B. The fundamental truths (principles) of the covenant declared in section two.

1. The decree of election is the "sole cause and fountain" of all salvation, of all the gifts of grace, and particularly of faith.

a. Positively, this declaration affirms that salvation in the covenant; the blessings of the covenant, for example, union with Christ and justification; the grace of the covenant; and the covenant of grace itself have their source in election and are wholly determined by and bestowed according to election. That is, election governs the covenant of grace.

1. Implied is that, since election is unconditional, that is, does not depend on anything in the one who is elected but only upon the gracious good pleasure of God, so also are the covenant and its blessings unconditional.

2. There is special emphasis on the fact that election is the cause and fountain of faith, that is, the faith of covenant children. The faith of covenant children is the gift of God to them, flowing to them from the fountain of God's eternal election of them.

b. Negatively, this declaration refutes these errors of the defenders of a conditional covenant:

1. Various gifts and blessings of the covenant come to all baptized children alike, that is, also to reprobate children, Esau as well as Jacob.

2. The beginning of covenant salvation is bestowed by God upon all the baptized children alike at their baptism.

3. The covenant, its grace, its blessings, and its salvation are

not governed by election, so that the gracious covenant, the grace of the covenant, and the blessings of the covenant *are wider in extent than the elect.*

4. Especially that in the covenant, with regard to baptized children, faith is a condition upon which the covenant and its salvation depend, rather than the gift of God to the elect children.

c. Concerning the election that is the cause and fountain of all salvation, these truths must be kept in mind.

1. Election, which is taught by the confessions as the sole cause and fountain of salvation, is the eternal decree of God, "unconditional and unchangeable."

Defenders of a conditional covenant view election as a conditional, changeable decision of God in history, dependent upon the children's performance or nonperformance of conditions.

2. Election is the cause and fountain of all *covenant* salvation and of all the gifts of *covenant* grace.

Defenders of a conditional covenant illegitimately restrict what the confessions teach concerning election's being the sole fountain of salvation and of the gifts of grace to salvation on the mission field, as though the doctrine of the confessions does not apply also to covenant salvation and covenant grace among the physical offspring of believers.

3. Election is the decree of God appointing "a certain number of persons" to salvation in Jesus Christ. This "certain number" applies to the physical children of believers: Only some, not all, are elected.

Defenders of a conditional covenant teach that all the children of believers are elect until some refuse to perform the condition of faith, whereupon they become reprobate.

d. The confessions on election as the sole cause and fountain of salvation and of the gifts of grace, including faith.

1. Appeal is made to Canons 1.6–7 (explained above).

2. The Heidelberg Catechism, Question 54 proves that the entire work of saving the church, including the bestowal of all the gifts of grace and referring to the saving of the

children of believers as well as to the saving of men and women in missions, has its source in and is wholly governed by God's eternal election ("a church chosen to everlasting life").

3. The baptism form proves that the fullness of salvation, conceived as "an eternal covenant of grace," proceeds from election. The phrase "till we shall finally be presented...among the assembly of the elect in life eternal" implies that election is the fountain and cause of the eternal covenant, of adoption, of redemption, of union with Christ, of justification, and of sanctification. That election is the source of the fullness of salvation applies particularly to the children of believers.

4. Strangely, the Declaration does not appeal at this point to Canons 1.9, where the phrase "election is the fountain of every saving good" occurs: "Election is the fountain of every saving good; from which proceed faith, holiness, and the other gifts of salvation, and finally eternal life itself, as its fruits and effects."[14]

2. Christ died for the elect and for the elect only, so that the saving power and benefit of his death, which is efficacious, extend to the elect and to the elect only.

a. In explanation of this declaration, which on the face of it must seem self-evident to every Reformed Christian and noncontroversial.

1. The reference is specifically to baptized infants of believers: Christ died only for the elect infants, and God extends the saving efficacy of Christ's death only to the elect infants.

2. It is the doctrine of the defenders of a conditional covenant that at baptism God graciously extends the (inefficacious) saving power and benefit of the death of Christ *to all the baptized children alike* in a certain, important respect. Defenders of a conditional covenant describe this respect as "objective." That is, even though many of the children never

---

14 Canons of Dordt 1.9, in Philip Schaff, ed., *The Creeds of Christendom: With a History and Critical Notes*, 6th ed. (New York: Harper and Row, 1931; repr., Grand Rapids MI: Baker, 2007), 3:583.

enjoy forgiveness and righteousness in their experience (because they refuse to perform the condition of faith), God on his part ("objectively") applies the death of Christ in a gracious manner to them. He does this by promising them covenant salvation, by establishing his covenant with them, and even by bestowing on them some benefits of the death of Christ, for example, justification (all of which they will forfeit and fail to enjoy ["subjectively"] by refusing to perform the condition upon which this objective grace depends).

The inescapable implication is that the death of Christ is ineffectual.

b. The confessions on the death of Christ for the elect infants only, so that God on his part extends the saving efficacy of the death of Christ only to the elect infants (whether objectively or subjectively).

1. Canons 2.8 proves not only that Christ died for the elect children of believers and for them only, but also that it is God's sovereign, gracious purpose that the saving power of the cross, which is effectual, and the benefits of the cross, which include all the aspects of grace—objective as well as subjective—extend to the elect children, and to the elect children only.

Significantly, this article describes the death of Christ as Christ's confirmation of the new covenant, that is, his actual grounding and making sure the covenant with all the elect, and the elect only. The heretical alternative is the teaching that Christ's death merely enabled God to make the covenant with all the children alike, conditionally. Such a covenant is not sure and steadfast. This doctrine of the relation between the death of Christ and the covenant, the Canons reject in Canons 2, Errors 2–4.

The appeal to Canons 2.8 is accompanied by explanation of the quotation. The explanation takes issue with the teaching of the defenders of the conditional covenant that God makes his covenant promise to all the baptized children of believers alike; that this promise bestows on all the children alike "the objective right of salvation" (in distinction, presumably, from the "subjective" right, which is obtained by the children who perform the condition of faith); and that the covenant promise to all the children is conditional.

The explanation of Canons 2.8 contends that God can promise to persons only that which Christ merited. But Christ merited—objectively—salvation only for the elect. Only the elect children, therefore, have the right (whether objectively, subjectively, or any other category) to covenant salvation. Thus the covenant promise of God is unconditionally to the elect infants, and to them only.

All the confessional proof that follows in section two grounds the declaration that the covenant promise is for and to the elect children only and that the covenant promise is unconditional. The basis of the affirmation of an unconditional promise to the elect only is the death of Christ for the elect only, as clearly and conclusively confessed in Canons 2.8: "God cannot promise what was not objectively merited by Christ."

2. The Heidelberg Catechism, Questions 65–66 prove that since the content of the promise of the gospel is the benefits of the death of Christ, the promise of the gospel is only for and to believers, that is, the elect, for whom alone Christ earned these benefits. The sacraments declare and seal this particular promise only to and for believers, that is, the elect.

3. The Heidelberg Catechism, Question 74 is extremely important in the controversy over the covenant. Defenders of a conditional covenant understand the infants of Question 74 as all the physical offspring of believers. They explain the promise of the seventy-fourth answer as a conditional promise to all the baptized infants alike—a promise of redemption by the blood of Christ and of the Holy Spirit on condition of faith.

The argument of the Declaration at this point indicates the importance of a right understanding of this question and answer.

This argument against the explanation of Question 74 of the Catechism by the defenders of a conditional covenant is devastating of that doctrine and conclusive on behalf of the doctrine of the unconditional covenant.

First, the covenant promise is to infants, who are incapable of performing conditions. The promise therefore must be unconditional.

Second, since the death of Christ was for the elect only (as Canons 2.8 teaches), the promise of the application of this death must be to and for elect infants only.

Third, the promise to the infants of believers includes the gift of the Holy Spirit, who is deliberately identified as the "author of faith." The gift of faith is part of the promise, not a condition upon which the fulfillment of the promise depends. To whomever God makes the covenant promise, he promises to give faith. The covenant promise to infants of believers, therefore, is made by God to the elect infants only, and he makes it unconditionally.

An important truth in the controversy over the covenant is implied here: The (genuine, spiritual) children of believers, whom the confessions refer to whenever they speak of the children of believers as the object of divine grace, *are not all the physical offspring, but those, and those only, whom God has elected.*

4. The Belgic Confession, Article 33 proves that the promises of the gospel, which are sealed by the sacraments, are made by God to "us," that is, believers, according to election.

5. The Belgic Confession, Article 34 proves that the people, particularly the infant children, in view in the sacrament of baptism and therefore also in view in the promise of the gospel, which baptism seals, are God's elect. For the sacrament signifies and seals the saving efficacy and benefit of the death of Christ, and Christ died only for the elect. In the language of Article 34, Christ did not "shed his blood" for all the children alike, reprobate as well as elect.

6. The Belgic Confession, Article 35 proves that the grace of God in the sacrament of the Lord's supper and therefore the gracious promise of the gospel, which the supper seals,

are only for the elect ("those whom he hath already regenerated") and that both the sacrament and the preaching of the gospel are for the condemnation of the reprobate unbelievers who may partake of the supper and hear the gospel.

7. Canons 1.10 proves that just as election is unconditional, so also is all salvation unconditional, including the salvation of covenant children. Implied is that the promise of salvation is likewise unconditional. The unconditional good pleasure of God is the "sole cause" of election, and election is the sole cause and fountain of all salvation.

That the covenant promise of salvation, with regard to the children of believers, is for and to the elect children only is conclusively proved by Romans 9:11–13, the biblical passage quoted by Canons 1.10.

8. Canons 1, Error 2 repudiates as Arminian heresy the teaching that there is an election unto grace and eternal life that is "general and indefinite...incomplete, revocable, non-decisive, and conditional." This is the position of the defenders of a conditional covenant (and of the federal vision). Implied by this article of the Canons is that there is no general, incomplete, revocable, nondecisive, and conditional covenant salvation because of a conditional covenant promise.

9. Canons 1, Error 3 repudiates as Arminian heresy the teaching that "faith...[with] its incomplete obedience...[is] a condition of salvation." Although the reference is specifically to a corrupting of the doctrine of election, the repudiation applies broadly to every form of the false doctrine that makes God's grace and salvation depend on the sinner's faith as a condition.

10. Canons 1, Error 5 repudiates as Arminian heresy the teaching that faith is a condition unto final glory, rather than the fruit of an unchangeable election unto glory.

11. The baptism form proves that when it and the other creeds teach the grace of God toward and the salvation of the children of believers, they refer to the elect children. Only the elect children "are...again received unto grace in

Christ," in their infancy and without their knowledge. Their salvation, in infancy, is certainly unconditional and so also is the promise to them unconditional.

3. The third fundamental truth declared in section two of the Declaration is that faith is not a condition unto salvation, specifically regarding the covenant salvation of the children of believers, but a gift of God and the means—*only* the means—by which the elect children receive and take to themselves the salvation God has decreed for them and Christ has earned for them.

a. In explanation of this principle of the covenant.

1. Basic to the false doctrine of a general, conditional, covenant promise and of a conditional covenant established graciously by God with all the physical offspring of believers alike is the teaching that the faith of the child is the condition for the realization and fulfillment of the promise in the salvation of the child and for the continuing of the covenant with the child. That is, faith is the work, or act, or effort, of the child upon which the promise and the covenant depend. The promise is God's covenant grace to all the children alike; faith is the demand upon the children, upon which the promise depends for its fulfillment in the everlasting salvation of the children. The grace of the covenant promise depends upon faith as a demanded condition.

2. Damning against this basic element of the doctrine of a conditional covenant are these two truths of the confessions regarding faith, particularly the faith of covenant children.

Faith is the gift of God to the elect children; it is not a work of or a contribution by little children. Although faith is a demand (God calls for faith in his word to little children), it is not a demand *contrasted with the gracious promise and supposedly constituting a second element of the covenant with the gracious promise, as though the covenant consists of the gracious promise on the one hand and the demand of faith on the other hand. Faith is part of the content of the gracious promise, and it is as much a gift to elect children as forgiveness and eternal life.*

Equally significant, faith is the means or instrument by which covenant children receive and appropriate Christ. It is not a human act upon which God's grace depends, or that makes one worthy of God's grace, or by which one child distinguishes himself from another, equally the object of God's grace.

3. The critically important truth regarding faith in the controversy over the covenant is this: When faith is made the condition of a gracious promise, of a gracious covenant, and of covenant grace, *which are wider in extent than election*, faith has, by virtue of this fact, become a human work upon which God's grace depends, so that the entire doctrine of covenant salvation is a form of the false gospel of salvation by the sinner's will and works (see Rom. 9:16).

b. The confessions on faith as both a gift and a means (and not a condition).

1. The Heidelberg Catechism, Question 20 teaches that faith is essentially union with Christ; the work in those who are saved of God alone (the elect *"are* ingrafted" into Christ; they do not and cannot graft themselves); and the means—*means by which*, not *condition upon which*—to receive the benefits of salvation that are in Christ.

2. Belgic Confession, Article 22 proves that faith is the gift of God: "The Holy Ghost kindleth in our hearts an upright faith." The article proves also that faith is only a means by which the believer receives Christ and his salvation: The article calls faith "an instrument."

The article applies the truth that faith is the means of receiving the blessings of salvation, and not a human work (condition) upon which grace depends, to the blessing of justification. Those today who are developing the doctrine of a conditional covenant teach that justification depends upon the condition of faith, so that justification is by faith and works, that is, justification is *on account of* faith and *on account of* works.

3. The Belgic Confession, Articles 33–35 on the sacraments present faith as the means by which elect believers receive

Christ: "hand and mouth of our soul."[15] These articles also teach that faith is the gift of God, both in its beginning and in its continuance and strengthening.

4. Canons 3–4.10 condemns the doctrine that explains the conversion of some children of believers as their own distinguishing of themselves (by performing the condition of faith) from other children, equally the objects of covenant grace. The article insists rather that God converts some children of believers by giving them faith, according to his election of them. Implied is that he withholds grace and faith from the other children, according to his eternal decree of reprobation.

5. Canons 3–4.14 teaches that faith is the gift of God, both regarding the power to believe and regarding the activity of faith.

The article exposes and condemns the scheme of salvation, including salvation in the covenant, that presents faith as the sinner's part in a bargain, agreement, or contract, upon which God's part depends: "consent to the terms of salvation."

Evident in this article is the fact that the doctrine of a conditional covenant and the doctrine of an unconditional covenant are two essentially different gospels of salvation. For the doctrine of a conditional covenant, salvation is a cooperative effort of God and the sinner as both carry out the terms of salvation, which evidently both parties have hammered out and agreed to. This is a New Testament covenant of works. For the doctrine of the unconditional covenant, salvation is God's gift and God's work. This is the New Testament covenant of grace.

IV. SECTION THREE

A. Section three draws important conclusions concerning the controversy over the covenant from the confessional proof given in the preceding sections. In the characteristically Reformed manner, the conclusions are both negative ("we repudiate") and positive ("we maintain").

---

15 Belgic Confession Article 35, in ibid., 3:429.

1. This section clarifies the fundamental issue in the controversy as the unconditionality or conditionality of the covenant *promise*.

If the covenant promise is general and conditional, so also are the covenant and covenant salvation conditional; if the covenant promise is particular and unconditional, so also are the covenant and covenant salvation unconditional.

2. Although there is some repetition in the negations and affirmations, the expressions of the truth and of the errors concerning the covenant are sharpened.

3. In addition, the significance of this section is that it wards off false charges against the doctrine of the unconditional covenant, prevents misunderstandings of the doctrine by other Reformed and Presbyterian churches, and guards against any abuse of the doctrine by the PRC.

B. The repudiation of errors.

1. The teaching that God makes the covenant promise to all the baptized children alike, conditionally, that is, that God swears to every child at baptism, "I will be your God and Savior in Jesus Christ on condition that you believe."

a. Implied by the doctrine of a conditional promise to all who are baptized is that God establishes his covenant with all alike, but that the continuation of the covenant with children and the everlasting covenant salvation of children depend upon their performance of the condition, namely, faith.

b. It is this doctrine that the men of the federal vision are developing at the beginning of the twenty-first century by teaching that all the baptized children alike are united to Christ and begin to enjoy his life and the benefits of salvation (including justification), but that the children's continuing in Christ and the everlasting salvation of the children depend upon conditions they must perform.

2. The teaching of presupposed regeneration.

a. This is the doctrine supposedly taught by the Dutch Reformed theologian Abraham Kuyper. According to this doctrine, the church supposes the regeneration of all the baptized children, and this supposition is the basis of infant baptism.

b. The PRC reject this teaching; their doctrine of an unconditional covenant with the elect children in no way countenances the teaching of presupposed regeneration.

c. Scripture, history, and experience explode the presupposition that all circumcised children in the Old Testament and all baptized children in the New Testament are regenerated.

Scripture teaches that a circumcised Esau was reprobate and unregenerated—a profane child and a profane man (Gen. 25:19–34; Gen. 26:34–35; Gen. 27:41; Rom. 9:6–13; Heb. 12:16–17). The history of the church of the new dispensation shows that many baptized children of godly parents lived and died in unbelief and disobedience. The present experience of the people of God corroborates the grievous testimony of Hebrews 10:29, 31 that some who have been "sanctified" by (infant) baptism insult the Spirit of grace and fall everlastingly into the hands of the living God.

d. The reason for the mention of the error of presupposed regeneration in section three is that the advocates of a conditional covenant are insistent and noisy that the alternative to their doctrine is presupposed regeneration. They make this a "bogey" in their effort to discredit the doctrine of the unconditional covenant.

The charge against the doctrine of the unconditional covenant that it is the teaching of presupposed regeneration is false. Persistence in making the charge, in the face of the PRC's explicit rejection of presupposed regeneration and careful demonstration of their rejection, must be viewed as merely an attempt to divert attention from the real and vital issue in the controversy.[16]

e. Concerning the error of presupposed regeneration, it should be noted:

---

16 For a thorough explanation and refutation of the error of presupposed regeneration, see Hoeksema, *Believers and Their Seed*, 29–56.

1. The basis of infant baptism is not, and may not be, an uncertain presupposition, whether of regeneration or of anything else. The basis must be the certain, revealed word of God. What the basis is, section three will state at the end.

2. Although the PRC do not presuppose the regeneration of all the baptized infants, they do believe (not presuppose) that ordinarily God unites to Christ by the bond of faith and regenerates the elect infants of believers in earliest childhood, often when they are yet in the womb of their mother, as was the case with John (see Luke 1:41, 44).

3. The confessional proof of these rejections.

a. Canons 1.6–8, which has already been referred to in section one, proves that election is the source of and governs the gracious covenant promise and regeneration, so that neither is the promise (as distinguished from the *preaching* of the promise) broader in its address than election, nor is regeneration to be presupposed of all the children (since Scripture and experience prove that not all the children are elect).

Canons 1.6–8 deny that faith is a condition unto covenant salvation; faith, rather, is the gift of God to the elect.

These articles refute the implication of the doctrine of a conditional covenant that the saving call of God in the covenant is ineffectual and resistible ("effectually to call and draw"), and the implicit teaching of the doctrine of a conditional covenant that there is an election of God unto grace that is not unto glory.

b. The baptism form.

As the Declaration's brief explanation of the quotation of this form indicates ("the prayer refers only to the elect," etc.), the point here of the long quotation of the baptism form is to demonstrate that the reference throughout the form to God's saving of the children of believers does not have, and cannot have, all the baptized children in view, but only the elect children—*who are the true, spiritual children of Abraham and of believers.*

The doctrine of a conditional covenant with all the children alike views the children mentioned in the form as all the baptized children, those who perish as well as those who are saved.

The defenders of a conditional covenant contend that every statement in the form concerning God's gracious will and acts regarding the salvation of the children must be explained as conditional: The Father makes an eternal covenant of grace with all the children, *conditionally*; the Son washes all the children from their sin, *conditionally*; the Spirit assures all the children that he will dwell in them, *conditionally*; all the children are "sanctified in Christ," *conditionally*; etc.

But this explanation of the form is an utter impossibility; it is a wresting of the form on behalf of a covenant doctrine that militates against the doctrine of the form. Indeed, this explanation denies the gospel of salvation by sovereign (irresistible) grace with regard to the offspring of believers. According to this explanation of the form, God on his part is gracious to all the physical offspring of believers alike. From beginning to end, the salvation of the children of believers depends upon the children's performing the condition. If this is what the baptism form teaches, it is doctrinally corrupt. It is a thoroughly Arminian creed. It contradicts the theology of the Canons of Dordt.

The contemporary heresy of the federal vision is a natural, logical, inevitable development of this explanation of the baptism form.

But the baptism form teaches no such thing. The baptism form teaches the establishment of a covenant of grace, not a covenant of conditions: The Father makes an eternal covenant of grace with his chosen people, *by sovereign grace*; the Son washes the chosen people in his blood, *in sovereign grace*; the Spirit indwells the chosen people and sanctifies them, *by sovereign grace*.

Especially the prayer after baptism refutes the explanation foisted upon the form that the children who are the objects of grace are all the children *conditionally*. The prayer thanks God for forgiving the baptized children, working in the baptized children by the Holy Spirit, uniting the baptized children to Jesus Christ, and adopting them as his children. Therefore, the baptized children can be "piously and religiously educated, increase and grow up in the Lord Jesus." This is true only of the elect children. Thus, the prayer makes plain that the form regards the elect children as the true, spiritual, covenant children of believers, which is the viewpoint of Scripture (see Rom. 9:6–13; Gal. 3:16, 29).

Neither is the baptism form *presupposing* that what it affirms of the children of believers—their salvation in Christ—is true of all the physical offspring of believers. The form does not say, "We *presuppose* that all the baptized children again received into grace in Christ are sanctified in Christ, forgiven," etc. (even though we know better). But it says of the children of believers that they *are* received into grace in Christ, sanctified in Christ, etc. This is true only of the elect children, whom the form rightly regards as the true, spiritual children of Abraham and of believers.

4. Section three also repudiates the teaching of the defenders of a general, conditional, covenant promise that this promise is an objective bequest to every child of a right to Christ and salvation.

The Declaration exposed this error also in section two. Here, the Declaration flatly rejects this teaching.

The teaching that God bestows upon every child, objectively, a right to Jesus Christ is both confusing and erroneous. The teaching is confusing. What does it mean that God gives covenant grace and covenant blessing objectively? Evidently, by the word *objectively* the defenders of a conditional covenant with all the children intend to recognize that God does not give covenant grace and salvation to all the children *subjectively*, that is, presumably, by working grace in their hearts. (However, the men of the federal vision are developing the doctrine of a conditional promise by teaching that God also gives grace and blessing to all the children *subjectively*. That is, God actually unites all the baptized children to Christ, so that they all share the resurrection life of Christ.) If *objectively* means anything at all, it proposes a gracious attitude of God toward all the children alike and a gracious desire of God to save them all. This the confessions deny, insisting that election is the source and cause of all God's grace in Christ, whether objective or subjective. Besides, the notion of an objective covenant grace toward all the children has God at loggerheads with himself. Objectively he is gracious to all, but subjectively (in which respect grace alone saves a child) he withholds grace from some.

In addition, the doctrine of the bestowal upon reprobate children of a right to Christ is false. None of fallen mankind has a right to Christ, or any good, except those for whom Christ merited this right by his death. But as Canons 2.8 teaches, Christ died not for all humans, nor for all the physical offspring of believers, but for the elect only.

If God's covenant promise assures reprobate, unbelieving children of believers that they have a right to Christ *in any sense whatever*, the promise lies or is mistaken. And if the promise lies or is mistaken, the promising God lies or is mistaken.

C. Affirmation of covenant truths.

1. God surely fulfills his promise to the elect. This "principle" of the covenant is richer than might appear.

a. The covenant promise of God is and must be certain, that is, truthful; the veracity of God is at stake. In contrast, the covenant promise of God in the doctrine of a conditional covenant is highly uncertain: It fails in numerous instances—it fails because the objects of the promise refuse to perform the condition upon which the promise depends, *but it fails.*

b. The covenant promise of God is not merely the expression of God's willingness to save. The promise also consists of the sure realization and fulfillment of the solemn oath of God. That is, the promise to a baptized child, "I swear by myself that I will be your God in Christ and save you, and you will be my child," is not merely a strong statement of what God would like to do, or even of what he is willing to do (if only the child will perform the condition upon which the fulfillment of the promise depends). If this is all the covenant promise is, it is as empty and useless as a human's promise to a corpse that he is willing to raise the corpse from the dead. But the promise of God assures the accomplishment of the content of the promise in the one to whom the promise is made: covenant salvation, the resurrection of the body, and eternal life in communion with God in the new world. In contrast, the covenant promise in the doctrine of a conditional covenant consists merely of the well-meaning willingness of God to save (all the children alike); it does not include, and assure, the fulfillment of itself in any of the children (for fulfillment of the promise depends on conditions that the children must perform).

c. The covenant promise is a thing of sovereign power: It itself, by itself, accomplishes itself. In contrast, the covenant promise of the conditional covenant is an inherently weak thing. In many cases, it fails to realize itself, because realization depends on the children's performing conditions. By implication, in those cases in which it is realized (in the everlasting salvation of the children), it is not realized by virtue of its own power, but by virtue of the children's performing the condition. (A conditional promise is worthless.)

d. God makes the covenant promise only to the elect children, and in every case he fulfills the promise, by the sovereign power of the promise itself. Here, it might be wished that the Declaration had departed from its rule of appealing only to the confessions. Galatians 3:16 and 29 teach that God made the covenant promise to Abraham's seed, Jesus Christ, as head of the covenant of grace, and that therefore the covenant promise is extended to those who are in Christ by faith (according to election), and to them only. "Now to Abraham and his seed were the promises made. He saith not, And to seeds, as of many; but as of one. And to thy seed, which is Christ...And if ye be Christ's, then are ye Abraham's seed, and heirs according to the promise."

2. The second, lengthy, and manifold affirmation wards off objections against the doctrine of the unconditional covenant, prevents misunderstandings, and guards those who confess the doctrine of the unconditional covenant against abuse of the doctrine.

a. The various objections and errors guarded against and warded off may be summarized as antinomianism, that is, the teaching and practice of lawlessness as the implication of salvation by grace (*antinomianism* means "against the law"), and hyper-Calvinism, that is, such an understanding of divine sovereignty as denies human responsibility (*hyper-Calvinism* means "above and beyond [true] Calvinism").

There is a charge, or misunderstanding, or abuse, that the doctrine of the unconditional covenant implies carelessness of life on the part of the member of the covenant, or at least the denial of demands in the covenant for a holy life.

There is a charge, or misunderstanding, or abuse, that the truth of a particular promise (for elect believers only) implies a restriction upon the *preaching* of the promise (as though those who hold the unconditional covenant, particularly the PRC, preach only to the elect).

There is a charge, or misunderstanding, or abuse, that the truth of a particular promise implies the denial of God's serious command to all who hear the preaching, whether regenerated or unregenerated, believer or unbeliever, elect or reprobate, to believe and repent, and that it implies the denial of the promiscuous proclamation of the (particular) promise that all who believe will be saved.

All of these and similar charges, the PRC reject; all of these and similar misunderstandings, the PRC clarify; all of these and similar abuses, the PRC warn against—*in the Declaration.*

Consistent Calvinism, or better, the Reformed faith consistently held and practiced, is not antinomian or hyper-Calvinistic.

b. Against these charges, misunderstandings, and abuses, the PRC maintain, positively:

1. The promise of God, which saves the objects of the promise as rational and moral creatures (not treating them as puppets or as stocks and blocks), works with irresistible power in the children of the promise, so that they live a holy life of thankfulness. Such is the working of the promise that it confronts the elect believer with the obligation to love God and the neighbor, to live a holy life, and to pray. Noteworthy is the following.

Rather than the promise being conditioned by the covenant faithfulness of sinners, the promise itself produces covenant faithfulness.

Covenant faithfulness is an obligation, rather than a condition upon which the covenant depends.

The motive of the covenant life is thankfulness for grace and salvation, about which one is assured, rather than an anxious desire to perform conditions, upon which an uncertain salvation depends.

Against the all-too-familiar fear, or charge, on the part of those who are ignorant of grace, that the teaching of covenant salvation by sheer, sovereign grace may make children (and grown-ups) careless and profane, the Declaration here breathes the certainty that it is "impossible" that grace not produce holiness as its fruit.

In its sanctifying work, the covenant promise uses warnings, particularly the warning that those who walk impenitently in sin are under divine wrath and outside the kingdom. This warning also renders the reprobate in the sphere of the covenant inexcusable.

2. Although the grace and the gracious promise of the gospel are for the elect only, the *preaching* of the gospel is, and must be, to all without any restriction, limitation, or hesitation. In the promiscuous preaching of the gospel of Jesus Christ, God himself seriously commands all hearers, unregenerated as well as regenerated, reprobate as well as elect, to believe on Jesus Christ and to repent of their sins. At the same time the preaching announces to all hearers the promise that everyone who believes will be saved (as well as the warning that all who refuse to believe will be damned).

Here, the PRC clearly and deliberately distinguish their doctrine of particular grace in the preaching of the gospel, whether in the sphere of the covenant or on the mission field, from the (real) error of hyper-Calvinism. Hyper-Calvinism restricts the preaching of the gospel to those who show themselves regenerated and denies that the serious, external call of the gospel by God himself, "Believe! Repent!" comes to the reprobate unbeliever.[17]

---

17 On hyper-Calvinism and the Protestant Reformed Churches' rejection of

3. The confessional proof of these affirmations evidently applies to the affirmations concerning the impossibility of a careless life on the part of the object of the promise; concerning the truth of obligations in the covenant; and concerning the preaching of the gospel to all and sundry.

a. The third part of the baptism form teaches that the member of the covenant has a "part" in the covenant, which consists of obedience as an obligation.

b. The Lord's supper form teaches that the member of the covenant who is living by faith shows his thankfulness to God by holiness in his whole life. It warns the unthankful and unholy that while they continue impenitently in this condition they have no part in Christ's kingdom and are barred from the supper, which "Christ hath ordained only for the faithful."

c. The Heidelberg Catechism, Question 64 states that it is "impossible" that the doctrine of grace makes men careless. Profane men and women will abuse the doctrine, but the doctrine of salvation by grace alone, particularly the doctrine of justification by faith alone, always produces holiness in the believer. It is noteworthy that covenant faithfulness is not a condition of the covenant, but the "fruit" of it.

d. The Heidelberg Catechism, Question 84 teaches that the preaching of the gospel goes out to all, unbelievers as well as believers; that the preaching commands all to believe and repent; and that the preaching announces to all, unbelievers as well as believers, that whoever believes will be forgiven (as also that those who remain unconverted are exposed to wrath and condemnation).

e. The Heidelberg Catechism, Question 116 teaches that God commands his covenant friends to pray. The Catechism teaches also that the way of salvation is a way of sincere,

---

this error, see David J. Engelsma, *Hyper-Calvinism & the Call of the Gospel: An Examination of the "Well-Meant Offer" of the Gospel*, rev. ed. (Grand Rapids, MI: Reformed Free Publishing Association, 1994).

diligent, spiritual activity. Sovereign grace does not nullify responsibility; it maintains responsibility (in the words of the Declaration, "He realizes in us as rational and moral creatures") and enables and empowers the godly exercise of responsibility.

f. Canons 3–4.12, 16–17 teach that the grace of God in Jesus Christ (which is covenant grace), treating men and women as rational, moral creatures ("not...as senseless stocks and blocks"), irresistibly makes the objects of this grace spiritually alive and willingly, actively holy. In this work of sanctification, God uses the means of the gospel, with its "precepts" and its "admonitions." This confessional proof guards against misunderstanding and abuse of the truth that the covenant promise is unconditional to the elect children of believers. Thus godly parents, trusting God's promise to save their children, will not avoid sharp warnings to their children (as though warnings would compromise grace) but will use them in the rearing of their children (as grace employs warnings to accomplish the purpose of the salvation of the children). The same holds true of good Reformed pastors with regard to their congregation. The notion that admonitions are unnecessary is a form of the antinomianism and hyper-Calvinism that the Declaration rejects.

g. Canons 3–4, Error 9 rejects as a form of the heresy of Pelagianism the explanation of conversion and holiness that suspends conversion and holiness on the will of the sinner.

Exactly this is the error of the doctrine of a conditional covenant: The grace of covenant conversion and of continued covenant salvation is made to depend on the baptized child's faith and faithfulness as conditions that he must perform.

Of great importance is the appeal by this article of the Canons to 1 Corinthians 4:7: "For who maketh thee to differ from another? and what hast thou that thou didst not receive? now if thou didst receive it, why dost thou glory, as if thou hadst not received it?" Since all children alike are objects of the gracious covenant promise, are in the covenant by a gracious act of God at baptism, and even have the covenant blessings, objectively, according to the advocates of a conditional covenant, that some children believe and are saved, in distinction from others, is their own distinguishing of themselves from the others.

h. Canons 5.14 teaches that God maintains and perfects the work of grace in all in whom the work is begun by means not only of the promises of the word, but also of the threatenings and exhortations of the word, and that God works in such a way as causes his people to be active.

i. Belgic Confession, Article 24 denies that grace, specifically justification by faith alone, makes the justified sinner impious and carelessly unholy. On the contrary, grace always renews and sanctifies the believing and justified sinner. The faith by which alone one is justified, since it is union with Christ by the Holy Spirit, always produces good works.

This article is powerful in its warning that a holy life and good works are not conditions of salvation ("we do not found our salvation upon them"), but "fruits" and themselves the work of God's grace in his people.

4. A third affirmation of this section of the Declaration states the ground of infant baptism: God's command, rising from and reflecting his gracious covenant will to gather his church from the families of believers, "in the line of continued generations." (Earlier in this section, the Declaration has rejected presupposed regeneration as the ground of infant baptism.)

a. No confessional proof is offered for this affirmation. The confessional proof has been given in the preceding sections, for example, the Heidelberg Catechism, Question 74; the Belgic Confession, Article 34; and the baptism form.

b. This affirmation concerning the ground of infant baptism wards off the charge that for the PRC the ground of infant baptism is presupposed regeneration. It also rejects the position that the ground of infant baptism is a conditional promise to all the children, so that the covenant is established conditionally with all the children alike.

The ground of infant baptism is God's covenant in the line of generations, not his covenant with all the physical offspring of all believing parents. (As Romans 9:6–13 clearly teaches, indeed as it is the express purpose of the passage to teach, the sovereignty of God in salvation includes that predestination, reprobation as well as election, applies to the physical offspring of believers as well as to audiences on the mission field.)

V. SECTION FOUR

A. The fourth section of the Declaration, which declares and demonstrates from the confessions the Protestant Reformed belief and practice of the autonomy of the local congregation, is an anomaly in the document.

1. The autonomy of the local church is not related materially to the doctrine of the unconditional covenant or to the truth of particular grace.

2. The autonomy of the local church is an aspect of proper Reformed church polity (or government).

3. No doubt, the explanation for the inclusion of this affirmation of the autonomy of the local church is that the Reformed Churches in the Netherlands (liberated), with whom the PRC were in contact at the time of the Declaration and with whose immigrant members in Canada the PRC were working, are strong proponents of the autonomy of the local church.

This affirmation, after the long, sustained repudiation of the conditional covenant doctrine of the liberated, indicates some common ground between the liberated and the PRC in a forlorn hope that some contact might be maintained. (If this is the explanation of the final section of the Declaration, the hope was immediately and completely dashed.)

B. The autonomy of the local church means that each (true) congregation, with its offices of pastor, elder, and deacon, is a complete, self-governing manifestation of the body and bride of Jesus Christ (autonomy means "self-governing"). To the congregation are given the keys of the kingdom, consisting of the preaching of the pure doctrine of the gospel (confirmed by the pure administration of the sacraments instituted by Christ) and of the exercise of Christian discipline upon those who show themselves unbelieving and disobedient in doctrine or life.

1. This doctrine of the church, with its corresponding practice of church polity, particularly opposes the hierarchical doctrine and practice that view the denomination as the church; regard the local congregation merely as part of the church; and give the denomination the authority to preach, administer the sacraments, and, especially, exercise discipline. Thus the hierarchical church, of which the Roman Catholic Church is the chief (but by no means only) example, lords it over the local congregation.

2. The PRC were formed as a denomination on the occasion of the practice of this hierarchical church polity by the CRC: The denomination, functioning through its major assemblies, exercised the discipline of deposition and excommunication upon (faithful) office bearers.

C. That the affirmation of the autonomy of the local church does not imply independentism, or congregationalism, that is, the teaching that the local church is not called by God to federate with likeminded congregations in a denomination and that, if it does federate, the decisions of the federation (classis and synod) are not binding on the local church, is evident from the history, fact, and purpose of the Declaration itself. The Declaration was adopted by the Protestant Reformed denomination at a synodical assembly; was intended to be the instrument of the denominational mission committee; and is "settled and binding" for all the congregations in the denomination, indeed all the members of the denomination, according to Article 31 of the Reformed Church Order of Dordt (the church order of the PRC).

1. A congregation is duty bound to belong to a denomination—a federation of churches, that is, a covenantal union—by virtue of

its calling to manifest the unity of the church of Christ.

2. In the denomination, the denomination, through its major assembles—classis and synod for the Reformed—has a certain "jurisdiction" over the consistory of the local church, according to Article 36 of the Church Order.

D. Confessional proof of the autonomy of the local church.

1. The Belgic Confession, Article 31 teaches that "the church" is the local congregation, which chooses its own officebearers and governs itself by these officebearers. The article condemns hierarchy in the basic form of one minister's having power over other ministers ("lording it over" the others), obviously with reference to the Roman Catholic hierarchy of the lordship over all ministers by the bishop of Rome.

> The evil of all forms of hierarchy is the denial, whether explicit or implicit, of the rule over his church by Jesus Christ, "the only universal Bishop and the only Head of the church.

2. The Church Order, Article 36 proves the autonomy of the local church by its significant omission to grant jurisdiction by the denominational major assemblies over the local congregation. As the brief explanation of the Declaration states, "Only the consistory has authority over the local congregation."

3. The Church Order, Article 84 is the outstanding anti-hierarchical article in the Reformed Church Order of Dordt. Implied by the appeal of the Declaration to this article is that a doctrine of the church that views the denomination, rather than the local congregation, as the church is, by virtue of this fact, illegitimate hierarchy. In addition, the article places the government of every congregation in the hands of the minister(s), elders, and deacons of the congregation. For other officebearers to presume to govern a congregation would be "lording it over" the congregation.

4. The Form for the Installation of Elders and Deacons (a minor creed, referred to at the beginning of the Declaration as a liturgical form) views each local congregation as "God's church," not merely as part of God's church. And God rules in the local

congregation, particularly in the important choosing of office bearers, not from above by a higher body or overlord, but by the decisions of the local church itself.

Appendix Four

Covenant Salvaticn: "Contingent on What We Do"

Not of Works: Norman Shepherd and His Critics, by Ralph F. Boersema. Minneapolis, MN: NextStep Resources, 2012. Pp. xxxi + 235. $15 (paper).

The heresy of the federal vision is not going to disappear anytime soon. Not only do prominent, aggressive proponents of the theology remain in the Reformed and Presbyterian churches, but also influential theologians continue to arise for the public defense of the teaching.

In 2011, Presbyterian theologian Ian A. Hewitson published a vigorous, book-length defense of Norman Shepherd and his theology, which is essentially the theology of the federal vision. The book is *Trust and Obey: Norman Shepherd & the Justification Controversy at Westminster Theological Seminary*. I critiqued this book in an appendix of my *Federal Vision: Heresy at the Root*.[1]

Now, Reformed theologian Ralph F. Boersema comes out with a book defending and promoting the theology of Shepherd and the federal vision: *Not of Works: Norman Shepherd and His Critics*.

With the publication of *Not of Works*, the truth concerning the federal vision becomes even clearer to the conservative Reformed reading public, and more intriguing.

For Boersema is a minister and theologian in the Canadian Reformed Churches, the denomination in North America descended from the Reformed Churches in the Netherlands (liberated) and disciples of the covenant theologians Schilder, Holwerda, Veenhof, and others.

---

1 David J. Engelsma, *Federal Vision: Heresy at the Root* (Jenison, MI: Reformed Free Publishing Association, 2012), 219–238.

THE ROOT OF SHEPHERD'S THEOLOGY

Boersema locates the source of the theology of Shepherd and the federal vision in the covenant doctrine of the liberated churches, exactly where the source is. The Protestant Reformed Churches have called the attention of the Reformed churches to the root of the federal vision in the covenant theology of Schilder and the liberated Reformed for a long time. But the purported critics of the federal vision have stubbornly refused to recognize this root and to condemn the federal vision in terms of it.

Apart from the charge by the Protestant Reformed Churches, apart from the obvious similarity of the doctrine of the federal vision to the covenant theology of the liberated Reformed, and apart from the very name of the heresy (federal means "covenant"), the refusal of the Reformed critics of the federal vision to consider the covenant root of the federal vision has been inexcusable. As Boersema notes, Canadian Reformed theologian Jelle Faber rose to the defense of Norman Shepherd on the pages of the Canadian Reformed magazine *Clarion* already when the Shepherd controversy at Westminster Theological Seminary became public in 1982 (59).

Also, liberated theologians Cornelis Van Dam and Nelson Kloosterman gave high praise to Hewitson's defense of Shepherd and his theology. Of Hewitson's book, Van Dam exclaimed on the back cover of the book, "highly recommended." On one of the opening pages of the book, Kloosterman, despite his avowed aversion to polemics ("very harmful to the truth"), recommended Hewitson's defense of Shepherd as a "compelling study."

Boersema makes it even harder, if not impossible, for would-be critics of the theology of Shepherd studiously to ignore that the theology of Shepherd and the federal vision is the natural, inevitable development of the covenant doctrine of Schilder and the liberated Reformed.

Taking note of Shepherd's teaching that God makes his gracious covenant with all the baptized children alike, but conditionally, because the covenant is not founded on or governed by election—the very heart of the theology of the federal vision—Boersema states that "Shepherd has adopted" the "solution" to the issue of the relation of covenant and election of men "like S. Greijdanus

270

and K. Schilder." This "solution" holds that God's covenant "is not only with the elect. The covenant is not unconditional." By promise to all alike, the covenant is graciously established with all the children alike. But for the continuation of the covenant, issuing in eternal salvation, there are "obligations," that is, conditions. Failure on the part of some children to perform the "obligations"/conditions results in those children's being "cut off" (84–85).

Although Boersema's book concentrates on Shepherd's doctrine of justification (the sub, subtitle is "The Justification Controversy Laid to Rest Through Understanding"), Boersema is explicit that the root of Shepherd's and the federal vision's theology is his and its doctrine of the covenant: "He [Shepherd] is only seeking to do justice to the dynamic of historical covenant language" (148).

Shepherd himself writes an important foreword to the book. In the foreword he approves Boersema's analysis and defense of his theology. Shepherd also offers a brief defense of his own. Almost at once he explains his doctrine of justification as an aspect of his theology of the biblical doctrine of the covenant (xvii–xxiii).

The theology of Shepherd and the federal vision is a distinct doctrine of the covenant of grace. If it is not critiqued with regard to its teaching about the covenant, not only will it not be understood, but also in the end it will not be condemned by Reformed and Presbyterian churches even regarding its erroneous teaching on justification.

A CONDITIONAL COVENANT, CUT LOOSE FROM ELECTION

What the distinct covenant doctrine of Shepherd and the federal vision is, its defender—liberated theologian Ralph Boersema—and Shepherd himself make plain. It is the doctrine of a (saving) covenant love and grace of God in Jesus Christ for all baptized children alike. (I place "saving" in parentheses not because the covenant love and grace of federal vision theology actually save anyone. They do not. They are impotent. But the covenant love and grace in federal vision theology are saving *in nature*; they are not merely a non-saving, common love and grace.) In this (saving) love, God establishes his covenant with all the children alike.

Indeed, the covenant theology of Shepherd is the doctrine

of a (saving) covenant love and grace of God in Jesus Christ for all humans alike, baptized or unbaptized. Refusing to identify the "seed" of Abraham in the covenant promise to Abraham as Christ and the elect in him, and therefore refusing to identify the "nations" in the covenant promise to Abraham as the elect in every nation, Shepherd explains the covenant promise to Abraham as referring to all humans without exception. If the universal covenant promise does not imply that God makes his covenant with every human, it does imply that he desires to bless every human with the blessings of the covenant.

> The Lord made a covenant with Abraham, one by which he would bless all the families of the earth. The Good News proclaims the covenant to all nations. This is not just a manner of speaking. God really does desire all men to repent and know Christ. He does not make his covenant with all, but he does lovingly offer it to all....He does pledge to all of them that he will be their God and they his people so long as they keep his covenant (138–39).

In his covenant love and grace, God sends out the federal vision evangelists, including Norman Shepherd, preaching John 3:16 and telling every hearer that God loves him, that Christ died for him, and that God desires to save him.

> From the perspective of the covenant...all of the words of John 3:16 mean exactly what they say. The Reformed evangelist can and must preach to everyone on the basis of John 3:16, "Christ died to save you." (87).

> John 3:16 is embedded in the covenant documents of the New Testament...John 3:16 is covenant truth. Its specific application...in the declaration, "Christ died for you" [to every human], is a demonstration of the grace of our Lord Jesus Christ opening the way to fellowship with God (88).

> God so loved the world that he gave his only Son so that whoever believes in him may have eternal life. This is true love for all persons (138).

Specifically now with regard to all the baptized infants of believers, the covenant grace of God toward them and the covenant bond itself are conditional. That is, they depend for their ability to continue with an infant and to bring an infant finally to eternal life upon the individual, sinful infant himself. God's (saving) covenant love and grace are contingent upon the child's performing the work of believing and upon his performing the work of lifelong obedience to the law of God.

It is possible, indeed reality in multitudes of instances, that one who is the object of covenant love and grace and truly in covenant relationship with God fails to perform the conditions, so that he frustrates the love and grace of God, is separated from God, and perishes forever. So do Shepherd and the men of the federal vision emphasize the real possibility of falling away from covenant grace and of breaking the covenant, which was truly established with one, that the doctrine of falling away from grace must be regarded as a favorite doctrine of theirs.

Thus one's covenant election is resisted. Indeed, covenant election becomes reprobation.

Explaining and defending Shepherd's doctrine, Boersema denies that election governs the covenant. In a defense of this denial that staggers a Reformed Christian, Boersema argues that "if the covenant is really only with the elect, there can be no possibility of falling away" (137). To say nothing of the terror that this doctrine casts into the soul of every believer until his last breath, are Boersema and Shepherd ignorant that the Reformed churches have struggled through this issue to the comforting confession of perseverance in the fifth head of the Canons of Dordt? "God, who is rich in mercy, according to his unchangeable purpose of election, does not...suffer them [the elect] to...forfeit the state of justification... and to plunge themselves into everlasting destruction."[2]

Boersema correctly relates what it means for Shepherd and the federal vision—and for Boersema and the liberated Reformed— that God makes his covenant with all the baptized babies alike, regardless of eternal predestination.

> This covenant love is that of a Father for his children and is bestowed on all members of the covenant people. It is not addressed only to the elect, nor does it merely bring

---

2   Canons of Dordt 5.6, in Schaff, *Creeds of Christendom*, 3:593.

a people into the pale of the Gospel. Baptism symbolizes union with God in Christ, not just the offer of union (137).

This love that is ineffectual in many children is the implication of an oath to save them all that is never fulfilled with many. God establishes his covenant by oath-bound promise. According to Shepherd and Boersema, God swears to every baptized child that he will be the child's God and that the child will be God's covenant friend. This is an oath-bound promise to save every child. "Election should…not be allowed to mute the fact that the Lord has established a legally binding bond with his people in the form of a covenant in which he really swears an oath to be a God and Father to his people." That the oath-bound, covenant promise is addressed to every baptized child, Boersema makes plain by stating that the truth of a covenant bond formed by the promise "does not only apply to the elect" (138).

THE WELL-MEANT OFFER

Bravely (for a theologian who confesses the Canons of Dordt) picking up on a teaching of Shepherd that most of Shepherd's purported critics deliberately ignore (lest their dear doctrine of the well-meant offer be exposed), Boersema recognizes and defends Shepherd's doctrine that God has promised his covenant to all humans without exception, so that he loves them all, desires the salvation of them all, and graciously offers Christ to them all in the well-meant offer.

> Salvation through Christ is sincerely offered to all people. If we look at history only from the perspective of predestination, it is illogical to think that God truly calls the reprobate to partake of Christ's love or that his love is revealed to them in Christ. However, God so loved the world that he gave his only Son so that whoever believes in him may have eternal life. This is true love for all persons…God really does desire all men to repent and know Christ. He does not make his covenant with all, but he does lovingly offer it to all (138).

Accurately expressing Shepherd's and the federal vision theology, Boersema establishes the connection between the well-meant offer and the conditional covenant: "The well-meant Gospel offer is spoken to all men in the same kind of language as the covenant, language that expresses God's sincere commitment and heart's desire, without predicting the outcome" (139). The outcome cannot be predicted, of course, because the grace both of the well-meant offer and of the covenant efforts of God is conditional.

Despite some misgivings, Boersema cannot condemn Shepherd's explanation of John 3:16: "The Reformed evangelist can and must preach to everyone on the basis of John 3:16, 'Christ died to save you'" (87). This is the doctrine of universal atonement, in flagrant contradiction of Canons 2.8, which is binding on both Shepherd and Boersema. But Boersema cannot condemn universal atonement in the theology of Shepherd and the federal vision, because Shepherd's doctrine of universal atonement is based on Shepherd's and Boersema's covenant theology. Cut loose, like the covenant, from election, the proclamation of the gospel is "a genuine offer of grace to the whole world, not just to the elect. God's grace is good news for everyone" (88).

Boersema has enough Reformed sensibility at this point to be stricken by the awareness of the contradiction of the Reformed doctrine of reprobation. "God loves the world even as he hates Esau before he was born" (88).

Boersema's defense of the contradiction? "There is mystery here" (88).

Boersema's "mystery" is not the "mystery" of Scripture: a deep truth that had been hidden but is now revealed by divine inspiration. Boersema's "mystery" is a semantic cover-up of sheer, diametrical, irreconcilable contradiction regarding a fundamental truth of the gospel of grace. It is therefore also the obscuring, indeed the corruption, of the gospel of grace. If God loves Esau as well as Jacob and graciously swears his covenant of grace into existence with them both alike, the reason Jacob is saved in distinction from his brother is not the grace of God. Rather, the reason for Jacob's salvation is that Jacob performed the conditions and made himself to differ. The glory of his covenant salvation is Jacob's, not God's.

Contrary to Boersema's insistence that Shepherd "treasures the five points of Calvinism" (as confessed in the Canons—xxviii; 83), Shepherd denies the five points and rejects the Canons of Dordt as openly as any avowed Arminian *with regard to the gracious covenant, covenant grace and love, and covenant salvation.* Defending Shepherd and the theology of the federal vision as he does, the liberated theologian makes, or shows, himself guilty of the same evil.

Another instance of this open opposition to the Canons is Shepherd's teaching that there are "various decrees of election," one (covenant) decree of election unto grace and the way of salvation, and another (eternal) decree unto salvation and glory. Canons 1.8 flatly condemns this teaching.

> There are not various decrees of election, but one and the same decree respecting all those who shall be saved both under the Old and New Testament; since the Scripture declares the good pleasure, purpose, and counsel of the divine will to be one, according to which he hath chosen us from eternity, both to grace and to glory, to salvation and the way of salvation, which he hath ordained that we should walk therein.[3]

The root of the heresy of Shepherd and the federal vision is the doctrine of a conditional covenant, which is cut loose from election.

SALVATION "CONTINGENT ON WHAT WE DO"

What this heretical root amounts to, both Shepherd and Boersema freely acknowledge.

In his foreword Norman Shepherd describes his theology in these words: "The New Testament as well as the Old makes our eternal welfare contingent in some way and to some extent on what we do" (ix).

Having read Shepherd's description of the essence of his theology, Boersema both approves it and uses it to describe his—Boersema's—own: "Many Scripture passages...condition our eternal well-being on what we do" (187). What these passages of Scripture are, neither Shepherd nor Boersema informs the reader. Among them is not Romans 9:16: "[Salvation] is not of him that willeth, nor of him that runneth, but of God that sheweth mercy." Neither is Ephesians 2:8–9 on the list of the two defenders of a

---

3   Canons of Dordt 1.8, in ibid., 3:583.

conditional covenant: "For by grace are ye saved through faith; and that not of yourselves: it is the gift of God: Not of works, lest any man should boast."

According to Shepherd and Boersema, our eternal salvation depends on what we do.

I doubt that Jacob Arminius, or indeed a Jesuit, would be so bald and bold in confessing their theologies of man saving himself.

This is the message of the doctrine of a conditional covenant.

And this is why most purported critics leave strictly alone the covenant root of the theology of Shepherd and the federal vision. Most of them wholeheartedly share Shepherd's and Boersema's doctrine of a conditional covenant. For them to take up the issue of the conditional covenant would mean exposing themselves as committed to the teaching that, with regard to covenant salvation and well-being, our salvation and well-being are "contingent in some way and to some extent on what we do," as committed to this gross heresy as are Shepherd, the federal vision, and Ralph Boersema.

Purported critic Cornelis P. Venema is quoted by Boersema, at great length, as approving Shepherd's doctrine of a conditional covenant (151–58). Among "Shepherd's...evident strengths," according to Venema (as quoted by Boersema), is his insistence on the "conditionality of the covenant relationship...The covenant of grace is...conditional in its administration" (151).

According to Venema, *in a critique of Shepherd*, to view salvation "in terms of God's sovereign and unconditional electing grace" would make it impossible to do justice to "human responsibility" and to ward off "the error of antinomianism" (152).

Venema goes on to approve "Shepherd's advocacy of a covenant-evangelism approach" (152). This, as I have demonstrated from Shepherd himself, consists of saying to every human, on the basis of John 3:16, "God loves you with the (saving) love that gave his Son, desires to save you, had Christ die for you, and now graciously offers you salvation, if only you will perform the condition of accepting the offer." That is, Shepherd's approach to evangelism, warmly approved by Cornelis Venema, is the expression of the fundamental conviction that everyone's eternal welfare is contingent on what he himself does.

Not content with approving Shepherd's conditional-covenant

approach to evangelism, Venema must take a swipe at the approach to evangelism that is founded on and faithful to the decree of election. "Because the electing grace of God in Christ is unconditional, evangelism that is oriented to the decree of election also suffers… from an inordinate fear of emphasizing the gospel's condition of faith and obedience" (153).

The Arminians were right after all: Predestination cannot assure; leads to antinomianism; and cannot evangelize.

Convinced as they are of the fatal and deplorable weaknesses of the Reformed faith, why do these theologians still want to identify themselves as Reformed, and why do they still make a pretense of representing this faith?

It will be interesting to observe whether a single non-Protestant-Reformed critic of Shepherd will offer any objection to Shepherd's bold statement that our eternal welfare is contingent on what we do. And if one does, it will be still more interesting to see how he reconciles his objection with the doctrine of a conditional, that is, contingent, covenant.

CONDITIONAL JUSTIFICATION

Since Shepherd's and the federal vision's doctrine of justification is merely the effect and symptom of their doctrine of a conditional covenant, the reviewer of Boersema's book can be briefer in his analysis of this aspect of Shepherd's theology as vigorously defended by Ralph Boersema.

Boersema does *defend* Shepherd's doctrine of justification.

That aspect of the federal vision heresy that is too much even for some of the most devoted sympathizers with Shepherd's doctrine of a conditional covenant finds approval in the liberated theologian.

Boersema's defense of Shepherd's doctrine of justification by faith and by good works, like Shepherd's own defense, is the contention that Shepherd is only concerned that the faith that justifies be a true and living faith.

But this defense fails.

It is the doctrine of Shepherd and the federal vision that in justifying the believing sinner God takes the good works of the sinner himself into account. Thus it is also Shepherd's instruction to the sinner seeking justification that, for his justification, he present his own good works to God the judge.

Shepherd therefore teaches justification by faith *and by (faith's) good works*, in contradiction of the apostle in Romans 3:28: "Therefore we conclude that a man is justified by faith without the deeds of the law."

Shepherd denies that the good works excluded from justification in Romans 3:28 are all good works whatever. He insists that Romans 3 and 4, particularly Romans 3:28, have in view only those works that were part of the "old, Mosaic covenant," for example circumcision and those works performed with the purpose of meriting salvation. "These 'works of the law' are not any and all good works" (xii).

According to Shepherd's own explanation of the text, therefore, Romans 3:28 must be read as follows: "Therefore we conclude that a man is justified by faith without any works belonging to the Old Testament, Mosaic economy and without any works performed in order to merit, but definitely and emphatically *with* good works performed by true faith." That is, justification is by faith *and by (faith's) good works*.

Because, as all agree, in Romans 3:28 the apostle is teaching justification as the forensic act of God the judge, that is, God's declaration or verdict changing the legal standing of the sinner from guilt to innocence by forgiving his sins and imputing to him the righteousness of Christ, Shepherd's doctrine is that justification *as a forensic act of God* is by faith and works.

That he teaches justification by faith and works, Shepherd confirms by his exegesis of Romans 2:13, "For not the hearers of the law are just before God, but the doers of the law shall be justified." Luther, Calvin, and the Reformation explained the text as teaching what would have to be the case if justification were by the law (which it is not and cannot be). If justification were by the law, hearing the law would not be sufficient for justification. But one would have to do the law. Doing the law is utter impossibility. No totally depraved sinner can do the law. No regenerated, believing child of God can do the law. Doing the law consists of perfect love of God and perfect love of the neighbor every moment and regarding every thought, desire, and feeling, as well as regarding every word and every deed, all one's life long. One slip-up, one sin, in a lifetime of otherwise perfect obedience would make justification by the law impossible.

In Romans 2:13, according to the Reformation's (and the correct) interpretation, the apostle is laying the groundwork for his doctrine of gracious justification—justification by faith only—on the basis of the perfect obedience and atoning death of the substitute for elect sinners, Jesus Christ.

But Shepherd, his federal vision cohorts, and Ralph Boersema dissent from this Reformation exegesis (which is not only that of Luther, but also that of Calvin). For Shepherd, "the Pauline affirmation in Romans 2:13, 'the doers of the Law will be justified,' is not to be understood hypothetically in the sense that there are no persons who fall into that class, but in the sense that faithful disciples of the Lord Jesus Christ will be justified" (198). Boersema defends Shepherd's interpretation (198–201).

What this interpretation of Romans 2:13 affirms concerning justification is that justification is by doing the law.

In harmony with this Roman Catholic, Arminian, and Judaistic self-righteous theology is Shepherd's explanation of James 2.

In James 2 the apostle exposes a false, dead faith. This is a certain intellectual knowledge of Christian doctrine and a profession of salvation in Jesus Christ that is devoid of good works, especially works of love on behalf of the needy members of the church. Though a church member says he has faith, if his faith does not work by love, his faith is "dead, being alone" (James 2:14–17). In the context of this warning against false faith, James declares that "by works a man is justified, and not by faith only" (James 2:24).

At the Reformation the Roman Catholic adversaries of Luther's, Calvin's, and the Reformation's doctrine of justification by faith only made James 2 the decisive passage on (forensic) justification, the chief bulwark with which to withstand the Reformation's gospel of justification by faith only, and the main catapult with which to demolish the Reformation's gospel of grace.

Shepherd and the federal vision do the same, thus showing their colors.

The issue regarding James 2 is simply this: Does James 2 mean by "justification" the same truth as does Paul in Romans 3 and 4? Beyond all doubt and question, Paul speaks of justification as the forensic act of God the judge. That is, justification in Romans 3 and 4 is God's declaration pronouncing the sinner righteous, changing his legal standing from guilt to innocence. In Romans 4:5 justification is God's counting, or reckoning, faith for righteousness. According to Romans 4:6–7 justification is the imputation of righteousness, thus forgiving iniquities. According to Romans 4:8 justification is the non-imputation of sin. Counting, reckoning, imputing, and forgiving are forensic terms, describing the legal declaration that effects a change in one's standing before the law and the judge.

If James 2 speaks of justification in the same sense, James contradicts Paul with regard to a fundamental truth of the gospel. Whereas Paul teaches that justification is by faith only, apart from good works, James now teaches that justification is by faith and by good works, expressly denying that justification is by faith only.

This is impossible. Two apostles of Christ cannot contradict each other on the pages of inspired Scripture. Scripture does not contradict itself, least of all regarding such a fundamental truth as justification.

There are only two conceivable ways of harmonizing Paul and James. One is that Paul and James have two different kinds of works in mind. James refers to genuine good works. Paul refers to ceremonial works and to works that intend to merit salvation. According to this way of harmonizing Paul and James, justification—the forensic act—is by faith and by faith's genuine good works.

This is the explanation of Shepherd, the federal vision, and Ralph Boersema. "Shepherd favors the forensic justification exegesis of James 2" (168).

And, let us not forget, this is the explanation of the Roman Catholic Church, to the overthrow of the sixteenth-century Reformation of the church.

The other, and correct, harmonizing of Paul and James is that the two apostles speak of justification in two different senses. "Justification" does not have the same reference in James 2 that it has in Romans 3 and 4. Paul refers to the forensic act of God, beyond dispute. James, in contrast, refers to the *demonstration* of justification. Or, to say it differently, James refers to justification as it shows itself to be genuine. Just as a faith devoid of good works shows itself to be a dead and false faith, so an alleged justification by such a dead faith is shown to be a spurious justification by the lack of good works as the fruit of justification.

This was the explanation not only of Luther but also of Calvin, indeed of all the reformers.

It is significant that, eager as Shepherd, the federal vision, and Boersema are to support their doctrines by selected quotations of Calvin, at this critical point there is no reference to Calvin. The same is true regarding Shepherd's interpretation of Romans 2:13.

CONDEMNED BY THE CREEDS

If the contradiction of Calvin at the crucial points is significant, the contradiction of the Reformed creeds by Shepherd and his federal vision colleagues is damning.

Shepherd publicly teaches and defends justification by faith and by works in open defiance of Questions and Answers 59–64 of the Heidelberg Catechism, his own creed: "righteous only by faith."[4]

Against the teaching that is fundamental to Shepherd's and the federal vision's doctrine of justification, namely that the works excluded from justification by Paul in Romans 3 and 4 are only ceremonial works and works performed with the motive of meriting, stands the clear teaching of Question and Answer 62 of the Catechism. Here the Catechism excludes from justification *all* our good works, not only ceremonial works that a Jew might perform. "Why can not our good works be the whole or part of our righteousness before God?" The answer is not that ceremonial works have passed away, nor that the motive of works performed in order to merit is obnoxious to God. But the answer is that "the righteousness which can stand before the judgment-seat of God must be perfect throughout, and wholly conformable to the divine law; whereas even our best works in this life are all imperfect and defiled with sin."[5]

Thus the authoritative, binding doctrine of the creed is that the works excluded from consideration in justification include the good works of the believing child of God. In fact, the Catechism excludes from justification our "best works," which would include

---

4   Heidelberg Catechism Q 61, in ibid.3:327.

5   Heidelberg Catechism Q&A 62, in ibid..

feeding the hungry and clothing the naked, that is, all the good works James 2 exhorts upon us.

Lest there be any question about the good works excluded by the Catechism, Question 63 identifies them as works that "it is God's will to reward."[6] Surely these are not Old Testament ceremonies or works done to merit.

It is the creedal doctrine of the Reformed faith that justification by faith only means that all good works are excluded from consideration in the justifying act of God, "also...our best works." The reason is that even the best works of a believer, those that proceed from true faith, are "all imperfect and defiled with sin."

It is the creedal doctrine of the Reformed faith also that the denial of justification by faith only, by introducing good works into the act of justification—as Shepherd does—is in fact making those good works "the whole or part of our righteousness before God."[7]

It is irrelevant that Shepherd denies that the good works by which the sinner is justified are meritorious. It is irrelevant that Shepherd denies that the good works by which the sinner is justified are the ground of justification.

To introduce works into the forensic act of justification, to read Romans 3:28 thus, "A man is justified by faith *and by the genuine good works that faith performs*," is, by virtue of the introduction of works into the act of justification, to be guilty of teaching that "our good works [are]...part of our righteousness before God."[8]

Similar is Shepherd's disregard of the creeds in his teaching that good works do not follow justification (as works of thankfulness for the forgiveness of sins), but accompany justification and even precede justification. Determined as he is to have good works be a necessary aspect of justification, indeed necessary for justification, Shepherd argues at length that good works precede and accompany justification, rather than follow justification as fruit. His purpose is to establish that good works cannot be excluded from justification.

In a folksy manner, Boersema sums up Shepherd's opposition to

---

6   Heidelberg Catechism Q 63 in ibid.

7   Heidelberg Catechism Q 62, in ibid.

8   Ibid.

the teaching that good works follow justification and Shepherd's reason for opposing the teaching.

> What some people don't like is that Shepherd says that works are necessary for justification. They say that works are the fruit and evidence of faith and always follow faith, but Shepherd says more than that. For him, works are not only necessary for sanctification, but also for justification (214).

Both Shepherd and his liberated defender Ralph Boersema blithely ignore the doctrine of the Reformed creeds, particularly Article 24 of the Belgic Confession.

> Works, as they proceed from the good root of faith, are good and acceptable in the sight of God, forasmuch as they are all sanctified by his grace: howbeit they are of no account towards our justification. For it is by faith in Christ that we are justified, *even before we do good works, otherwise they could not be good works any more than the fruit of a tree can be good before the tree itself is good* (emphasis added).[9]

The theology of Norman Shepherd includes a heretical doctrine of justification. Openly, Shepherd teaches justification by faith and by the good works that true faith performs.

This doctrine of justification stands condemned by the Reformed creeds, specifically by Questions and Answers 59–64 of the Heidelberg Catechism and by Articles 22–24 of the Belgic Confession. Shepherd's doctrine stands condemned by the Reformed creeds, regardless that Shepherd denies that the works are meritorious, and regardless that Shepherd denies that these works are the ground of the verdict. To teach (forensic) justification by faith and by works is heresy, regardless of any and all mitigating explanations.

CONCLUSION

Some Reformed theologians, not all, as liberated theologian Ralph Boersema evidences, take issue with this aspect of Shepherd's and

---

9   Belgic Confession Article 24, in ibid., 3:411.

the federal vision's theology. They criticize Shepherd's doctrine of justification by faith and works.

But their opposition to this glaring error in Shepherd's theology will not be successful to root his theology out of their own denominations or out of the Reformed community. Nor will their opposition prevent the theology of the federal vision from spreading.

For, as also this latest defense of Shepherd by Boersema recognizes (with the express approval of Shepherd), justification by good works is only one expression of the fundamental theology of Norman Shepherd. The fundamental theology of Shepherd is the doctrine of a conditional covenant, a covenant that does not have its source in eternal election, nor is governed by election.

And the essence of this covenant theology, in Shepherd's own words, is the doctrine that our eternal welfare is contingent on what we do.

This covenant doctrine, the root of the heresy, the notable critics of Shepherd and the federal vision will not touch with the proverbial ten-foot pole.

The reason is that they are committed to the doctrine of a conditional covenant. Therefore they share with Shepherd the conviction that our eternal welfare is contingent on what we do, although they are less candid than is Shepherd in acknowledging this conviction.

How can a Reformed theologian who himself preaches John 3:16 as a universal love of God and a Christ proceeding from this universal love, graciously offered to all in the sincere desire of God that all accept his love and his Christ, but contingent—all of it, the love of God, Christ, and the offer—on acceptance by the sinner, engage in serious theological battle with Shepherd and the men of the federal vision?

The sixteenth-century Reformation, obviously at stake in the heresy of justification by good works, is now being undone in the reputedly conservative Reformed and Presbyterian churches, while the theologians, ministers, and elders—appointed watchmen on the walls of Zion—either stand idly by or, as is the case with Boersema, promote the overthrow of the Reformation.

God have mercy on the Reformed people!

And arise for the defense of the precious Reformed faith, his own gospel of grace!

Appendix Five

Yet Again Shepherd and the Federal Vision: "The Issue [is] Contingency"

Obedient Faith: A Festschrift for Norman Shepherd, ed. P. Andrew Sandlin and John Barach. Mount Hermon, CA: Kerygma Press, 2012. 312 pages. $21.95 (paper).

There comes another defense of Norman Shepherd and his theology. In fact, the book is a vigorous promotion of the theology of Shepherd, of the federal vision, and of a conditional covenant, severed from election.

This defense of Shepherd's theology is in the form of a "festschrift for Norman Shepherd." Inasmuch as festschrifts are books honoring theologians who have distinguished themselves as defenders and developers of the faith, it is evident that the men of the federal vision become bolder and that the movement becomes increasingly aggressive. Instead of defending Shepherd against the charge that he is a heretic, whose heresy is the grave false doctrine denying the gospel-truth that was the heart of the sixteenth-century Reformation of the church and that is the fundamental difference of Protestantism from the false church of Rome—justification by faith alone—the men of the federal vision now extol Shepherd as a notable, praiseworthy Christian and Reformed theologian. The theology of Norman Shepherd opens up to Reformed and Presbyterian churches new, splendid, necessary, "lasting" insights into the truth of divine revelation.

The end of this development will be that Shepherd will be reinstated with honor in the Orthodox Presbyterian, Presbyterian Church in America, and United Reformed Churches denominations, his theology will be declared the standard of orthodoxy, and all those who oppose it will be either disciplined or marginalized.

No doubt, this boldness of Shepherd's disciples and allies is due to the inability of Reformed theologians and churches to issue a damning verdict upon Shepherd's theology, beginning with the faculty of Westminster Theological Seminary in Philadelphia and the Orthodox Presbyterian Church.[1] In addition, prominent, influential Presbyterian and Reformed theologians publicly defend Shepherd's theology, including Richard Gaffin, John Frame, Ian Hewitson, and Ralph Boersema.

Nor is it lost on Shepherd's supporters that none except the Protestant Reformed Churches take hold of the root of the heresy of the federal vision—the doctrine of a gracious, but conditional, covenant with all baptized infants alike, if not with all humans, a covenant with its salvation divorced from election.

Thus the heresy goes from strength to strength. The end will be the loss in the Reformed churches of the gospel of grace in all its particulars, especially justification by faith alone and the five doctrines of grace confessed by the Canons of Dordt, and eventually a return to Rome, which has taught justification by faith and works and conditional salvation since the Reformation.

The contributors to the festschrift are John Barach, formerly minister in the United Reformed Churches; Ralph F. Boersema, Canadian Reformed theologian; Don Garlington, a Baptist professor of theology; Ian A. Hewitson, a Presbyterian Church in America minister; James B. Jordan; Peter J. Leithart; Rich Lusk; and P. Andrew Sandlin. The last four are leading figures in the movement known as Christian reconstruction.

Chiming in with praise for Shepherd and his theology, in a section of the book headed "Tributes," are John H. Armstrong; John M. Frame; Charles A. McIlhenny; Michael D. Pasarilla; Steve M. Schlissel; Jeffery J. Ventrella; and Roger Wagner. These tributes involve the Orthodox Presbyterian Church and Reformed Theological Seminary in Florida, among other denominations and religious organizations, in support of Shepherd and the theology of the federal vision.

---

1 Ian A. Hewitson, *Trust and Obey: Norman Shepherd & the Justification Controversy at Westminster Theological* Seminary (Minneapolis, MN: NextStep Resources).

SHEPHERD ON SHEPHERD

In a revelatory opening chapter Shepherd outlines his career, sketches the controversy at Westminster seminary over his teaching, and indicates the main elements of his theology of covenant.

He suggests that his rejection of eternal election as the source of the covenant, covenant salvation, and covenant life was due to the disregard, if not fear, of election in his Presbyterian circles.

> It is helpful to reflect on how the doctrine of election, and more broadly the doctrine of the decrees, functions in the life of the congregation. We can bring these doctrines out of the closet from time to time to examine and admire them and to reaffirm our acceptance of them as Scriptural truth. But then we put them back in the closet because they don't seem to have any practical application. We are afraid that they might actually have a paralyzing effect on the people of God (47).

The fountain and cause of all salvation may have a "paralyzing effect on the people of God"! In churches that claim to be Presbyterian and Reformed!

Where election is not preached but kept in the "closet," because it is not loved but feared, it will be denied. This is at the root of the heresy of the theology of Norman Shepherd and of the federal vision.

Evidently, Shepherd shares this disinterest in and suspicion of election. The result is a doctrine of the covenant that ignores, dismisses, and in reality denies election.

This raises the questions: How does such a theologian get an appointment to teach systematic theology in a creedal, Presbyterian seminary? Why do Reformed people allow themselves to be influenced by such an election-disparaging theologian? And why does every book promoting the theology of Norman Shepherd carry the recommendations of theologians and professors of theology who claim to be, and are widely regarded as being, outstanding Reformed teachers and churchmen?

Speaking for myself, no theologian who has little use for election will ever get my ear, much less my heart. Scripture is too clear, the Canons of Dordt are too loud, and the glory of God is too demanding.

Shepherd states that in James 2 justification does not have a "demonstrative sense" but has the "ordinary soteric sense...the sense that predominates in the teaching of Paul" (50). This commits Shepherd to teaching that justification, in the forensic sense—the forgiving of sins and the verdict declaring the sinner righteous before God the judge—is by the good works of the sinner. This has Shepherd necessarily overthrowing the sixteenth-century Reformation of the church; contradicting Questions and Answers 60–64 of the Heidelberg Catechism; and expressing agreement with the fundamental doctrine of the Roman Catholic Church. Evidently, none of this troubles the contributors to the festschrift, or those who pay tribute to Shepherd in the book, in the slightest.

In explanation of his heresy, Shepherd is bold to affirm that "our ultimate destiny [is] contingent upon what we do in this life" (51). This is the God-dishonoring, comfort-robbing implication of the doctrine of a conditional covenant. The Reformed confession is radically different. Our ultimate destiny is dependent on God's election and the death of Christ. For persevering in salvation is "a fruit of election [and] a gift of God gained by the death of Christ." Persevering in salvation, thus obtaining heaven as our ultimate destiny, is not "a condition of the new covenant." [2]

Shepherd is at pains to inform the reader of the book, which will certainly circulate widely throughout all the reputedly conservative Presbyterian and Reformed churches in North America, that he and his theology were approved by the faculty of Westminster seminary, by the board of trustees of Westminster seminary, by the Philadelphia Presbytery of the Orthodox Presbyterian Church, and by Classis Hackensack of the Christian Reformed Church, when Shepherd left the Orthodox Presbyterian Church for the Christian Reformed Church. "None of these bodies ever found my views to be contrary to either Scripture or Confession. I left the Orthodox Presbyterian Church by the front door as a minister in good and regular standing, and I entered the Christian Reformed Church by the front door as a minister in good and regular standing" (56).

Shepherd is clear and emphatic that his theology is covenant theology. He titles his chapter in the book "A Theological

---

2 Canons of Dordt 5, Error 1, in *Confessions and Church Order*, 176.

Autobiography: Growing in Covenant Consciousness" (25–63). He characterizes his "theological development...as a growing covenant consciousness and a consciousness that I wanted to share with my students and with anyone willing to listen...I had come to the conclusion that what is distinctive about the Reformed faith is its understanding and appropriation of the Biblical teaching on the covenants that the Lord God has made with his people, with believers and their children" (37–38). Specifically, his doctrine of justification, on which his purported critics concentrate, is in Shepherd's mind a "covenant perspective on justification" (50).

No one can doubt that what motivates Shepherd as a theologian is the conviction "that the church today stands in desperate need of discovering what it means to live in covenant with the Lord" (63). Accordingly, no one can doubt that a critique of Shepherd's theology that ignores his doctrine of the covenant is an exercise in futility.

The distinctive doctrine of the covenant that Shepherd propounds and develops, however, is that of the Reformed Churches in the Netherlands (liberated) and of their daughter in North America, the Canadian Reformed Churches. Hewitson notes Shepherd's indebtedness to Dutch theologian S. G. De Graaf (104). Cornelis Vonk supported Shepherd during the controversy at Westminster, expressly praising Shepherd's doctrine of justification (142–43).

"THE ISSUE [IS] CONTINGENCY"

Ian Hewitson, ardent supporter of Shepherd, is correct, therefore, when he writes concerning the controversy over the theology of Shepherd and of the federal vision that "the outstanding issue was, and remains to this day, the issue of contingency" (110). Contingency is conditionality, that is, the dependence of God for the salvation of the sinner upon the sinner himself. And the covenant doctrine of the liberated Reformed makes the covenant promise, the covenant, and covenant salvation contingent on the works of the baptized, sinful baby, rather than dependent on the sovereign work of the faithful covenant God.

It comes as no surprise that one of the chapters extolling Shepherd is written by Canadian Reformed theologian Ralph F. Boersema. Boersema has written an entire book defending the theology of Shepherd.[3] In his encomium to Shepherd in *Obedient Faith*, Boersema defends Shepherd's heresy regarding justification. The works that Paul excludes from justification are "works that seek to establish self-righteousness," not all works, absolutely. And James 2 teaches justification as a forensic act of God taking place "by works and not by faith alone…This is true because, as human functions, faith and works exist together as surely as do body and soul" (161).

The doctrine of a conditional covenant implies a conditional justification, as it also implies a conditional election, a conditional atonement, and a conditional perseverance. That is, the doctrine of a conditional covenant is the overthrow not only of the sixteenth-century Reformation of the church, but also of the seventeenth-century confession of the gospel of grace by the Synod of Dordt.

JUSTIFICATION BY GOOD WORKS

Much of the defense of Shepherd, throughout the book, on the part of all the contributors, consists of justifying Shepherd's doctrine of justification. Thus continues the error on the part of Shepherd's defenders, as well as his would-be critics, of concentrating on the fruit of Shepherd's theology—justification contingent on works—while ignoring the root—his theology of a conditional covenant.

This is not to suggest that the treatment of justification is not significant. The writers are bold in repudiating the Reformation's (and the Reformed creeds') doctrine of justification by faith alone, apart from any and all good works of the justified sinner, and in making the good works of the justified sinner part of his righteousness in his justification, especially in the final judgment.

At the same time their treatment of justification is either seriously confused or deliberately misleading.

Rich Lusk intends to prove that Romans 2:13 ("For not the hearers of the law are just before God, but the doers of the law shall be justified") teaches an actual, in distinction from hypothetical, justification of sinners. For Lusk "justifying works are…a necessary condition of final justification" (251). He quotes with approval Simon

---

3   Ralph F. Boersema, *Not of Works: Norman Shepherd and His Critics* (Minneapolis, MN: NextStep Resources, 2012).

Gathercole affirming that "the final vindication of God's people [is] *on the basis...* of their obedience" (emphasis added). Gathercole adds that Romans 2:13 teaches "justification as for the *doers...* It will not do to write this off as a hypothetical reference" (292).

P. Andrew Sandlin shows which way the winds of doctrine are blowing in the churches that will not condemn the theology of Shepherd and the federal vision. Sandlin is open to the charge of the new perspective on Paul that Luther misrepresented Paul (244). Sandlin goes further. He proposes that the message of the Protestant Reformation, specifically "*sola fide*" (by faith alone), was culturally conditioned and that its time has passed. The Reformation's message is no longer relevant. "In this cultural ambiance [of AD 2012], *justificatio sola fide* [justification by faith alone] is not 'the article by which the church stands and falls' or 'the principal hinge of religion'" (248).

Justification by faith alone and therefore the gospel of salvation by grace alone, of which justification by faith alone is an essential element, are not today *the* message of the gospel of Scripture. If they are not the message of the gospel today, they never were, for the message of the gospel of Scripture is unchanging. Thus is undone the sixteenth-century Reformation of the church. Thus is the way paved back to the Roman Catholic Church.

Can Reformed theologians and churches, indifferent though they are to sound doctrine, tolerate this attack on both the Reformation and the gospel?

But serious confusion runs through the book's defense of Shepherd, blurring the real issues in the controversy of creedal Reformed orthodoxy with Shepherd and the theology of the federal vision.

This confusion characterizes much of the defense of Shepherd's doctrine of justification. For one thing, the Bible's teaching that the final judgment of the elect believer will be a judgment "*according to* works" is not the same as a teaching that the final judgment will be "*on the basis of* works." The public justification of the elect believer in the final judgment will be based solely on the obedience of Jesus Christ, especially his lifelong suffering and his death, imputed to the account of the elect, believing sinner. This judgment will accord with the elect sinner's life of good works, which are themselves the fruit of election and the gift of God.

To argue from the biblical teaching that the final judgment will be *according to* good works to the unbiblical and anti-biblical conclusion that the final judgment will be *based on* the believer's good works, as do the contributors to *Obedient Faith*, is confused and fallacious. "In accordance with" is not the same as "on the basis of." My love for my wife is in accordance with her behavior of love toward me, but it is not based on her love for me. It is based on Christ's command to me as a Christian husband to love my wife. Basis is one thing; "in accordance with" is another.

In addition, with regard to the inheritance that will be the outcome of the final judgment for the elect believer, that salvation will not be based on the good works of the believer, although it will be in harmony with his life of good works, indeed a reward of his life of good works. The inheritance of salvation will come to the believer as a gift of God, originating in his (unconditional) decree of election and earned by the obedience of Jesus Christ. It will be a reward of the believer's life of good works, but the reward will be "of grace," that is, not based on our works, not what our works have coming as a debt God owes to them.[4]

Rich Lusk's understanding of his many quotations of Calvin is similarly confused. Lusk quotes Calvin to prove that Calvin taught justification by faith and by good works (253–59). This project is doomed from the start by the clear, forceful doctrine of Calvin in every place in his writings where he directly treats justification. Lusk might as well attempt to collect quotations proving that Calvin denied double predestination.

The point of all the quotations of Calvin on pages 253–59 of *Obedient Faith* is not that justification is by faith and works, which is what Lusk is trying to prove, but, in Calvin's own words in one of the quotations, that "by faith alone not only we ourselves but our works as well are justified" (259).

Calvin's comment demolishes Lusk's (and the book's) project. So far is it from being the case that the believer's good works justify the believer, or enter into the divine verdict upon him, that our good works themselves need to be justified. As tainted with sin,

---

4   Heidelberg Catechism Q&A 63, in Schaff, *Creeds of Christendom*, 3:327.

our good works need to be forgiven and declared righteous, not by virtue of any inherent righteousness, but on the ground of the perfect obedience of Jesus Christ. If my good works need to be justified, they cannot justify me. To look to them for justification is as foolish as it would be for a beggar to seek monetary help from a fellow pauper. This is the foolish theology of Norman Shepherd and the contributors to *Obedient Faith*, except that this theology is wicked besides, since "going about to establish their own righteousness, [they] have not submitted themselves unto the righteousness of God. For Christ is the end of the law for righteousness to every one that believeth" (Rom. 10:3–4).

Lusk's summation of Calvin's doctrine of justification is proved false, therefore, by the very quotation that Lusk thinks to summarize. Lusk's summation is: "For Calvin, justification by faith paves the way for justification by works" (259).

In truth, Calvin's doctrine of justification was: "By faith alone not only we ourselves but our works as well are justified."

In support of Shepherd's and his own doctrine of justification by works, Lusk appeals also to the decision on justification of the Regensberg Colloquy of 1541. This was an ecumenical conference of Protestants, headed by Martin Bucer, and Roman Catholic theologians. Calvin was present but had nothing to do with the statement on justification that resulted from the conference.

The Regensberg declaration on justification was a compromise. Like all compromises regarding doctrine, it favored the lie, in this case the Roman Catholic doctrine of justification as infused righteousness.

Regensberg identified justification with regeneration, allowed for a "justification of works," spoke of one's being "increasingly justified," acknowledged that justification is "always enlarged and promoted by good works," confessed that "the regenerate are... justified through this kind of works of faith and love," and failed outrightly to condemn the Roman Catholic doctrine of justification as a denial of the gospel of grace.

Luther, who was not a participant at the conference (he and his kind are always excluded from such conferences, which, though it may be understandable, puts the church and the truth at risk), damned the Regensberg statement on justification, indeed the entire compromising document, heartily. "We hate the book [containing the compromise of justification and other doctrines] worse than a dog or a snake...that utterly wretched book."

Luther was irate with Bucer, the one chiefly responsible for the Regensberg debacle. "Bucer, the rascal, has absolutely lost all my confidence. I shall never trust him again, he has betrayed me too often."[5]

Lusk must not appeal to Regensberg in defense of Shepherd's doctrine of justification. Rather, the opposite is the case. He must view Regensberg as a warning to Protestants not to compromise the truth of justification by faith alone.

Don Garlington does not so much confuse the issue as misrepresent it, whether wittingly or unwittingly. The issue in the controversy of Reformed orthodoxy with Norman Shepherd is not that the royal Jesus Christ commands, works, and receives willing obedience from and in his conquered, saved people. This is not the issue whatever. I cannot imagine that anyone could emphasize too strongly for Reformed orthodoxy the lordship of Christ over and in the lives of his people or the calling of Christ's people to lead holy lives. Genuine Calvinists love the truth of sanctification as a grand, necessary work of the Spirit of the Lord Jesus, always following the divine act of justification.

But the issue is whether King Jesus' saving work of justification, which is basic to his people's obedience, is by their own good works. The issue is whether their own good works enter into the verdict of God acquitting them of their sins and reckoning them righteous before him.

To defend Shepherd by contending that the Bible teaches that the gospel "entails not simply belief...but unconditional submission to his [Jesus Christ's] lordship" is both beside the point and deceiving (203–4). It leaves the impression that opposition to Shepherd arises from some form of antinomianism.

Utterly confused is Gathercole in regarding the Gentiles of Romans 2:14–15 as justified. "Paul goes on directly afterward [that is, after his statement in verse 13 that not the hearers of the law but

5   See David J. Engelsma, "Martin Bucer: 'Fanatic of Unity,'" *Mid-America Journal of Theology* 4, no. 1 [Spring 1988]: 32–53.

the doers of the law are justified, *if justification were by the law,* which it is not] to provide instances of these doers of the law who will be justified: the Gentiles who have the law written on their hearts" (292).

First, the apostle did not write that the Gentiles have the *law* written on their hearts. He wrote that they have the *work* of the law written on their hearts, that is, the law's work of distinguishing right from wrong. Second, the passage does not teach that the Gentiles are justified by thus having the work of the law written on their hearts. On the contrary, his doctrine is that this work of the law *condemns* them: "their conscience also bearing witness, and their thoughts the mean while accusing or else excusing one another" (v. 15).

POSTMILLENNIALISM

Of no little importance in the defense of Shepherd is the contention that Shepherd's theology promotes the postmillennial conception of the last things. When Sandlin dismisses the doctrine of justification by faith alone, and by implication the entire gospel of salvation by sovereign grace as confessed in the Canons of Dordt, as outdated, he proposes instead, as the message of the gospel demanded by our age, the gospel of the Christianizing of the world. Indeed, according to P. Andrew Sandlin the main message of the gospel of Scripture has always been that the church must "'set things straight' in God's world, not merely to save sinners" (244).

Significantly, Sandlin immediately appeals to Abraham Kuyper as the Reformed theologian who saw the cultural mandate as the central message of the Bible.

> Over a century ago...Abraham Kuyper argued that the glorification of God in the world and the extension of his kingdom, not personal salvation or justification by faith, is the goal of God's redemptive work in the world. God redeems sinners in his scope of redeeming all of creation...This cultural mandate is woven into the fabric of humanity...For too long the evangelical church has limited the goal of the gospel to the individual and the church (243–47).

Sandlin urges the calling of the church to redeem and reconstruct culture as the article by which the church stands and falls in our day (248).

James B. Jordan takes leave of his allegorizing interpretation of Scripture long enough to (mis)inform the reader that the Reformed reformers of the sixteenth century were "postmillennial" (167).

This eschatological aspect of Shepherd's theology is commonly overlooked. Shepherd himself is an avowed postmillennialist. His universalistic theology of covenant, a theology of covenant divorced from election, has God desirous of establishing his covenant with all humans; Christ dying for all humans; and evangelists graciously offering Jesus Christ in the name of God to all humans. Involved is at least the hope that a majority of mankind will in the end be converted and saved.

Then the good works that justify will also redeem and reconstruct the world into the earthly kingdom of Christ, prior to the second coming of the Lord. The running of the saints, in the language of Romans 9:16, saves both the sinner himself and the world.

This postmillennial element in Shepherd's theology explains in part Shepherd's attraction to the Christian reconstructionists—Jordan, Sandlin, Wilson, and others.

AGAINST THE ROOT OF SHEPHERD'S THEOLOGY, THE PROTESTANT REFORMED CHURCHES

Although Sandlin certainly does not intend it so, he honors the Protestant Reformed Churches by observing that these churches teach "'unconditional salvation,' including even the condition [sic] of faith" (240–41).

The undiscerning Reformed and Presbyterian public will undoubtedly take the statement as Sandlin meant it: *in malem partem.*

But there may be the stray thinker who reflects on the fact that, regarding a heresy fundamental to which, according to its proponents, is the "contingency of salvation," there is a denomination of Reformed churches confessing that salvation is unconditional. That is, salvation is gracious. Or, in the language of heaven, "Salvation to our God which sitteth upon the throne, and unto the Lamb" (Rev. 7:10).

And even in this apostate age, there may yet be the Reformed or Presbyterian Christian who remembers and takes seriously the condemnation by the Canons of Dordt of the teaching that "faith… [is] a condition of salvation."[6]

---

6   Canons of Dordt 1, Error 3, in *Confessions and Church Order*, 160.

Heritage Recordings

Remembering the Schism of 1953
An Audio Collection

Visit www.rfpa.org and listen to a commemorative audio set regarding the schism of 1953 within the Protestant Reformed Churches (PRC).

Two of the warriors of the controversy were Rev. Herman Hoeksema (defending an unconditional covenant, the view upheld and taught within the PRC and promoted by the Reformed Free Publishing Association) and Rev. Hubert De Wolf (defending a conditional covenant). **The sermons and lectures given by these two men at the time of the schism have been preserved and are part of the Heritage Recordings audio collection.** They are now available to you at www.rfpa.org in the form of **free audio downloads.** Also available is a PDF timeline of important events and dates pertinent to the schism of 1953.

Please take the time to visit our site and listen to these valuable pieces of the history of the Reformed Free Publishing Association and the Protestant Reformed Churches!

http://rfpa.org/pages/remembering-the-schism-of-1953

OTHER WORKS BY THE AUTHOR

In addition to writing, *Battle for Sovereign Grace in the Covenant*, David J. Engelsma has authored, coauthored, and edited numerous other books and written countless articles for the *Standard Bearer* magazine and several pamphlets pertaining to Christian life.

RFPA PUBLICATIONS WRITTEN BY DAVID J. ENGELSMA

Better to Marry: Sex and Marriage in 1 Corinthians 6 and 7
Bound to Join: Letters on Church Membership
Common Grace Revisited: A Response to Richard J. Mouw's
　He Shines in All That's Fair
Covenant and Election in the Reformed Tradition
The Covenant of God and the Children of Believers: Sovereign
　Grace in the Covenant
A Defense of the Church Institute: Response to the Critics of
　Bound to Join
Federal Vision: Heresy at the Root
Hyper-Calvinism and the Call of the Gospel: An Examination of
　the "Well-Meant Offer" of the Gospel
Marriage, the Mystery of Christ and the Church: The Covenant-Bond
　in Scripture and History
Prosperous Wicked and Plagued Saints: An Exposition of Psalm 73
Reformed Education: The Christian School as Demand of the Covenant
The Reformed Faith of John Calvin: The Institutes in Summary
Reformed Worship (coauthor with Barrett Gritters and Charles Terpstra)
Trinity and Covenant: God as Holy Family
Unfolding Covenant History: Judges and Ruth

RFPA PUBLICATIONS EDITED BY DAVID J. ENGELSMA

Always Reforming
Communion with God: Reformed Spirituality
Peace for the Troubled Heart: Reformed Spirituality
Righteous by Faith Alone: A Devotional Commentary on Romans
The Sixteenth-Century Reformation of the Church